The Democratic Potential of Charter Schools

Studies in the
Postmodern Theory of Education

Joe L. Kincheloe and Shirley R. Steinberg
General Editors

Vol. 136

PETER LANG
New York • Washington, D.C./Baltimore • Boston • Bern
Frankfurt am Main • Berlin • Brussels • Vienna • Oxford

Stacy Smith

The Democratic Potential
of Charter Schools

PETER LANG
New York • Washington, D.C./Baltimore • Boston • Bern
Frankfurt am Main • Berlin • Brussels • Vienna • Oxford

Library of Congress Cataloging-in-Publication Data

Smith, Stacy.
The democratic potential of charter schools / Stacy Smith.
p. cm. — (Counterpoints; vol. 136)
Includes bibliographical references (p.) and index.
1. Charter schools—United States—Case studies. 2. School choice—Social
aspects—United States—Case studies. 3. Citizenship—Study and teaching—
United States—Case studies. 4. Educational equalization—United States—
Case studies. I. Title. II. Counterpoints (New York, N.Y.); vol. 136.
LB2806.36.S65   371.01—dc21   99-055972
ISBN 0-8204-4909-1
ISSN 1058-1634

Die Deutsche Bibliothek-CIP-Einheitsaufnahme

Smith, Stacy:
The democratic potential of charter schools / Stacy Smith.
–New York; Washington, D.C./Baltimore; Boston; Bern;
Frankfurt am Main; Berlin; Brussels; Vienna; Oxford: Lang.
(Counterpoints; Vol. 136)
ISBN 0-8204-4909-1

Cover design by Joni Holst
The paper in this book meets the guidelines for permanence and durability
of the Committee on Production Guidelines for Book Longevity
of the Council of Library Resources.

© 2001 Stacy Smith

Printed in the United States of America

To the members of Winthrop Academy Charter School—
for having the courage to breathe life into democratic ideals.

Table of Contents

List of Tables

Acknowledgments

The support of many people is reflected in the pages of this book. I wish to thank the faculty and students at Winthrop Academy Charter School (pseudonym)—this study would not have been possible without their co-operation and assistance. I also want to thank my graduate school advisors—Dr. Kenneth Strike, Dr. Deborah Trumbull, and Dr. Don Barr—for their guidance and critical feedback. I am indebted to my friends and colleagues Alexis Kaminsky, Rob Reich, and Anne Dodd for their careful reading and exchange of ideas. I am grateful for the support of the Charlotte W. Newcombe Doctoral Dissertation Fellowship from the Woodrow Wilson National Fellowship Foundation. And, finally, the unflagging encouragement of my husband, Matthew Arrants, provided me with the wherewithal to complete this project.

I have presented some of the arguments of this book previously in other forms. The introduction, chapter 1, and chapter 5 each include expanded and/or adapted versions of segments of "The Democratizing Potential of Charter Schools" which appeared in *Educational Leadership* 56, no. 2 (1998): 55–58 and "School Choice: Accountability to Publics, Not Markets" which appeared in *Journal of Maine Education* 25 (1999): 7–10. Portions of chapter 2 are adapted from "Voluntary Segregation: Gender and Race as Legitimate Grounds for Differential Treatment and Freedom of Association," which appeared in *Philosophy of Education 1996*, ed. Frank Margonis, 48–57 (Urbana, IL: University of Illinois at Urbana-Champaign, 1997), "Democracy, Plurality, and Education: Deliberating Practices of and for Civic Participation" which appeared in *Philosophy of Education 1997*, ed. Susan Laird, 338–347 (Urbana, IL: University of Illinois at Urbana-Champaign, 1998), and "Charter Schools: Voluntary Associations or Political Communities?" which appeared in *Philosophy of Education 1998*, ed. Steve Tozer, 131–139 (Urbana, IL: University of Illinois at Urbana-Champaign, 1999). Each of these selections is used by permission of the publisher.

Introduction

Since Minnesota first enacted legislation in 1991, charter school reform has swept the country. Within the span of eight years, thirty-six states and the District of Columbia have passed charter legislation, and many other state legislatures are now considering proposed bills. Charter schools are unequivocally public entities—they must provide a free education to all eligible public school students and they are funded by public moneys, often based upon a per pupil expenditure from the state. But charters blur the boundary between "public" and "private" schools in a few different ways. First, they are similar to private schools in that they are schools of choice with distinct missions. Second, charter schools are autonomously managed by groups of parents, teachers, or community members; but unlike private schools, they are under contract with a public agency. Finally, charters are freed from many bureaucratic structures governing public schools at the state and local levels; they make most of their own decisions about budget, personnel, and curriculum.

Because charter schools blur traditional boundaries between public and private schools in a variety of ways, they revive questions of balancing public and private interests in education which we in the United States have struggled with since public education became compulsory early in the twentieth century. In large part because of tensions particular to this public/private struggle, debate about charter schooling has been lively, and often heated and contentious. Many supporters tout charters as the best hope for public education, while equally vocal critics insist that charters will bring about its demise.[1]

Although their stances are vastly different, both proponents and opponents of the movement emphasize the *privatizing* aspects of charter school reform. Proponents draw heavily upon language associated with the marketplace. They refer to students and parents as *consumers* and *clients*, play up the attributes of bringing *competition* into the public educational sphere, and often refer to charter school founders as *entrepreneurs*. It is precisely this market orientation that concerns skeptics and critics of the charter movement. Alex Molnar, for example, claims that charters threaten the common purposes traditionally associated with public education:

> Charter schools, like private school vouchers and for-profit schools, are built on the illusion that our society can be held together solely by the self-interested pursuit of our individual purposes. Considered in this light, the charter school movement represents a radical rejection not only of the possibility of the common school, but of common purposes outside the school as well. The struggle is not between market-based reforms and the educational status quo. It is about whether the democratic ideal of the common good can survive the onslaught of a market mentality that threatens to turn every human relationship into a commercial transaction.[2]

Molnar's critique illustrates a common tendency among naysayers to charter school reform—they frame the entire movement as inherently antidemocratic. To the extent that charter schools are conceived of only in terms of a "market mentality" such concerns about the rejection of common purposes are quite valid. But what this position overlooks is the possibility that there might be more to the charter school reform movement. The tendency to emphasize the privatizing, market-oriented aspects of charter reform is overly simplistic. Consequently, virtually all debate on the topic neglects, or at best downplays, the *democratizing* potentials of charter schools.

Educators and others concerned with preserving the "public" nature of public education should not summarily write off charter school reform as a move toward privatization. The alternative organizational model of charter schools raises some interesting possibilities for fulfilling public interests in education. Before outlining these possibilities I will briefly explain some of the primary, and often conflicting, interests in the education of children in the United States.

Two fundamental types of interests are at stake in educating future generations of Americans. The first type can be referred to as *particular* or *private interests* in education. These private interests have to do with parents' stakes in transmitting specific identities and values to their children. A Jewish family, for instance, may wish to pass on cultural traditions, religious values, and a sense of identity to its children. The family is interested in such cultural transmission because it views a Jewish way of life as an exemplar of "the good life" and hopes to prepare its children to take part. The family is also interested in preparing the children to carry on a religious and cultural tradition; cultural survival is ensured through the education of future members.

The second type of interests at stake in educating future Americans are *common* or *public interests*. These interests are also known as "public goods" and simply refer to our collective concerns regarding the education of future members of our society. As a democratic society, we as citizens are interested in perpetuating a form of governance "by, for, and of the people." The "people" in this instance share a civic identity as fellow citizens. In addition, we call upon shared democratic values, such as liberty and equality, or at least a shared set of institutional practices, with which to make collective decisions. Some degree of common education ensures that schooling will be equally in the interests of all and will prepare children for their future roles as citizens.

In some fairly homogenous societies private and public interests in education may converge. In the United States, however, the situation is more complicated, and balancing the two sets of interests poses a perpetual challenge. The U.S. is a pluralistic society in many senses of the word. We are a society of many distinct individuals. We are a society of multiple sociocultural groups who share various beliefs, values, traditions, and religious faiths. And we are a society composed of numerous associations and organizations representing the interests of such individuals and groups.[3] These dimensions of difference give rise to identity-based, value-based, and interest-based pluralism. Individuals claim many different identities and have a stake in attaining different, and often diverging, ends.

Balancing private and public interests amidst social pluralism is no easy task. Pluralism complicates the cultivation of a shared civic identity as citizens of a democratic society. Pluralism complicates processes of reaching collective agreements and casts doubt on whether "common interests" can even be identified. And pluralism complicates the straightforward application of principles of equality. Thus, within the realm of education, we are persistently faced with the question: In a pluralistic democracy such as our own, what kinds of educational structures and practices balance private and public interests in a manner that is equally in the interests of all?

In 1925 the Supreme Court offered one answer to this perennial question in its *Pierce v. Society of Sisters* decision. This case came before the Court because the state of Oregon had passed a law requiring all of its children not only to attend school, but to attend public schools. The Court overturned the act on the grounds that:

[W]e think it entirely plain that the Act of 1922 unreasonably interferes with the liberty of parents and guardians to direct the upbringing and education of children under their control. . . . The fundamental theory of liberty upon which all governments in this Union repose excludes any general power of the State to standardize its children by forcing them to accept instruction from public teachers only. The child is not the mere creature of the State; those who nurture him and direct his destiny have the right, coupled with the high duty, to recognize and prepare him for additional obligations.[4]

The Court, in this instance, protected the private interests of families in educating their children and preparing them for "additional obligations" to those of democratic citizenship. Yet the Court also stressed public interests in the education of all students and authorized public oversight:

No question is raised concerning the power of the State reasonably to regulate all schools, to inspect, supervise and examine them, their teachers and pupils; to require that all children of proper age attend some schools, that teachers shall be of good moral character and patriotic disposition, that certain studies plainly essential to good citizenship must be taught, and that nothing be taught which is manifestly inimical to the public welfare.[5]

The *Pierce* decision balanced public and private interests in education by protecting a private sphere of educational choices for parents or guardians. In its wake, particularistic views about the appropriate upbringing of children or the additional obligations that they should be prepared for are pursued in this private sphere.[6] In terms of public education, on the other hand, the state provides a standardized education that attempts to remain neutral toward a plethora of private ends.

The pressing question over seventy years after the *Pierce* decision is whether this solution has proved satisfactory. David Tyack contends that public education at the end of the twentieth century is at the same time too homogeneous and too heterogeneous. Public education is too homogeneous in that schools teach similar curricula in similar ways with similar textbooks. But it is also too heterogeneous in that educational resources and the quality of schooling vary greatly from district to district and from school to school.[7] Both the homogeneity and the heterogeneity suggest that the present organizational structure of education is not equally in the interests of all.

Multiculturalists, among others, charge that curricular homogeneity in public education does not represent neutrality, but rather the cultural domination of mainstream over marginalized groups. On another front, those interested in moral education argue that homogeneous or neutral approaches to values education can quickly lead toward value relativism.

Many families with children in the public schools must contend with pressures of assimilation and relativism as they attempt to transmit their own particular values. To escape these pressures, or to be assured a certain quality of education, some families choose educational alternatives in the private sphere. But only those who can afford to pay private school tuition can avail themselves of this option. Thus, families whose values are not represented in the mainstream culture and low- to middle-income families are each at a disadvantage in the present structure of public education.

Charter schools offer an alternative organizational structure for balancing public and private interests in education. They provide one model of what Tyack refers to as "public schools of choice [where] like-minded parents and public educators could together create schools . . . within public education that seek to honor different ideals of character . . . [and] different ethical outlooks."[8] Because they are privately organized according to specific educational missions, charters broaden opportunities for the transmission of particularistic values. At the same time, because they are public and accessible to all families, they also have the potential to equalize opportunities for quality schooling within public education. Thus, charter schools may address negative aspects of both homogeneity and heterogeneity within the present system.

The prevalent discourse around charter school reform, however, tends to conceptualize our prospects for balancing public and private interests in a limited fashion. Proponents of charter schools emphasize the goods of privatization and market competition. Critics, on the other hand, tend to view any move toward privatization as antidemocratic and equate what is "public" about public education with existing institutional structures. Consequently, debate surrounding the desirability of charter schools is needlessly narrow and overlooks some of the most interesting possibilities posed by charter reform.

In this book I explore the potential of charter schools to cultivate strong educative communities that represent a variety of particular interests while simultaneously fulfilling shared public interests. In order to convey a clearer picture of this democratic potential of charter schools, I will outline a few key areas where charters reconfigure traditional approaches to public education. I will refer to these areas—distribution, governance, and civic education—as three central aspects of "democratic education."[9]

First, there is the issue of distributing public education. *Distribution* is generally thought of in terms of "equal access" or "equal opportunity." Given differences in families' educational interests and in students' identities and needs, it is difficult to determine what constitutes equal treatment in the educational sphere. Questions surrounding equitable distribution of educational opportunities come to the fore in arguments about racial segregation versus integration, for instance, and in more recent debates over whether girls and boys should be taught in separate math classes.

The charter school debate is polemicized between two very different models for distributing educational opportunities. Charter school supporters extol a model of market choice. Choice is identified as a form of "empowerment" whereby low-income families in particular can demand the types of educational options that were previously available only in the private sector. Skeptics, on the other hand, worry that disenfranchised parents will not have the resources at their disposal to make good choices for their children.[10] This concern leads some critics to prefer the current model of geography-based schools that students are assigned to attend. Each side of this polemic limits the terms of this debate. In the first instance, parents' and students' status as citizens is overlooked in favor of their status as consumers; in the latter instance, their capacity for human agency and self-determination is devalued in favor of public oversight. I will argue that charter schools have the potential to expand and equalize choices available for all citizens within the sphere of public education.

Second, there is the issue of *governance* of public education. This simply has to do with how educational institutions are governed. How are decisions made about education? What structures are used—representative legislatures, direct forums with face-to-face deliberations, or other manifestations of democratic decision making? In this area, the charter debate vacillates between decision-making models of private management as opposed to interest-based, highly bureaucratized political structures. Supporters argue that autonomy and accountability will bring efficiency and effectiveness into a failing system. Opponents charge that contracting responsibility to a charter school board is a move toward privatization that is antidemocratic and threatens public interests in education. Yet another message lurking behind this rhetoric is concerned with the political bargaining power of teachers' unions, professional associations, and local bureaucracies composed of school boards, superintendents, and administrators.[11] Charters threaten the power of each of these groups. This political maneuvering raises the question: To what extent does these groups' stake in the present system represent "the public interest"?

I will argue that charter schools, as specific types of public institutions, have the potential to move beyond the privatization versus public bureaucracy dichotomy by functioning as multiple forums for localized and inclusive democratic decision making. Essentially, charters represent "multiple publics" within our civil society, where collective decisions are made surrounding all aspects of public education. As such, the authors of a recent study claim that charters have the potential to "shift power from bureaucracies to the schools themselves and ultimately to the individuals responsible for them—educators, parents, and students."[12]

Finally, there is the issue of *civic education*. This has to do with preparing students to become future citizens. More concretely, civic education emphasizes cultivating the shared values and civic capacities that are necessary for citizenship in our democratic society. In terms of charter school reform, there is not much public debate about our shared public interest in preparing future citizens. Civic education is rarely talked about in relation to charter schools or, for that matter, in most debates over public education reform in general. But the fact that civic education is a neglected topic does not lessen its importance in a democratic society. We all have an interest in preparing citizens who will actively and effectively participate in a system "by, for, and of the people." Perhaps our failure to keep this interest in mind has something to do with declining voting rates and the general apathy of our population when it comes to politics. Public education is an avenue for us to encourage civic participation—not only for future citizens, but also among current citizens as we make collective decisions about the education of our young people.

Philosopher Amy Gutmann advises in her book *Democratic Education* that we think about cultivating citizenship as a means of "conscious social reproduction." Within our democratic society, conscious social reproduction refers to:

> the ways in which citizens are or should be empowered to influence the education that in turn shapes the political values, attitudes, and modes of behavior of future citizens. Since the democratic ideal of education is that of conscious social reproduction, a democratic theory focuses on practices of deliberate instruction by individuals and on the educative influences of institutions designed at least partly for educational purposes.[13]

I will argue that charter schools provide us with an opportunity to reconsider civic education in terms of both "practices of deliberate instruction" and the "educative influences of institutions." Charters are places where pedagogical practices are intended to vary and be innovative. And the institutional structure of charters raises unique questions about the possible influences of schools that are distinct from one another as well as bastions of localized decision making.

In the following chapters I set out to broaden public discourse surrounding charter school reform in terms of our public interests in three central aspects of democratic education—distribution, governance, and civic education. I undertake this broad endeavor by focusing my attention on the final aspect, civic education, and the ideal of "conscious social reproduction." I consider the first two aspects, distribution and governance, primarily in terms of what Gutmann would call their "educative influences" on the preparation of future citizens.

In Chapter 1, I start out by defining charter schools and outlining the most common arguments for and against them. I then discuss in greater depth some of the overlooked potentials raised by charter schools and consider their implications in terms of democratic education. I hypothesize that key features of charter schools—namely their voluntaristic, particularistic, and associational nature—heighten the likelihood that they will become distinct school communities. In terms of our public interests in education, this raises the seldom-discussed potential of charters as *local democratic associations with distinct school communities.* I urge us to consider seriously the desirability of such school communities in terms of conscious social reproduction.

Chapter 2 takes up the question of desirability by drawing upon normative political theory. I turn to Jurgen Habermas's "discourse theory of democracy" for an idealized model of public life in late-twentieth-century, complex, pluralistic societies such as our own. Advocates of this brand of "deliberative democracy" claim that it offers the "most adequate conceptual and institutional model" for our times.[14] I find this claim compelling because the theory attempts to overcome the traditional liberal/communitarian debate, sustains pluralism while holding out the possibility of shared political norms, and stresses participatory over integrationist, political communities. In a nutshell, the theory's principles of inclusion, equality, and participation are attractive as democratic ideals for public school communities within a pluralistic society. I contend, however, that the ultimate challenge for any normative theory is its capacity for translation into day-to-day practice. Charter schools provide deliberative democratic theory with a testing ground for its viability in educational practice.

I end Chapter 2 by considering how the principles and procedures of deliberative democracy apply to education. Whereas Habermas's theory offers "legitimate conditions" for democratic decision making, education is about more than making decisions. In order to begin theorizing a deliberative model of civic education, I distinguish between *practices of* and *practices for* democratic decision making. *Practices of* refer to what Gutmann describes as ". . . the ways in which citizens are or should be empowered to influence the education that in turn shapes the political values, attitudes, and modes of behavior of future citizens." In this case, Habermas's ideal procedure translates rather easily into the public sphere of education. *Practices for* democratic decision making, on the other hand, have to do with the "deliberate practices of instruction" and the "educative influences" of institutions that comprise civic education. Here, questions of legitimacy are not so straightforward. Students, for example, are not necessarily equals within school communities. Charters, because they are particularistic, may not include everyone. Thus, deliberative democracy's ideal procedure for decision making requires careful translation into "legitimate conditions" for civic education.

Chapters 3 and 4 inform legitimate educational conditions within charter schooling through an ethnographic case study of one school's experiences with civic education. I employ a case study in order to demonstrate how deliberative democratic principles can be used as "critical yardsticks" for assessing whether charter school policies and practices fulfill public interests. Winthrop Academy Charter School in Eaton, Massachusetts educates high school students with an emphasis on democratic citizenship that is clear from its mission:

> Winthrop Academy is dedicated to rekindling the passion for democracy, the commitment to public service, the respect for hard work, and the hunger for learning in urban youth. This [civic education] mission will inform our curriculum, our pedagogy, our attitudes, and our management structure, and guide our efforts to teach students to be thoughtful and active citizens.
>
> Today, this mission is increasingly urgent. Many of our students are unconcerned with what is happening in the world, much less in their city. . . . The habits of tolerance, of thoughtful debate, of community involvement necessary for a democracy to flourish are not innate. They must be taught, exercised, and owned. The time has come for a new Winthrop Academy, a school which prepares students to understand, practice, and embrace the principles and habits of democracy.[15]

Because of this civic education mission, Winthrop Academy provides an optimal setting for investigating how the ideals of deliberative democracy—participation, inclusion, and equality—are fostered and hindered through specific, deliberate practices of civic education. I focus on deliberate practices of civic education in order to consider two issues surrounding charters as public school communities. First, I seek to illustrate the complexities surrounding how charters fulfill public interests in civic education within the particular context of their own school communities. And, second, I aim to illuminate tensions in the relationship between the ideal deliberative model and concrete practices of civic education.

Chapter 5 concludes the book by synthesizing the case study findings and theoretical considerations into insights that aspire to be useful for at least three audiences. First, I hope that the case study will serve as a vehicle for Winthrop Academy faculty to reflect on and assess the implementation of their curricular objectives surrounding civic education. Second, I offer the case as "vicarious experience"[16] for those interested in education reform broadly, or charter schools in particular. And, third, I intend for policy makers and regulators to make use of information garnered from Winthrop Academy's experiences to inform the ways in which they define and evaluate whether charter schools are satisfying public interests in education. Finally, I hope that this book will vitalize public discourse surrounding charter school reform and, more generally, the educational prospects we offer future democratic citizens.

Notes

1. Joe Nathan, *Charter Schools: Creating Hope and Opportunity for American Education* (San Francisco: Jossey-Bass, 1996), 93–118 cites detractors who consider charters "just plain bad public policy," a far-right plot, a costly hoax, "partisan, anti-government and racist, a ploy promoted by 'arch conservatives' and the 'religious right'" and evidence that "elitists [are] out to destroy public education." For some of these arguments see also R. E. Astrup, "Charter Schools: A Dissenting View," *Education Week,* 23 September 1992, 29. For arguments in support of charter schools see Ted Kolderie, "Chartering Diversity," *Equity and Choice* 9, no. 1 (1992): 28–31 and Nathan, 1–19.

2. Alex Molnar, "Charter Schools: The Smiling Face of Disinvestment," *Educational Leadership* 54 no. 2 (1996): 15.

3. With these three levels of individual, group, and organizational pluralism I am thinking of alternative conceptions of "plurality" between individuals, ethical or values "pluralism," and "pluralist democracy." Hannah Arendt defined plurality as "the condition of human action because we are all the same, that is, human, in such a way that nobody is ever the same as anyone else who ever lived, lives, or will live" in *Human Condition* (Chicago: University of Chicago Press, 1958), 8. Ethical, moral, or values pluralism is often referred to as the "fact of reasonable pluralism" by Rawls and other modern liberals. See John Rawls, *Political Liberalism* (New York: Columbia University Press, 1993), 36–37. And "pluralist democracy" is Robert Dahl's term for "the existence of a plurality of relatively autonomous (independent) organizations (subsystems) within the domain of a state" In *Dilemmas of Pluralist Democracy: Autonomy vs. Control* (New Haven: Yale University Press, 1982), 5. See also William E. Connolly, *The Ethos of Pluralization* (Minneapolis: University of Minnesota Press, 1995). I address the issue of pluralism in greater detail in Chapter Two.

4. *Pierce v. Society of Sisters*, 268 U.S. (1925). See Mark G. Yudof, David L. Kirp, and Betsy Levin, *Educational Policy and the Law*, 3rd ed. (St. Paul, MN: West Publishing Company, 1992), 12.

5. Yudof et al., 12.

6. This stance represents a fairly typical modern liberal view that particularistic traditions or conceptions of the good life are created and carried on in the private spheres of civil society. See, for example, Rawls, *Theory of Justice* (Cambridge, MA: Harvard University Press, 1971) and *Political Liberalism*, and K. Anthony Appiah, "Culture, Subculture, Multiculturalism: Educational Options," in *Public Education in a Multicultural Society: Policy, Theory, and Critique*, ed. Robert K. Fullinwider (New York: Cambridge University Press, 1996), 81–82.

7. David Tyack, "Can We Build a System of Choice That Is Not Just a 'Sorting Machine' or a Market-Based 'Free-for-All'?" *Equity and Choice* 9, no. 1 (1992): 16.

8. Tyack, 15–16.

9. These three aspects are not intended to provide an exhaustive account of the
    ways in which democratic interests are at stake in public education. Public fund-
    ing and school finance, for example, involve public interests and intersect with
    each of the three areas I have outlined. I emphasize distribution, governance, and
    civic education because these are three key features of concern regarding charter
    school reform. For more in-depth discussion of democratic public interests and
    education see John Dewey, *Democracy and Education* (New York: The Free
    Press, 1966 [1916]); R.S. Peters's chapter entitled "Democracy and Education"
    in *Ethics and Education* (Atlanta: Scott, Foresman, and Co., 1967), 195–218;
    Israel Scheffler, "Moral Education and the Democratic Ideal," in *Reason and
    Teaching*, ed. Israel Scheffler (Indianapolis and New York: The Bobbs-Merrill
    Company, 1973), 136–45; Amy Gutmann, *Democratic Education* (Princeton:
    Princeton University Press, 1987); and Kenneth A. Strike, "The Moral Role of
    Schooling in a Liberal Democratic Society," in *Review of Research in Education*
    17 (1991): 413–83.

10. For concrete articulations of these concerns see Bruce Fuller and Richard F. Elmore,
    eds. with Gary Orfield, *Who Chooses? Who Loses?: Culture, Institutions, and
    the Unequal Effects of School Choice* (New York: Teachers College Press, 1996)
    and Amy Stuart Wells, *Beyond the Rhetoric of Charter School Reform: A Study
    of Ten California School Districts* (UCLA: UCLA Charter School Study, 1998),
    particularly Finding #9. For a discussion of the complexities within charter school
    reform between empowerment and marginalization, for example, see also Amy
    Stuart Wells, Alejandra Lopez, Janelle Scott, and Jennifer Jellison Holme, "Char-
    ter Schools as Postmodern Paradox: Rethinking Social Stratification in an Age of
    Deregulated School Choice," *Harvard Educational Review* 69 (1999): 172–204.

11. See Nathan, 75–118.

12. Brunno V. Manno, Chester E. Finn, Jr., Louann A. Bierlein, and Gregg Vanourek,
    "How Charter Schools are Different: Lessons and Implications from a National
    Study," *Phi Delta Kappan* 79 (1998): 498.

13. Gutmann, 14.

14. Seyla Benhabib, "The Democratic Moment and the Problem of Difference," in
    Democracy and Difference: Contesting the Boundaries of the Political
    (Princeton: Princeton University Press, 1996), 6.

15. Beth Taft and Cathleen Eichler, "Winthrop Academy Charter School Applica-
    tion" (submitted to the Massachusetts Executive Office of Education, Boston, MA,
    February, 1994), 1. The name of the school, the city where it is located, and the
    names of all faculty members and students are pseudonyms in order to protect
    the identity of the research site and participants. Eaton is a large city in Massa-
    chusetts with both racial/ethnic and socio-economic diversity. Winthrop Acad-
    emy was among the first charter schools to open in Eaton, and in the state of
    Massachusetts as a whole.

16. The concept of research as "vicarious experience" is discussed by Robert Donmoyer, "Generalizability and the Single-Case Study," in *Qualitative Inquiry in Education: The Continuing Debate*, eds. Elliot W. Eisner and Alan Peshkin (New York: Teachers College Press, 1990), 175–200 and Reba Page and Linda Valli, eds. *Curriculum Differentiation: Interpretive Studies in U.S. Secondary Schools* (Albany: State University of New York Press, 1990), 7–8.

PART ONE

CHARTERS, PUBLIC LIFE, AND DEMOCRATIC EDUCATION

Chapter 1

Charter School Reform: Broadening the Terms of Debate

School choice has become a buzzword of education reform over the past decade. Intra-district choice plans, magnet schools, pilot schools, charter schools, and voucher schemes represent only a few of the many forms that school choice iniatives can take. Although each form of school choice offers specific advantages and disadvantages, and raises particular questions and concerns, some common threads run throughout the choice movement. As Peter Cookson explains,

> [the] common denominator is that [choice plans] encourage or require students and their families to become actively engaged in choosing schools. Whereas previously most American families simply sent their children to their neighborhood schools, the implementation of choice plans makes it possible for students to attend schools inside or outside their district, and sometimes even outside their city or town.[1]

Debate about various school choice options also exhibits some commonalities. Advocates of choice, for instance, emphasize parental rights and the benefits of a marketplace of competition and diversity. Critics of choice, on the other hand, worry that among other things the common mission of public schools is being abandoned and that choice will resegregate schools along any number of demographic characteristics.

Within the context of a wider school choice movement, this book is concerned first and foremost with the *democratizing potential of charter school reform*. This book does not assess whether school choice as a monolithic entity is desirable, nor does it compare charter school initiatives directly with other choice options such as vouchers. Rather, this book investigates education reform discourse in its particular manifestation within debates surrounding charter schooling.[2]

I will attempt to broaden and inform charter school discourse in two ways: first, by drawing upon normative political theory relevant to institutions within civil society; and, second, by applying this theoretical framework to a case study of one charter school that is particularly interested in the relationship between charter reform and the revitalization of both public education and public life in our democratic society. This chapter sets the stage for my agenda by defining some basic features of the charter school movement and by outlining some of the most common arguments for and against charter schools. After pointing out that the debate surrounding charter school reform is needlessly narrow in its focus, I suggest a few overlooked aspects of charter schooling that highlight its democratizing potential.

I. Introduction to Charter Reform

During the 1990s charter school reform spread across the nation. Following Minnesota's 1991 lead, by 1999 thirty-six states and the District of Columbia had approved charter school legislation.[3] Under these laws, over 1,500 charter schools had opened or been approved to open by the spring of 1999.[4] These pioneer charter schools are vastly different from one another. Some schools focus on a back-to-basics curriculum while others emphasize alternative approaches to learning; some emphasize math, science, and computer technology while others stress the fine arts; some require parental involvement whereas others aim to provide individual high school students with a flexible program for attaining a diploma; some emphasize critical thinking skills while their peer institutions are more interested in character development. The list of stark differences between the educational philosophies and missions of charter schools goes on and on. This is precisely the diversity of options that early charter advocates hoped to achieve. And the diversity exists not only because charters are autonomous public schools, but because charter school laws themselves are so diverse among the states.

Specific provisions regulating charter schools vary within each state's legislation, but a few features provide the defining characteristics of the movement. At a general level, charter schools are *publicly-funded* schools of choice that are *autonomous* from local school districts and are outcomes- or results-oriented.[5] Charter schools are public schools in that they cannot select students on the basis of merit; and they are funded by public moneys, often based upon a per pupil expenditure from the state. They differ from traditional public schools in that they are fairly independent of direct administrative control from the local educational establishment: they make most of their own decisions about budget, personnel, and curriculum. A charter school's accountability comes in terms of living up to the outcomes it promises within its mission and original charter documents.

Beyond these shared characteristics there is a great deal of variation between charters from state to state. For instance, the sponsoring agency, or the public body that grants the charter, differs. In some states local school boards grant charters; in others, this power is exercised at the state level completing bypassing districts. In many states charters are subject to the same standards of assessment as all other schools in the state, but in others they are not. Taken together, a range of characteristics form what advocates refer to as strong or weak charter legislation.[6] Strong legislation is characterized by a law that allows or encourages the formation of a significant number of fairly autonomous charter schools in a given state. Autonomous charter schools enjoy a high level of relief from public school regulations. In other words, such regulations are waived for charter schools. Weak laws are those that produce few charter schools or charters that are not much different from existing public schools. Proponents of charters prefer strong laws whereas critics oppose all charter legislation, but they sometimes influence the formulation of weak laws as a political compromise.[7]

Rather than analyzing the implications of various aspects of state laws, or the veracity of claims put forward by proponents or critics of such laws, this chapter explores at a more general level the discourse surrounding charter reform. I am interested in identifying some "emancipatory promises" of charter schooling that have been squelched within current terms of the debate.[8] In the following section I outline a few of the most common arguments for and against charter legislation. Then, I suggest that the charter debate lacks careful attention to models for the organization and governance of public education that transcend strict dualisms between public versus private schools, or market-based versus bureaucratic institutions.

II. Common Arguments For and Against Charter Reform

Proponents of charter schooling stress a few key themes: choice, autonomy, innovation, and accountability. They argue that schools freed from the control of the existing public educational bureaucracy will be able to offer innovative methods of teaching and learning. The authors of

the 1997 Hudson Institute report *Charter Schools in Action*, for example, assert that "the charter concept is simple but powerful: *sound
school choices can be provided to families under the umbrella of public education without micromanagement by government bureaucracies*" [emphases in original].[9] Innovative choices that work will attract
parents and students. Because families will have choices, market competition and an entrepreneurial spirit will encourage change in other public
schools.

   These joint emphases led the authors of *Charter Schools in Action* to
refer to charter schools as "consumer-oriented institutions." According to
the report,

> Charter schools spring from the impulse to meet educational needs that are not
> now being fulfilled. They respond to frustrations, demands, and dreams that the
> regular system—for whatever reason—is not satisfying. In that sense, they are
> consumer-oriented, with their consumers including parents, voters, taxpayers,
> elected officials, employers, and other community representatives. This orienta-
> tion is the opposite of conventional public education, which is producer-oriented
> and inclined to take the interests of its employees more seriously than those of its
> customers.[10]

The report continues on to quote an assistant principal from Arizona
who says, "I see parents as my boss—and their children as my product."[11]
   The words used by the authors of this report are just one example of
the way in which advocates of charter schools draw heavily on the language of business and the marketplace. Such market-based rhetoric tends
to emphasize concepts such as customer satisfaction, competition,
entrepreneurialism, and the quality of educational products. Within this
framework charter supporters contend that accountability to the consumers of education will increase public school efficiency and effectiveness.[12]
   Opponents of charter schools, on the other hand, are concerned about
the impact of charters on the existing educational system. One primary
area of concern centers around the "ghettoization" of resources from
existing schools. Ghettoization refers to two types of resources: money
and students. First, critics worry that charters will siphon off much-needed
funds from existing public schools as per pupil expenditures follow students to charter schools. Second, some critics charge that charters will
skim off the "cream" of public school students. These critics draw upon
research findings like those published in the 1998 UCLA study to argue
that charter reform will not serve all families equally. This study's authors
reported that enrollment and recruitment practices, combined with other

requirements, give charters a greater amount of control over who attends the school than that exercised by traditional public schools. They concluded that such practices raise questions as to whether all families will have equal access to educational choices as a result of charter school reform. The concern regarding inequitable access due to the "creaming" of desirable parents and students gives rise to the related charges that charters will resegregate public schools and that traditional schools will be left to deal with the neediest and most challenging students.[13] Linking the two possible forms of ghettoization, skeptics fear that existing schools will be faced with the neediest student population but less money with which to serve them.

Another primary area of concern vocalized by opponents of charters is that of privatization. These types of arguments against charters include the claim that charter reform takes attention away from "real" reforms such as debates over nation- or state-wide standards; union concerns over wages and working conditions of teachers; and charges that charters are actually private schools that lack public accountability.[14] Rather than weigh the verity of specific arguments on either side of this debate, I would like to point out some negative implications of the stark polemic between proponents and opponents.

What's Missing from the Debate

In the debate over charter school reform, arguments on both sides tend either to overlook, downplay, or narrowly conceive our public interests in democratic education. What is lacking on each side of the charter school debate is careful attention to the complexity of balancing various public and private interests in education. While one side touts a model of privatized market relationships as a panacea for public education, the other side defends existing structures as if the status quo is *ipso facto* preferable to radical organizational change. Each side downplays weaknesses within its preferred model for representing specific educational interests.

For example, proponents' emphases on things like competition, innovation, and efficiency privileges certain types of *market goods* over *democratic public goods* that might also be served by charter schools. Charter schools may lead to efficient and effective schools, but can the "quality" these schools produce be held accountable to other public goods? Proponents of charters tend to stress goods such as *productivity* and *efficiency*, spurred by competition, rather than goods like *collective debate* within democratic decision-making processes.

Democratic governance is often not the most efficient form of decision making, but its processes are valued nevertheless because the constituencies served by public education share a common stake in educating future members of our society. The administrative control of superintendents, for instance, is balanced by the authority of appointed or elected school boards that represent the varied interests of parents, business, religious organizations, and other local constituencies.

Similarly, the market rhetoric surrounding charters conceptualizes parents and students as clients or consumers rather than as citizens of a democratic community.[15] Take, for example, the claim of the authors of the Hudson Institute report that charter schools are "consumer-oriented institutions." Consumer sovereignty certainly represents one form of power that accompanies market choices. But philosopher of education Kenneth Strike points out that this form of consumer power is constrained by the nature of market relationships. He explains,

> To be a client is to be someone who is consulted and considered in decision making and who may have some rights to informed consent, but it is also to be someone who is not a full participant in decision making. Thus, the relationship is . . . one of unequal status and power.[16]

Democratic citizens, on the other hand, participate in decision making as equals before the law. Thus, the democratic choice wielded by citizens is more egalitarian in nature than the consumer choice exercised by clients and customers.

These distinctions between characteristics of the public as market versus public as "civic community" are crucial for democratic societies. In a democracy, citizens participate in decision making about how to live together collectively. One question that democratic citizens face collectively surrounds education—how are future citizens to be educated? Accordingly, public education must be a democratic enterprise—adults must make decisions surrounding public education democratically, and students must be prepared to make democratic decisions in their future roles as citizens.

Opponents of charter schools move a bit beyond the market rhetoric of advocates in that they implicitly invoke democratic principles of fairness and equality when they express concerns surrounding the impact of charter schools on families and on the existing system. Such concerns may well be legitimate ones; more time and empirical evidence will indicate whether the predictions voiced by critics are valid. But aside from the actual outcomes of charter schooling, the implication of the critics' stance is that decentralization of control over public education is inherently anti-democratic. This message is sometimes even explicitly stated in assertions that charters are "anti-government" or "elitist."[17] This position implies two controversial, and disputable, assumptions: first, that only traditional bureaucratic governance of public schooling is democratic; and, second, that anti-democratic practices within specific charter schools are generalizable to the entire reform movement.

These assumptions, and ensuing political tactics relied on by opponents of charters, narrow public discourse surrounding the governance of public education to its current manifestation. What we have now is a system of public education governed by state legislatures, or other representative forms of government such as local school boards, that vector the various interests at stake through bargaining or voting, decide policy, and then call upon hierarchical, bureaucratic structures to implement their decisions.

Perhaps, however, neither the advocates nor the critics of charter schooling are recognizing a key aspect of the reform movement's potential. Perhaps neither the market nor a bureaucracy is the best structural model for balancing democratic interests in public education. As Strike contends, "[t]he primary choice is not between market and state. It is how we can have schools that are educative communities that serve both the public and private functions that schools need to serve."[18] One consequence of neglecting to consider seriously democratic aspects of charter reform has been a failure to recognize some potentials of charter schooling as an alternative structural model for balancing educational interests. At this point, I would like to highlight briefly some overlooked potentials posed by charter schooling and the implications of these potentials for democratic education.

III. Overlooked Potentialities of Charter Schooling

Traditional public schools are usually institutions that students are assigned to attend based upon geographic proximity. Geographic assignment is intended to bring students from various social and cultural backgrounds together within a "common school." In the interests of state neutrality and educational equality, these schools then attempt to remain neutral toward students' various backgrounds and traditions by stressing a common American identity. In addition, authority over educational decision making is divided between the state and local bodies such as school boards, administrators, and teachers. Accordingly, the system tends to be both hierarchical and bureaucratic (see table 1.1).

Table 1.1 Traditional versus Charter Schools

	Traditional Schools	**Charter Schools**
Organization	Assignment	Choice
Basis for Association	Geographic	Common Interest
Mission	Neutral	Particularistic
Governance	Bureaucratic, Hierarchical	Autonomous, Local (School-level)

Each of these characteristics—geographic assignment, neutrality, and bureaucratic control—arguably serves some public good. The ideal of public education traditionally has been the common school where diverse groups of students are imbued with shared democratic values, such as tolerance for one another. Schools composed of diverse student populations are viewed as necessary for cultivating inter-group understanding, and preparing students, as Kenneth Clark puts it, to "interact constructively with their fellow human beings."[19] Geography-based school districts are also seen as a way to avoid Madisonian fears of political factionalism. Regional districts, like those created for voting purposes, are professed to ensure public institutions mediated by diverse interests and a concern for the common good.[20]

Neutrality, as many modern liberals argue, is the appropriate stance for state-sponsored public education because it is the only way to ensure that no single value orientation is privileged over another. The neutrality, or impartiality, of public schools is intended to represent equally the interests of all families and students. Impartial policies are arrived at through representative democratic structures, such as state legislatures or elected school boards. Strike explains that educational bureaucracies, then, "exist to implement democratically achieved policy. Such bureaucracies express the location of political sovereignty in legislatures."[21] In sum, a few of the public goods represented in the traditional structure of public schooling include protection against political factionalism, promotion of democratic values such as tolerance, equal protection of educational interests through neutrality, and legitimate structures for the expression of political sovereignty.

Although the present system attempts to fulfill public interests in the ways described above, there may also be negative consequences that flow from its organizational structure. Key characteristics of traditional schools can be usefully analyzed through a sociological model offered by the German sociologist Tönnies in the late 1800s. Tönnies employed the terms

Table 1.2 A Continuum of Socio-Political Relationships

Gesellschaft——————————————————————Gemeinschaft	
Contractual——————————————————————Communal	
Loose——————————————————————————Tight	
Thin———————————————————————————Thick	

gemeinschaft and *gesellschaft*. *Gemeinschaft* refers to *informal, collective relationships associated with community* whereas *gesellschaft* refers to more *formal, contractual institutional relationships.* Traditional public schools are primarily organized according to *gesellschaft*-type relationships (see table 1.2).

Some sociologists claim that *gesellschaft's* formal, contractual relationships produce negative consequences, particularly alienation and isolation, which arise at multiple social levels.[22] In this analysis, schools are but one set of social institutions—among those of religion, family, medicine, and government—all of which are struggling to maintain a satisfied constituency within the turmoil of our late twentieth century "disenchantment with modernity."[23] The current "crisis" in public education, then, is not a problem endemic to education, but a symptom of broader social discontent and a deep sense of alienation from virtually all social institutions.

Yet symptoms of alienation within public education do take on specific forms. One type of alienation comes in the form of exclusion from or marginalization within educational institutions. This type of alienation is suggested by the demands of cultural groups for greater representation within public school curricula.[24] Alienated groups call for ameliorative responses ranging from multicultural curricula, to the creation of Afrocentric schools, to separate math classes for girls. These demands are based at least in part upon a sense of exclusion from what is presented as "mainstream" approaches to knowledge and learning. Some theorists blame the liberal ideal of neutrality that undergirds contractual relationships for excluding and silencing certain groups.[25] They charge that what is defined as neutral or common tends to privilege the identities, perspectives, knowledge, and modes of discourse of dominant social groups. Consequently, the interests of non-dominant groups are not equally protected by a regulative norm of neutrality, but rather are marginalized and oppressed.

Additional symptoms of alienation from public schools may also stem from contractual relationships within bureaucratic institutions.

Disproportionately high numbers of students from marginalized social groups perform poorly in public schools and/or drop out.[26] In this manner, certain social groups are not only conceptually, but physically excluded from traditional schools. Thomas Sergiovanni argues that membership in gangs is another indication of teens searching for meaningful relationships that they are not finding within institutions like the family and schools. He cites gang membership as evidence that where there is a lack of functional communities, dysfunctional communities arise to take their place.[27] In addition, other critics assert that the bureaucratization of public schooling, particularly in the past twenty years, has "fostered student passivity and teacher alienation."[28]

Low achievement, dropping out, joining a gang, student passivity—these may all be symptoms of alienation from schools characterized by neutral, contractual, bureaucratic relationships that exclude students from, rather than integrate them into, the public education system. Some education reformers interpret these trends as evidence that public schools have become "solidly ensconced in the *gesellschaft* camp with unhappy results."[29] They urge the creation of more *gemeinschaft*-type relationships in schools to counter widespread alienation and dislocation within American society by providing youth with a sense of belonging within school communities (see table 1.2).

One particular strand of research into the effects of "schools as communities" focuses on the differences between Catholic schools and traditional public schools. This research indicates that school communities promote not only a sense of belonging, but educational equity across diverse social groups. James Coleman and colleagues initially introduced a "common school hypothesis" that "Catholic schools as a group were advancing greater educational equity" in the early 1980s. From this hypothesis, Coleman and Thomas Hoffer, as well as Anthony Bryk with a second research team, began to explore the impact of Catholic schools as communities on academic achievement.[30] Bryk and his colleagues concluded not only that achievement levels were higher for all students in Catholic schools, but that achievement was also distributed more equally across social groups within Catholic schools.[31] In addition, they found that drop-out rates were lower by one-quarter in Catholic schools as opposed to public schools (p. 272).

As a result of these findings, Bryk et al. espoused the "idea of a school as a 'voluntary community' . . . to serve current school improvement efforts, particularly for the disadvantaged (p. 312–13)." They stressed three key features of a school as a voluntary community. First, daily life in the school is structured by a "communal organization." Second, the school must possess "a relatively high degree of autonomy in managing its affairs . . . because much of the rationale for activity within a communal organization relies on traditions and local judgments." And, third, membership in the community is marked by the voluntary nature of the association and the idea that participation is "not an inalienable right. . . . Students who seriously or chronically violate the community's norms must leave" (p. 313).

Charter schools have the potential to embody each of these features. Accordingly, charters offer a possible corrective to some negative consequences of public education's current organizational structure (see table 1.1). Unlike traditional schools, charter schools are not "common" in that they do not attempt to serve all families and students. Instead, they are each based upon unique missions and encourage innovative approaches to teaching and learning. In addition, charters propose to replace a neutral one-size-fits-all approach to public education with particularistic approaches intended to meet the diverse needs of students. Charter schools are also based upon specific common interests that people associate around due to shared educational philosophies and/or values. In this sense, because they are based upon common interests in particular values or philosphies, charters may be more amenable to communal organization than are traditionally organized public schools.

Two quite different charter schools in Massachusetts, for example, illustrate the particularity of missions in individual schools. The Renaissance Charter School highly values technology whereas the Benjamin Franklin Charter School stresses virtues including honesty, moderation, and humility. Members of each school share a common interest in associating with one another based upon this educational mission. Moreover, because these charters each represents particularistic values they increase the types of schools available to students and families. In other words, they *pluralize* public education. Within this pluralized sphere people who are attracted to particular goals or values may then choose to affiliate with a certain school. Families, students, and educators come together to pursue a common mission by choice. In these respects, charter schools are particularistic and voluntaristic associations; these features increase the likelihood that charter schools will embody the features of school communities.

The potential of charters to foster a pluralized public educational sphere composed of particularistic, voluntaristic associations suggests a movement away from *gesellschaft* toward *gemeinschaft* (see table 1.2). Because charter schools share a common mission and are autonomously governed locally, often at the building level, they seem more amenable to the informal, collective relationships of *gemeinschaft* than do traditional schools. Charter schools embody at least two of the structural features Bryk et al. identified as crucial to the idea of voluntary communities: autonomy and voluntaristic membership. They also have the potential to embody the third feature of communal organization. Thus, charters combine structural with valuational features of school communities.

To the extent that charters foster pluralized school communities more closely approximating a *gemeinschaft* or voluntary community model, some alternative consequences to exclusion and alienation become apparent. And these potential consequences have implications for each of three aspects of democratic education—distribution, governance, and civic education.[32]

Implications of Charter Schooling for Democratic Education

As I discussed in the introduction to this book, citizens in a democratic society share a collective stake, or a public interest, in the education of future generations. Amy Gutmann refers to such interests in their broadest form as a collective interest in "conscious social reproduction." This concept includes not only "practices of deliberate instruction" intended to prepare young people for future citizenship, but also the "educative influences of institutions designed at least partly for educational purposes."[33] I am interested in investigating the potential of charter schools to fulfill our public interests in conscious social reproduction through the educative influences of their distribution and governance practices, as well as their practices of deliberate instruction of the realm of civic education.

In terms of *distribution*, critics of charter reform worry that educational opportunities for the neediest segments of the school population will be constrained as students are left behind in traditional schools with fewer fiscal resources. Although empirical data is still slim, the effect of charters on access to educational opportunities may be the opposite. First, the "schools as communities" research suggests that to the extent that specific charter schools are like communities, they will equalize outcomes across social groups. This literature indicates that strong school communities promote a sense of belonging and equalize academic success across a wide range of students.[34]

Second, because charters are particularistic, they are more likely to embody and foster the diversity of ideals that families and communities wish to transmit to their children.[35] Charters are places where the diverse values and educational philosophies of families and social groups can be institutionally represented. Increased representation is particularly significant for historically marginalized groups. A number of new charter schools in various states, for instance, are targeted toward African American history and culture, or simply promoting the academic success of African American students. Due to this mission, most of the students enrolled in these schools are African American students, many of whom previously attended other public schools. Within a pluralized sphere of charter schools, low-income families and culturally marginalized groups are presented with educational opportunities that previously were available only by purchasing them within the private sector. Thus, conjoined with the voluntaristic nature of charters, their particularism fosters representation for heretofore underrepresented groups.

In this manner, charter schools have the potential to *expand* and *equalize* choice options for all families within the sphere of public education. In addition to simply increasing the number of public schools available for families to choose from, charters also expand the types of choices. To the extent that charters make additional choice options available to a broader range of students—especially those from alienated and marginalized families—and increase the distribution of certain educational goods—such as a sense of belonging and academic success—they may transform public education into a more inclusive and egalitarian endeavor.[36]

As we consider these democratizing potentials of charter schools, however, we must also beware of some anti-democratic potentials of school relationships characterized at the *gemeinschaft* side of the spectrum (see table 1.2). Nel Noddings warns of a "dark side" of community.[37] For a community to be a community it must be somewhat tightly-knit, either around a common set of beliefs and values, or perhaps even a shared sense of identity. Because of this emphasis on what is shared or held in common, communities are prone to either excluding individuals and groups who do not subscribe to their vision or assimilating them to shared norms. In these ways, communities can be particularly homogenizing—Noddings refers to this as "homologizing"—whereby plurality and individuality are undermined.

It is not immediately clear that the homogenizing aspects of community represent a dark side for charter schooling. First, James Coleman suggests that if students are in a school that can by characterized as a "valuational community" by choice "it is less likely to be oppressive than a school serving a traditional value community based on [geography]."[38] Second, the exclusionary or assimilating tendencies of community are problematic for charter schools because they are "public" and subject to democratic norms. But in the case of charters as *multiple publics*, students may be excluded from one school because of a poor match with its mission but included in another; this is the point of rejecting a one-size-fits-all notion of public education. The important question becomes: on what grounds is exclusion from a particular school legitimate or not? If a charter school represents the educational interests of certain social groups, does that mean that it can exclude members of other groups? And, if so, on what grounds? A normative theory of democratic public life will help us to respond to these questions in a principled fashion.

Next, in terms of implications of charter schooling for educational *governance*, the autonomy and "private" character of charter school management raise questions surrounding democratic sovereignty, public authority, and accountability. A move away from bureaucracy is not necessarily a democratic move. Strike reminds us that "[w]hen [we seek] autonomy from bureaucratic control . . . we need to remember that we are also seeking autonomy from legislative authority."[39] This raises the question of where public authority over education is to derive from if not from legislative bodies? In addition, to the extent that each charter school is independent from direct administrative oversight, how can the school be held accountable for what and how much students learn?

Charter school advocates insist that accountability is ensured in at least two ways. First, parental choice dictates that unsuccessful schools will not be able to maintain a student population; parents will simply choose to send their children to another school. Second, the sponsoring agency can revoke or refuse to renew the charter of a school that is not performing. But in addition to these two forms of accountability—parental choice and bureaucratic oversight—charters are accountable to public interests in another way. As public institutions, charters are not *autonomous from public oversight*. Instead, charters are *autonomous publics where accountability is localized* rather than bureaucratized.

Perhaps rather than conceiving of charters as private or anti-democratic, they might be viewed as public institutions subject to localized forms of fairly autonomous democratic governance. Charter schools should be thought of as public institutions subject to norms of democratic governance just as traditional school districts are subject to such norms. In the latter case, these norms generally take the form of elected or appointed school boards; in the case of charter schools, these norms might be more usefully thought of in terms of face-to-face deliberations among a group of citizens who have come together to pursue educational issues of common concern.

Charters are in a strong position to successfully replace representative governance with direct democratic forums because they offer conditions amenable to face-to-face democratic decision making. The shared values of valuational communities heighten the likelihood that consensual decisions could be reached through processes of face-to-face deliberation. Some skeptics have overlooked this potential and expressed concern that charter school governance limits public participation in educational decision making. Heather Voke, for example, argues that charter schools "appear to *restrict* free public deliberation about matters of mutual concern. Unlike traditional public schools, which are open to public deliberation, charter schools are largely insulated from public deliberation and control" [emphasis in original].[40]

One could argue, however, that charter schools are not excluding the public from decision making. Rather, charter schools have the potential for *inclusive decision making.* According to the traditional, bureaucratic model of public school governance, the bulk of decision making is under the purview of elected officials (e.g., state legislators and school board members), administrators, and union representatives. With charter schools, groups of parents, teachers, and community members found and subsequently govern the schools. Thus, previously excluded groups who are not necessarily public officials but simply citizens, nor educational bureaucrats, but nevertheless professionals, are often included in the decision making structures and processes of charter schools. Through such processes the autonomous, localized democratic governance of charter schools may actually encourage public discourse and civic participation among students and adults alike.[41]

Finally, in terms of *civic education*, charter schools offer the potential that vibrant, local associations—associations that share a common mission and that encourage inclusive participation in democratic decision making—might be better places in which to cultivate citizenship than are traditional public schools. In light of this potential, and the others outlined above, charters raise an interesting set of questions for the democratic ideal of "conscious social reproduction." What types of educative influences flow from the structural model of charters that may influence civic education? For instance, might particularistic communities threaten democratic values such as tolerance and respect for diversity of opinions? How might such distinct school communities imbue shared values of democratic citizenship? Again, a theory of democratic public life in our complex pluralistic society will help us to answer some of these questions by providing norms to assess the extent to which particular charter schools and the movement in general are fulfilling their democratizing potentials.

IV. Conclusion

Charter schools offer some potential goods and some potential dangers in terms of fulfilling our public interests in education in new and innovative ways. My emphases on the democratizing aspects of expanded and equalized choice, inclusive decision making, and localized accountability highlight some overlooked potentials within the reform movement. Moreover, the organizational structure of charters might encourage a sense of belonging to replace alienation; institutional inclusion rather than exclusion, especially for historically marginalized groups; and increased civic participation and public discourse surrounding our common educational interests.

But the very notion of *potential* suggests that these prospects may not be realized. The organizational features of charter schools also pose potential tradeoffs. The vast majority of charter schools are not concerned largely with civic education. Nor are all, or even most, charter schools more democratic than their neighboring traditional public schools. Expanded choice among distinct schools may serve to segregate or factionalize public school populations. Decision making *among* schools may be inclusive of frequently marginalized groups. But decision making *within* schools will not necessarily be inclusive. And autonomous school communities might be difficult to hold accountable to public interests.

Each of these issues calls for careful attention to the role that charter schools should play in public education reform. Charter school reform raises all sorts of normative questions about *plurality, autonomy,* and *community* within the public educational sphere. In order to decide whether we are "for" or "against" charter schools, we need to consider carefully: Is a pluralized sphere of distinct and autonomous school communities something we might want to cultivate? And if so, under what conditions?

In this book I take advantage of the opportunity charter schooling offers to 1) envision an idealized model of democratic public life in our complex, pluralistic society, and 2) formulate concrete ways to institutionalize this ideal in the structures and practices of charter schools. Unlike scholars of education reform who are skeptical of charter schools' capacity to serve public interests—largely because they view charters as a market-based reform that is likely to sharpen social divisions, including inequality between the rich and poor—I am interested in exploring how the unique potentials of charter schools to fulfill public interests can be realized.[42] Therefore, I proceed by asking: How can we maximize the potential goods while minimizing the potential dangers of charter school communities?

To begin answering this question, I draw on a normative political theory in the next chapter to inform what charter schools as local democratic associations *ought* to be like. Normative political theory is useful in this context because it provides us with relevant norms or standards for making principled decisions as to whether charter schools are fulfilling public interests. I specifically turn to deliberative democratic theory because it informs how we might reach collective agreements about public education that are equally in the interests of all. In addition, deliberative theory offers a participatory vision of democratic politics and a model of "associative democracy" that closely correspond to the social realities and institutional arrangements of charter schooling. Finally, the theory and its models provide an evaluative framework with which to assess the legitimacy, and hence, desirability, of charter schools as public educational institutions.[43]

After laying out a normative framework for deliberative democratic politics, I translate the theoretical model into requirements for civic education. The unique institutional features of charter schools both foster and constrain the potential for charters to fulfill public interests in preparing future democratic citizens. So, finally, I embark on a case study of Winthrop Academy to inform the trials and successes of institutionalizing the deliberative model of democratic public life through charter schooling.

Notes

1. Peter Cookson, *School Choice and The Struggle for the Soul of American Education* (New Haven: Yale University Press, 1994), 14.

2. For a more thorough treatment of school choice in general, see Peter Cookson, ed., *The Choice Controversy* (Newbury Park, CA: Corwin Press, 1992); Amy Stuart Wells, *Time to Choose: America at the Crossroads of School Choice Policy*. (NY: Hill and Wang, 1993); Cookson, *School Choice*; Jeffrey Henig, *Rethinking School Choice: Limits of the Market Metaphor* (Princeton: Princeton University Press, 1994); and Bruce Fuller and Richard F. Elmore, eds. with Gary Orfield, *Who Chooses? Who Loses?: Culture, Institutions, and the Unequal Effects of School Choice* (New York: Teachers College Press, 1996).

3. States with charter laws as of July, 1999 include Arizona (1994), Alaska (1995), Arkansas (1995), California (1992), Colorado (1993), Connecticut (1996), Delaware (1995), Florida (1996), Georgia (1993), Hawaii (1994), Idaho (1998), Illinois (1996), Kansas (1994), Louisiana (1995), Massachusetts (1993), Michigan (1993), Minnesota (1991), Mississippi (1997), Missouri (1998), Nevada (1997), New Hampshire (1995), New Jersey (1996), New Mexico (1993), New York (1998), North Carolina (1996), Ohio (1997), Oklahoma (1999), Oregon (1999), Pennsylvania (1997), Rhode Island (1995), South Carolina (1996), Texas (1995), Utah (1998), Virginia (1998), Wisconsin (1993), and Wyoming (1995). The District of Columbia passed charter legislation in 1996. For current information see *Charter School Highlights and Statistics* compiled by The Center for Education Reform, Washington D.C. (http://www.edreform.com/pubs/chglance.htm).

4. Angela Dale, ed., *National Charter School Directory 1998–1999* (Washington, D.C.: The Center for Education Reform, 1999), 1.

5. For helpful definitions of charter schools and the essential elements of charter school reform, see Ted Kolderie, "Chartering Diversity," *Equity and Choice* 9, no. 1 (1992): 28–31; Cookson, *School Choice*, 15; and Joe Nathan, *Charter Schools: Creating Hope and Opportunity for American Education* (San Francisco: Jossey-Bass, 1996).

6. Charters differ in many respects including, but not limited to, legal status, funding structure, method of payment, assessment or reporting requirements, teacher certification, sponsoring agency, admissions requirements, cap on number of charter schools in the state, cap on number of students attending charter schools, and length of charter. Because this book highlights the experiences of one charter school in Massachusetts, I have included the state's original charter school legislation in appendix A. According to this legislation, charter schools in Massachusetts are distinct legal entities, funded according to a per pupil expenditure formula, subject to lottery-based admissions and statewide assessments, exempt from teacher certification requirements, and sponsored by the state's Department of Education. The length of a charter is five years.

For more detailed discussion of differences between charter school laws from state to state and the implications of these differences, see Donna Harrington-Lueker, "Charter Schools," *The American School Board Journal* 181, no. 9 (1994): 22–26; Priscilla Wohlstetter, Richard Wenning, and Kerri L. Briggs, "Charter Schools in the United States: The Question of Autonomy," *Educational Policy,* 9, no. 4 (December 1995): 331–58; Mark Buechler, *Charter Schools: Legislation and Results After Four Years* (Bloomington, IN: Indiana Education Policy Center, 1996); Ted Kolderie, *A Guide to Charter Activity* (St. Paul, MN: Center for Policy Studies, 1996); Nathan, *Charter Schools,* Chester E. Finn Jr., Bruno V. Manno, Louann A. Bierlein, and Gregg Vanourek, *Charter Schools in Action: Final Report* (Washington D.C.: Hudson Institute, 1997); and Bryan C. Hassel, *The Charter School Challenge* (Washington, D.C.: Brookings Institution Press, 1999).

7. Charter school advocate Ted Kolderie offers a "Model Charter School Law" that is intended as a template for state charter school legislation. Kolderie recommends that charter school legislation offer a "superwaiver" for regulatory relief from "rules" governing other public schools. For a full draft of this law, see appendix B in this book or Nathan, 203–18. In Massachusetts, charter schools enjoy regulatory relief from district-level requirements such as those put forward by the local school committee or unions. Charter schools, however, are not exempt from state-level regulations. This means that charters are autonomous in the areas of budget and hiring, for example, but remain subject to health and safety requirements, special education regulations, and state assessments, among other things (see appendix A for the Massachusetts legislation). Such restrictions on charter schools result in Massachusetts legislation falling in the category of "strong to medium" versus "weak" laws according to the Center for Education Reform's *Charter School Highlights and Statistics.* For further discussion of "strong" versus "weak" charter school legislation see Kolderie, *A Guide to Charter Activity* and Finn et al., *Charter Schools in Action: Final Report.* For an in-depth look at the relationship between political comprises, ensuing charter school legislation, and the implementation of charter school programs, see Hassel, 1999.

8. I am drawing the phrase "emancipatory promises" from Amy Stuart Wells, Alejandra Lopez, Janelle Scott, and Jennifer Jellison Holme in "Charter Schools as Postmodern Paradox: Rethinking Social Stratification in an Age of Deregulated School Choice," *Harvard Educational Review* 69 (1999): 172–204. They are skeptical that such promises will be realized within the age of postmodern global inequalities whereas I am interested in considering how we might maximize the potential of emancipatory promises within the charter movement.

9. Brunno V. Manno, Chester E. Finn, Jr., Louann A. Bierlein, and Gregg Vanourek, "How Charter Schools are Different: Lessons and Implications from a National Study," *Phi Delta Kappan* 79 (1998): 490.

10. Finn et al., *Charter Schools in Action: Final Report,* Part VI and Manno et al., 497.

11. Finn et al., *Charter Schools in Action: Final Report,* Part VI.

12. Some advocates also see charter reform as a decentralized, grass-roots initiative that will allow the public education system to be more dynamic and adaptive to the multifarious needs of students and their families. Tony Wagner, for example, contends that the primary mission for charters is to undertake educational research and development. See "Why Charter Schools?" *New Schools, New Communities* 11, no. 1 (1994): 7–9. But I find that market-based rhetoric is much more prevalent than the defense of charter innovations as educational research and development.

For additional specific examples of common arguments advanced by charter supporters, see Louann Bierlein and Lori Mulholland, "The Promise of Charter Schools," *Educational Leadership* 52(1) (September, 1994): 34–40; Harrington-Lueker, "Charter Schools"; Michael Mandel, "Will Schools Ever Get Better?" *Business Week*, (April 17, 1995): 64–68; Wohlstetter et al., "Charter Schools in the United States: The Question of Autonomy"; Joe Nathan and Jennifer Power, *Policymakers' Views on the Charter School Movement* (University of Minnesota: Center for School Change, Hubert H. Humphrey Institute of Public Affairs, 1996); Nathan, *Charter Schools*; Finn et al., *Charter Schools in Action: Final Report*; Thomas Toch, "Education Bazaar," *U.S. News & World Report*, 27 April 1998, 35–46; Gregg Garn, "The Thinking Behind Arizona's Charter Movement," *Educational Leadership* 56, no. 2 (1998): 48–50; and June Kronholz, "Charter Schools Begin to Prod Public Schools Toward Competition," *The Wall St. Journal*, 12 February 1999, A1 & A8.

Since my case study research took place in Massachusetts, I am most familiar with arguments specific to that state's legislation (see appendix A). Common arguments in favor of charters in Massachusetts were drawn in part from Steven F. Wilson, *Reinventing the Schools: A Radical Plan for Boston* (Boston: Pioneer Institute for Public Policy Research, 1992). They can also be found in Commonwealth of Massachusetts, *Charter School Application* (Boston: Executive Office of Education, 1995); *The Massachusetts Charter School Handbook* (Boston: Pioneer Institute for Public Policy Research, 1995); and Commonwealth of Massachusetts, *The Massachusetts Charter School Initiative 1996 Report* (Boston: Massachusetts Department of Education, 1997).

13. See Amy Stuart Wells, *Beyond the Rhetoric of Charter School Reform: A Study of Ten California School Districts* (UCLA: UCLA Charter School Study, 1998), especially findings #9 and #10. For similar concerns see Frank Margonis and Laurence Parker, "Choice, Privatization, and Unspoken Strategies of Containment," *Educational Policy* 9 (1995): 375–403 and Fuller and Elmore, eds., *Who Chooses? Who Loses?*

There is, however, other emerging evidence that charter schools are serving a disproportionately high number of "at-risk" and minority students as compared to traditional public schools. Based upon their findings and a report published by the U.S. Department of Education, Finn et al. assert that "One might suppose that the 'creaming' allegation could now be laid to rest. Put simply, a third of public school students nationally are minorities, while half of charter school students nationally are minorities." See Finn et al., *Charter Schools in Action: Final Report,* Part I; RPP International, *A Study of Charter Schools: First-year Report* (Washington, DC: U.S. Department of Education, 1997); and, for statistics particular to Massachusetts, Kate Zernike, "Study Rebuts Fears About Demographics at Charter Schools," *The Boston Globe* 17 July 1996, A1 & A13. Other studies indicate that charters are at least serving "a broad cross-section of students: gifted, low achievers, low income, limited English proficient, and minority students." See Lori A. Mulholland, *Charter Schools: The Research*, Policy Brief (Tempe, AZ: Morrison Institute for Public Policy, 1996). But there is also evidence that special education students are not being served equitably by charter schools; the RPP International study cited above reported that charter schools are serving fewer special education students than are traditional public schools.

14. For further elucidation of concerns surrounding privatization and lack of public accountability, see Henry Giroux, "The Business of Public Education," *Z Magazine*, July-August 1998; Richard Rothstein, "Charter Conundrum," *The American Prospect* no. 39 (1998): 46–60; and Terry Geske, Douglas Davis, and Patricia Hingle, "Charter Schools: A Viable Public School Choice Option?" *Economics of Education Review* 16, no. 1 (1997): 15–23. For a discussion of the tensions between charter schooling and standards-based reform efforts, see Evans Clinchy, "The Educationally Challenged American School District," *Phi Delta Kappan* 80 (1998): 272–77. For a sense of union concerns regarding charter schools in Massachusetts, see Meline Kasparian, "Reshape Charter Schools," *MTA Today,* 4 February 1997, 4–5 ("MTA" is the acronym for the Massachusetts Teachers Association, the state branch of the National Teachers Association).

15. This charge is leveled at school choice in general and restructuring efforts respectively in David Tyack, "Can We Build a System of Choice That Is Not Just a 'Sorting Machine' or a Market-Based 'Free-for-All'?" *Equity and Choice* 9, no. 1 (1992): 13–17 and Kenneth A. Strike, "Professionalism, Democracy, and Discursive Communities: Normative Reflections on Restructuring," *American Educational Research Journal* 30, no. 2 (1993): 255–75.

16. Strike, "Professionalism, Democracy, and Discursive Communities," 261.

17. See Nathan, 93–118. This concern is articulated a bit differently, and in a more complex fashion, by Elaine Halchin who views charter schools as a move toward institutionalizing education as a "private good." Although I share her concern about the preponderance of a market-based approach to charters that encourages such a shift, I think that she is overlooking the possibility that charter reform promotes alternative ways of institutionalizing education as a "public good." See Elaine Halchin "And This Parent Went to Market: Education as Public versus Private Good," in *School Choice in the Real World: Lessons from Arizona Charter Schools*, eds. Robert Maranto et al. (Boulder: Westview Press, 1999).

18. Kenneth Strike, "Centralized Goal Formation and Systemic Reform: Reflections on Liberty, Localism and Pluralism," *Education Policy Analysis Archives* 5, no. 11 (1997): next to last paragraph [journal online], accessed 18 May 1998 from http://olam.ed.asu.edu/epaa/v5n11.html.

19. Kenneth B. Clark, "The *Brown* Decision: Racism, Education, and Human Values," *Journal of Negro Education* 57 (no. 2 (1988): 129–130; see also Amy

Gutmann, *Democratic Education* (Princeton: Princeton University Press, 1987), 162.

20. Madison warns against factionalism in "*Federalist* No. 10," (see *Dogmas and Dreams: Political Ideologies in the Modern World*, ed. Nancy S. Love (Chatham, NJ: Chatham House Publishers, 1991), 59–65). He advocates a democratic republic of representative governance over the face-to-face decisionmaking of "pure democracy" to guard against the "mischiefs of faction."

21. Strike, "Professionalism, Democracy, and Discursive Communities," 257.

22. See Robert N. Bellah et al., *Habits of the Heart: Individualism and Commitment in American Life* (Berkeley and Los Angeles: University of California Press, 1985) and Thomas Sergiovanni, *Building Community in Schools,* (San Francisco: Jossey-Bass, 1994).

23. Seyla Benhabib borrows the phrase "disenchantment with modernity" from Max Weber in her *Situating the Self: Gender, Community and Postmodernism in Contemporary Ethics* (New York: Routledge, 1992), 68.

24. Such debates over cultural representation have been rampant in the efforts to create statewide Social Studies standards in California, New York, and Massachusetts, among other states. See Carol Cornbleth and Dexter Waugh, *The Great Speckled Bird: Multicultural Politics and Education Policymaking* (New York: St. Martin's Press, 1995) and Robert K. Fullinwider, ed., *Public Education in a Multicultural Society: Policy, Theory, and Critique* (New York: Cambridge University Press, 1996).

25. For a discussion of the inadequacies of liberal neutrality, see Benhabib, *Situating the Self* and Iris Marion Young, *Justice and the Politics of Difference* (Princeton: Princeton University Press, 1990).

26. Anthony Bryk, Valerie E. Lee, and Peter B. Holland, *Catholic Schools and the Common Good* (Cambridge, MA: Harvard University Press, 1993), 273.

27. Sergiovanni, xii–xiv.

28. Bryk et al., 290.

29. Sergiovanni, 5–14. Also see Bryk et al., 290 and Nel Noddings, "On Community," *Educational Theory* 46, no. 3 (Summer 1996): 245–67. The *gemeinschaft/gesellschaft* distinction roughly corresponds to Coleman and Hoffer's two orientations to schooling. The first orientation stresses individual mobility, the stripping away of social origins, and implanting a common American identity. The second orientation views the school as an extension of family and community and as an institution for transmitting the community's culture. See James S. Coleman and Thomas Hoffer, *Public and Private High Schools* (New York: Basic Books, 1987), 3–27.

30. See Coleman and Hoffer, *Public and Private High Schools* and Bryk et al., *Catholic Schools and the Common Good.* Bryk et al. undertook their study in

response to the "common school hypothesis" put forward in James Coleman, Thomas Hoffer, and S. Kilgore, *Public and Private Schools* (Washington, D.C.: US Department of Education, 1981).

31. Specifically, they found that "variation in student achievement is less strongly related to social class or racial background" in Catholic versus public schools. Bryk et al., 246–248. Subsequent page references in the text are to this essay.

32. It is important to note that much of the "schools as communities" research relates academic success with the organizational or structural features of community. One of my goals is to consider more carefully the interrelationship between structural and valuational features of community within charter schools. Attention to values is important for at least two reasons. First, the types of valuational communities promoted within charters is a tricky question because they are *public* schools. It seems clear, for instance, that a charter might be denied to a proposed Nazi school. Second, closer attention to values is merited because this aspect of school communities has not received much attention thus far in the literature. Both Bryk et al. and Strike call for greater attention to the "actual content of the values" in schools and their role as a kind of "social glue" that binds communities. See Bryk et al., 312 and Kenneth A. Strike, "The Moral Role of Schooling in a Liberal Democratic Society," in *Review of Research in Education* 17 (1991): 470.

33. Gutmann, 14.

34. See Coleman and Hoffer, *Public and Private High Schools* and Bryk et al., *Catholic Schools and the Common Good.*

35. In this respect charters might represent Coleman and Hoffer's "second orientation" to schooling, see note #29.

36. These goods pertain to students and families. In addition, charters offer professional opportunities for teachers including chances to try innovative methods and to take on management roles. These sorts of opportunities for control over one's work, combined with communal attributes, may increase teachers' sense of efficacy and morale. For a discussion of this, see Bryk et al., 276–88.

37. Noddings, "On Community."

38. Coleman and Hoffer, 13.

39. Strike, "Professionalism, Democracy, and Discursive Communities," 257.

40. Heather Voke, "Charter Schools: Particularistic, Pluralistic, and Participatory?" in *Philosophy of Education 1998*, ed. Steve Tozer (Urbana, IL: University of Illinois at Urbana-Champaign, 1999), 142.

41. My emphasis on stakeholders as citizens and/or professionals is adapted from Strike's discussion of teacher professionalism and schools as local democratic communities in "Professionalism, Democracy, and Discursive Communities." For an interesting discussion of possible links between the institutional arrangement of charter schooling and increased forms of "social capital," such as civic capacity,

see Mark Schneider, Paul Teske, Melissa Marschall, Michael Mintrom, and Christine Roth, "Institutional Arrangements and the Creation of Social Capital: The Effects of Public School Choice," *American Political Science Review* 91, no. 1 (1997): 82–93.

42. Among other skeptics of charter school reform, I am referring here specifically to Alex Molnar and Amy Stuart Wells and her colleagues at UCLA. Molnar characterizes charter schools as a "market-based" reform and charges that the market will continue to efficiently "dismantle the civic infrastructure necessary to sustain the kind of voluntary organizations that are the hallmark of a healthy civil society." I, on the other hand, am interested in the potential of charters as "multiple publics" to enhance the number and quality of such voluntary organizations, and thereby spur the creation of a vibrant public educational realm of civil society. See Alex Molnar, "Why School Reform Is Not Enough to Mend Our Civil Society," *Educational Leadership* (February 1997): 37–39. Like Wells et al., I am interested in "exploring both the potential and inherent danger of charter school reform from an equity perspective." Wells et al., "Charter Schools as Postmodern Paradox," 175. But whereas Wells and her colleagues seem to identify more concerns with charter reform than liberatory possibilities, I am less pessimistic. I argue that the normative standards provided by deliberative democratic theory could serve to heighten the likelihood that the liberatory potentials of charter reform will outweigh anti-democratic concerns.

43. For additional scholarship linking deliberative democracy with charter schooling, see Michael Mintrom, "Local Organizations as Sites for Deliberative Democracy: Learning from Charter Schools," presented at the Annual Meeting of the American Political Science Association, Boston, Massachusetts, September, 1998.

Chapter 2

Democratic Politics and Charter Schooling: A Deliberative Conception

I. Democracy, Community, and Pluralism

In order to consider the desirability of charter schools as local democratic associations that foster a sense of community among students, this chapter theorizes a viable normative model of democratic public life amidst social complexity and pluralism. A normative model of democratic politics informs both whether charter schools are serving public interests in educational distribution and governance as well as interests in the civic preparation of future citizens. After defending deliberative democratic theory as the normative model most capable of navigating social complexity and pluralism, I consider what the theory implies for public charter schools.

Democratic societies seek a form of governance, by, for, and of the people. This succinct phrase captures the essential questions of democracy: by what processes will democratic decisions be made? how can citizens ensure that decisions are for them, or in their interests? and who constitutes the people? Theories of democratic legitimacy posit that decisions made among a polity of free and equal citizens, regarding issues of collective concern, and in the common interest of all are fair and binding.[1] Decision-making processes are fair if they include all affected parties and treat them equally; outcomes are fair if they represent common interests. Thus, normative democratic theory offers principles of equality, the common good, and inclusion with which to evaluate the descriptive definition of democracy as by, for, and of the people.

But this normative answer is not clear cut, and its simplicity belies a plethora of underlying social complexities. Differences between individuals, social groups, and autonomous organizations are characteristic of heterogeneous modern societies. This social pluralism complicates democratic tenets of equality, common interests, and inclusion. And reconciliation is no easy task. The well-known democratic theorist Robert Dahl proclaims that the "problem of democratic pluralism . . . is nearly a description of political theory since antiquity."[2]

In the United States, the "problem" of democratic pluralism has been attacked from many different angles. Dahl, for instance, is interested in the wide variety of autonomous organizations within large-scale nation states and the question of balancing their autonomy against state control.[3] Other aspects of pluralism, particularly those revolving around differences between individuals and the relationships between individuals and groups, have been tackled under the guise of the "liberal/communitarian" debate. Where communitarians stress the embeddedness of individuals within particular communities, liberals stress the autonomous capacities of individuals to make their own choices. The debate between liberals and communitarians centers around the appropriate conceptual and normative model for political life in our democratic society.

Historically, liberal and communitarian conceptions of politico-social organization have held sway at different periods. New England towns of the eighteenth century, for instance, were characterized by widely shared religious beliefs and direct democratic forums that are more consistent with communitarianism.[4] Twentieth-century America, on the other hand, is a more fragmented society, yet it is shot through with a liberal ethic of individualism. Concrete historical experiences with communitarian and liberal models have resulted in each drawing criticism for its excesses. Robert Bellah and his colleagues eschew the exclusion of characteristic tight-knit communities while simultaneously calling for a curbing of what they see as a deleterious "radical individualism."

> We should not forget that the small town and the doctrinaire church, which did offer more coherent narratives, were often narrow and oppressive. Our present radical individualism is in part a justified reaction against communities and practices that were irrationally constricting. A return to the mores of fifty or a hundred years ago, even if it were possible, would not solve, but only exacerbate, our problems. Yet in our desperate effort to free ourselves from the constrictions of the past, we have jettisoned too much, forgotten a history that we cannot abandon.[5]

Bellah et al.'s exhortation to Americans to find a new model of community capable of mediating the ideals of liberalism and communitarianism demonstrates how by the late 1980s key questions in the liberal/communitarian debate turned from "whether community?" to "what sort

of community?" and from "whether individual freedom?" to "which free-
doms, guaranteed by what constraints, at what cost, and to whom?"[6]

By the early 1990s, a corresponding set of questions was circulating
regarding social pluralism. In response to increasing calls by cultural groups
for representation within the "canon" and public school curricula, Arthur
Schlesinger Jr. came out with a scathing critique of multiculturalism in his
Disuniting of America.[7] From within the Canadian context, Charles
Taylor wrote the essay "Multiculturalism and the Politics of Recognition."[8]
This essay proved an enduring launch pad for dialogue, among a very
diverse group of scholars, on issues raised by socio-cultural pluralism for
liberal democratic societies across the globe. The nature of the
multiculturalism debate has been driven not by the question "whether
pluralism?" but by "what sort of pluralism?" constituted by "what sort of
group recognition, at what cost, and to whom?"

In this chapter I respond to these broad issues with a theory of deliberative democracy that claims to "provide the most adequate conceptual
and institutional model for theorizing the democratic experience of complex societies."[9] Charter schools provide an opportunity for us to reflect
on the tenacious dilemma of liberal versus communitarian visions of public life in our democratic society. Charter schools embody many organizational features of voluntaristic communities. Yet, the "problem" of democratic pluralism—the simple fact that we have an increasingly diverse student
body to educate—poses some stubborn questions to an ideal of "schools
as communities." Is the ideal of community appropriate only for our private associations in places like churches and clubs? Are our public interactions better governed by neutral laws and rights to protect our conflicting interests? Or, might it be possible to cultivate thicker public communities
within our shared institutions? Public education being one of the few
institutions available to all of us, might it be possible to cultivate thicker
public school communities without abrogating the rights of individuals or
groups through exclusion or subordination?

Educators who advocate the creation of public schools as communities
do not say much about what these communities should be like. They
emphasize replacing the contractual relationships and radical individualism of liberalism with communal relationships and interdependence. They
extol a sense of belonging, caring relationships among students and faculty, and some shared values. But what values are to provide a basis for
distinctly *public* communities? Some proponents of civic education and
civic renewal call for a return to the American tradition of civic republicanism.[10] But I will argue that republicanism invokes a model of political

community that homogenizes plurality. Just as liberalism is too thin to sustain community, republicanism is too thick to sustain pluralism.

Jurgen Habermas's discourse theory of deliberative democracy attempts to retain the strengths of both liberalism and civic republicanism while discarding the weaknesses of each. According to Benhabib, Habermas's theory mediates between republican communities of civic virtue and liberal contracts of self-interest with a "participatory vision of the politics of communicative ethics." This participatory vision emphasizes political participation and the "democratization of decision-making processes in social life."[11] The participationist view of democratic politics avoids the "ethical overload" of republicanism by focusing more on cultivating a sense of political agency than a shared civic identity. Yet, as opposed to liberalism's thin view of politics, participation does serve a socially integrative function by giving rise to mutual understanding and reasoned agreement.

Liberals are suspicious of participatory democratic communities because they fear that a thick civic culture will encroach on distinct conceptions of the good life and accompanying virtues. Essentially, liberals are wary of the assimilating tendencies of civic republicanism whereby community is equated with the state. In order to guard against such encroachment, they seek to protect value- and identity-pluralism by delineating a private sphere of particularistic communities.[12] In response to such concerns, Benhabib insists that participatory democratic politics need not fall prey to republican tendencies. She argues:

> participationism does not entail dedifferentiation, value homogeneity, or even value reeducation . . . For on the participationist model, the public sentiment which is encouraged is not reconciliation and harmony, but rather political agency and efficacy, namely the sense that we define our lives together, and that what one does makes a difference.[13]

On this model, participation in democratic politics does not entail sharing the same value system. Nor is political community embodied with the state. Rather, participationist political communities exist in the public sphere of civic society. Deliberative democracy identifies a vibrant civil public life as crucial to the ideas of democratic freedom and consent; the ideals embodied in the sentiment of governance by, for, and of the people. Participation in the informal networks of opinion-formation, as well as the formal procedures of decision making, represent the consent of the sovereign polity. In this manner, the participatory model of democratic politics is particularly inclusive. Because the public sphere is unrestricted, and issues are not confined to any one sphere, both political membership and the public agenda are accessible to all. Democratic participation itself then plays an integrative role between civil and political public spheres and between citizens.[14]

Thus, deliberative democracy provides a normative model for public life that is neither exclusionary nor assimilating. In doing so, it provides a theory with which we might assess the potential for charter schools to balance a plurality of interests in public education. In order to flush out a relationship between the discourse model of deliberative democracy and charter schooling, I consider two issues in this chapter.

First, in so far as deliberative democracy offers a tenable model for making legitimate collective decisions in a pluralistic society, what are its implications for public charter schools? This questions gives rise to a plethora of others: how might charter schools build vibrant, participatory communities? Can charter school communities be built around an ethic of participationism without value homogeneity? How should charters go about educating a citizenry capable of participating in ideal decision-making procedures? What pedagogical practices instill a sense of political agency and efficacy?

Second, how do the challenges posed by plurality vary from the political to the educational arena? Since schools are not peopled by adults alone, but include minors, and because schools have an educative as opposed to a political mission, what are their unique conditions of legitimacy? In other words, how does the educative mission of public schooling change the requirements for producing legitimate outcomes? And, once determined, how do differences complicate the legitimacy of educational processes aimed to prepare students for democratic citizenship?

In order to address these questions, section II briefly sketches my approach to pluralism and the primary challenges it poses to democratic politics. Section III then describes civic republican and liberal stances toward pluralism. I critique each stance for exhibiting exclusionary and assimilating tendencies that fail to sustain pluralism. In section IV, I describe the project of deliberative democracy and its relative merits in rising to the challenges of pluralism. Deliberative democracy attempts to both reconcile the traditional dichotomy of the liberal/communitarian debate and respond to the challenges of pluralism. According to Benhabib, a deliberative conception of democratic politics aspires to accomplish these tasks by "allow[ing] the expression of difference without fracturing the identity of the body politic or subverting existing forms of political sovereignty."[15] I explore how the theory's concepts of procedural deliberation, generalizable interests, and "unity in difference" buttress a democratic politics by, for, and of the people against the multifarious challenges of pluralism.

Next, in section V I address charges that deliberative democracy might unwittingly undermine pluralism and threaten basic rights. Postmodern doubt about Enlightenment claims to freedom and equality urge us to be ever wary and vigilant against subtle ways in which relations of domination are [re]entrenched in new languages and political forms. Heeding these warnings, but hopeful that ideal theories can help us to create ourselves as more rather than less free, more equal than unequal, I explore the dangers and promises of deliberative democracy by asking: How is deliberative democratic theory susceptible to promulgating relations of exclusion and privileging that often characterize attempts to create commonality amongst difference? And, once attuned to these concerns, how might we maximize the possibilities of deliberative democracy for promoting both inclusiveness and equality across a pluralistic citizenry? After considering each of these questions, I offer suggestions for maximizing the inclusive and egalitarian possibilities of deliberative democratic politics.

Finally, in Section V I connect this normative framework back to charter school reform by translating a deliberative theory of democratic politics into a theory of political education. I define political education in terms of Amy Gutmann's notion of "conscious social reproduction." I first explicate the concept of conscious social reproduction into two distinct levels: *practices of* and *practices for* democratic participation in the public sphere of education. Next, I consider each level in terms of charter schools as sites of deliberative democracy. I explore *practices of* democratic distribution and governance within charters as "associative democracies." I end with a discussion of how educators might approach translating Habermas's procedural conditions for democratic legitimacy into preparatory conditions, or *practices for*, civic education.

II. Pluralism and Democratic Politics

The idea of pluralism encompasses so much and usage of the term is so varied that it is a very tricky concept to get a handle on. In the interests of clarifying my usage of the term, I now describe various forms that pluralism takes, note societal levels at which pluralism arises, and outline a few conceptual orientations toward pluralism. Pluralism within democratic societies takes a least three forms: value-, identity-, and interest-based pluralism.[16] Value-based pluralism refers to differences in values, beliefs, ideas, or moral perspectives. This type of pluralism is usually the topic when political theorists refer to the "fact of reasonable pluralism."[17]

Identity-based pluralism has more to do with one's identity as a member of a group than differences in value orientation. It has to do, for instance, with one's identity as a woman, or as a Catholic, or as a Native American. Many identity categories are based upon ascribed characteristics like race or gender. These are categories that one cannot change, but they carry social significance nevertheless. In addition, one's identity as a member of such groups is often related to societal power relations whereby one group locates a privileged or dominant position over others. Thus, identity-pluralism is closely linked to unequal power relations and histories of discrimination in a given society.[18]

Interest-based pluralism is due in large part to the roles one plays and one's relative status within various societal spheres. Students, for instance, have interests in attaining a level of education equal to that of their peers; teachers have interests in securing a salary and working conditions commensurate with those of colleagues and other professionals. In this case, students' and teachers' interests are not mutually exclusive. But interests frequently conflict and democratic procedures are called upon to determine a fair resolution.

Clearly, interest-based pluralism is closely linked and intersects in multiple ways with both value- and identity-pluralism. And each of these forms of pluralism arises at multiple social levels: within individuals, within socio-cultural groups, and within formal organizations. For example, the identity of a particular individual as an African-American likely draws upon values shared by African-Americans as a distinct cultural group. This individual may also be a member of the National Association for the Advancement of Colored Persons, an organization intended to represent the interests of African Americans, among others, and composed of a membership that also shares some cultural perspectives and values.

As intertwined and convoluted as these forms and levels of pluralism appear, one overarching concept captures a common thrust—distinctiveness of perspectives. Values, identities, and interests all give rise to distinct perspectives. Hannah Arendt refers to this distinctiveness as the "plurality" of the human condition. She contends: "plurality is the condition of human action because we are all the same, that is human, in such a way that nobody is ever the same as anyone else who ever lived, lives, or will live."[19] Although Arendt is describing plurality among individuals, her assessment easily applies to social groups and organizations; none are the same as any other that has existed, exists, or will exist at some future point.

Arendt's claim brings me to the issue of conceptual orientations toward pluralism. She asserts plurality as the "condition of human action." This appears to be an ontological claim. A claim, in other words, that makes a statement about the very nature of being human. William Connolly's insistence that "difference is fundamental" is another example of an ontological conception of pluralism. [20] Yet all conceptions of pluralism are not ontological: some are merely descriptive, others are normative. A descriptive conception of pluralism simply makes an observation about social reality. Dahl's concern with the "existence of a plurality of relatively autonomous organizations within the state" fits the bill here. [21] A normative conception differs from mere description in that it is concerned with questions of moral worth. Normative claims evaluate whether or not social pluralism is a desirable state of being. Or, a normative assessment might be conjoined with a sociological description resulting in something like the "*fact* of *reasonable* pluralism." [22] In this case, pluralism is described both normatively as reasonable and descriptively as a fact.

To summarize, I have outlined three distinguishable forms of pluralism—value-, identity-, and interest-based pluralism—and discussed how each arises at multiple social levels within individuals, social groups, and autonomous organizations. In addition, I have described three conceptual orientations to pluralism—descriptive, ontological, and normative. In the following sections I employ Arendt's concept of plurality when I refer broadly to all three types of pluralism. I take plurality as a descriptive fact of our social life in late twentieth-century American society. Given the vast complexity of forms and manifestations of plurality, I would side with the ontological pluralists who see difference as a fundamental aspect of the human condition. In terms of a normative assessment, I fail to see how individual autonomy or freedom can exist apart from plurality, so I also approach pluralism as a good. But the precise way in which pluralism functions as a good is a question to be pursued within the confines of specific theoretical frameworks.

Such a thick conception of plurality, with all of its descriptive, ontological and normative elements, suggests that even fairly homogenous democratic communities are pluralistic in some regard, and therefore subject to its challenges. Plurality complicates the democratic principles of equality, common interests, and inclusion that make government by, for, and of the people possible. Difference problematizes any straightforward approach to equal status as citizens or equal treatment under the law. Difference draws into question how common interests are to be identified, or, indeed, whether they even exist. And difference highlights the boundaries around who is included in the sense of civic identity that constitutes "the people." Connolly argues that while a democratic civic identity depends upon difference, it is simultaneously threatened by it:

There is no identity without difference. . . . The stronger the drive to the unified nation, the integrated community, and/or the normal individual, the more powerful becomes the drive to convert differences into modes of otherness. And the more implacable the cultural drive to convert difference into otherness the less feasible it becomes to build majority assemblages of democratic governance that can actually govern a diverse populace.[23]

In the following sections I evaluate the adequacy with which civic republican, liberal, and deliberative conceptions of democratic politics respond to the challenges and dilemmas posed by plurality.

III. Plurality in Civic Republican and Modern Liberal Traditions

The civic republican tradition dates back to Aristotle's vision of attaining freedom and the good life through active citizenship in the *polis*. In this classical conception of face-to-face democratic community, membership as one of the "people" was restricted to eligible males, denying access to groups such as women or slaves. Later, civic republicanism *a la* Rousseau identified common interests in terms of a "general will." The general will emerged out of harmonious social situations devoid of conflicts of interests. Lack of conflict in political life was achieved by strictly distinguishing "private" from "public" man and severely limiting the size of the political community.

More recent strands of civic republicanism stress normative consensus within a shared political community but reject exclusionary citizenship practices. Groups of people are not explicitly denied access to political participation, but a premium is placed upon a background of shared values and moral convictions. Political rights are thought of primarily in terms of positive liberties including the freedom to participate in political life and to communicate with fellow citizens.[24] A shared culture, participation, and communication provide the bases for forming a common "ethicopolitical self-understanding." This dialogic conception of politics as "civic self-legislation" blurs institutional lines that liberals draw between state and society; the processes of forming a common "will" constitute society as a political community.

Habermas criticizes this recent strand of civic republicanism for "ethical overload." He argues that the formation of a collective identity is not to be collapsed onto political processes, nor are political questions to be equated with ethical questions surrounding "who we are and who we would like to be."[25] For without some distinction between politics and the good life, plurality is forsaken in favor of one, overarching ethicopolitical identity and a corresponding set of ends. Moreover, the presumption of a broad background consensus leaves little room for substantive differences within such a community. Aspirations toward shared self-understanding privilege "normocentricity" over dissent, and conformity over diversity.[26] Thus, difference is ignored as homogeneity is either assumed or sought after through programs of assimilation toward shared norms. Such practices describe the "exclusionary and/or assimilationist tendencies"[27] of the republican ideal of a tightly-knit ethicopolitical community.

Liberalism, on the other hand, purports to prize difference; it takes for granted value pluralism and conflicts of interests. Protecting individual freedom and distinct visions of a good life, then, are the hallmarks of basic liberal rights. Basic liberties protect individual differences and minority rights from state coercion and tyranny of the majority. Liberties are guaranteed through such tools as a strict split between public and private spheres, universal rights of citizenship, and a principle of neutrality.

Liberals favor a "thin" notion of democratic politics embodied within the state. The state constitutes the public sphere, or the political community, and remains a fair arbiter between competing interests by relying upon principles of universality and neutrality. In the public sphere, persons *qua* citizens are equal and treated in a similar fashion vis-à-vis the rule of law. The public sphere is separated from a private sphere where "thicker" values and partial notions of the good life can flourish. This public/private distinction restricts political discourse to issues of common concern. Value pluralism is bracketed from issues of justice and viewed in terms of the priority of the right over the good. These ideas are exemplified in the notion of religious toleration, for example, and the doctrine of "separation of church and state." Within the private sphere, religious institutions are free to pursue their unique beliefs and value systems. While in the public sphere, toleration is achieved by remaining neutral toward various private doctrines.

Before exploring the ways in which a liberal model of democratic politics falls short in addressing issues of plurality, I want to distinguish two strands of liberalism. Classical liberalism posits a set of "natural" rights that all human beings share simply by virtue of being human. Citizens enjoy negative liberties from interference as they freely pursue their own conceptions of the good life within the market, the family, and other private associations. The state is conceived of in minimalist terms; its primary function is the protection of individual rights within the private sphere. The state's power derives from a general will formed through the aggregation or bundling of interests through processes such as voting.

A more modern liberal tradition emerged quite recently. In the early 1970s, John Rawls renewed interest in normative political theory in general with his seminal work *A Theory of Justice*.[28] His continued exploration of the liberal project throughout the ensuing decades has resulted in a conception of liberalism that he refers to as political, not metaphysical. Rawls's political liberalism relies on a reconstructivist approach to public reason that eschews the metaphysical foundations underlying concepts of natural rights. Instead, he defends a concept of justice and basic rights derived from practical reason and political processes that draw upon a shared background consensus among citizens.[29]

Despite these important differences, classical and modern, or Rawlsian, liberalism share some fundamental similarities. Both are social contractarian approaches to political membership and authorization. Both clearly distinguish a public sphere regulated by a principle of state neutrality. And both approach citizens as formal equals similarly situated toward universal rights. In the following section, I use the generic term "liberalism" when referring to traits similar to both traditions. Otherwise, I clearly indicate the object of my remarks with the labels classical or aggregrative liberalism versus modern, Rawlsian, or political liberalism.

Critiques of Liberalism

While liberalism seems to protect certain kinds of differences quite effectively, such as its paradigm case of religious freedom, other differences do not fare so well. Feminists are quick to point out how a strict separation of public versus private spheres has made it difficult for women to politicize issues such as domestic abuse that violate the very basic rights that liberalism hopes to protect. As specific issues are labeled private and bracketed out of public discourse, certain groups are effectively silenced in the public arena.[30] Some feminists also charge that prevailing public discourses of rationality, impartiality, or neutrality privilege male modes of expression and communication, disadvantaging women in yet another manner.[31]

Although many of these critiques are compelling, some overstate their case against liberalism in ways that may undermine the democratic project itself. First, some critics represent liberalism as though its principles of neutrality and universality erase plurality. Anne Phillips finds this critique "distinctly odd" since diversity and difference have been at the heart of liberalism's attempts to ground equality and political coherence within heterogeneous societies.[32] Second, other skeptics of liberalism entirely abandon Enlightenment ideals, such as equality and impartiality, as "illusory and pernicious" goals that can only be achieved by ignoring or denying differences.[33]

Yet another group of feminist theorists is wary of such overly simplistic and overly skeptical critiques of liberal ideals. They caution against a skepticism that leads toward nihilism and encourage a more sophisticated approach to difference with the goal of reformulating Enlightenment ideals. Benhabib, for instance, argues that a concept of democratic legitimacy is not sustainable without some notion of impartiality.[34] The task, then, is to conceptualize impartiality in such a way that outcomes are "equally in the interests of all," rather than products of exclusion or silencing. An initial step toward this goal entails a careful critique of the ways in which the liberal approach to impartiality has resulted in exclusions and silencing.

Feminist critiques of liberalism center around issues of difference that come in the forms of identity and interest-based pluralism. The issues at stake are not values per se, but gender and related, gender-based interests—the ways in which women are excluded from full citizenship and the ways in which issues of particular interest to women are confined to the private sphere. Liberals have not necessarily ignored plurality, but their conceptual and strategic responses have resulted in identity-based exclusion for some groups, which means that related interests are also excluded or downplayed. Phillips points out:

> Difference is not something we have only just noticed. What we can more usefully say is that difference has been perceived in an overly cerebral fashion as differences in opinions and beliefs, and that the resulting emphasis on what I will call a politics of ideas has proved inadequate to the problems of political exclusion.[35]

Phillips argument suggests that political exclusion may plague liberalism because its attention to value-pluralism has not been matched with satisfactory approaches to identity-based pluralism. She continues:

> when the politics of ideas is taken in isolation from what I will call the politics of presence, it does not deal adequately with the experiences of those social groups who by virtue of their race or ethnicity or religion or gender have felt themselves excluded from the democratic process.[36]

Identity-based exclusion from a liberal conception of democratic politics stems from at least two sources: liberal conceptions of equality and impartiality.

First, liberalism posits a concept of absolute equality based upon citizens as universal subjects. The concept of absolute equality exhibits both exclusionary and assimilating tendencies. Exclusion comes in the form of universalization of dominant identity-types whereby other identities are unseen and differences between those "others" and the dominant types are repressed.[37] In terms of gender identity, for example, masculinity functions as the norm for neutrality. As a result, women are either ignored as political subjects, as was the case in many historical contexts, or the ways in which women are different from men are overlooked or downplayed.

Alternatively, gender differences are assimilated within the public sphere rather than excluded. Differences are assimilated toward the dominant identity-type of political subjects. Gender-based assimilation results from the "generalization of the male into a neutral or universal being [whereby] the male subject becomes the paradigm of humankind as such." This sort of "homologization" disallows women from acting as political subjects *as women*, rather than based upon the ways in which they are like men.[38]

Second, liberalism's approaches to impartiality rely upon processes that fail to adequately account for complex plurality. Notions of impartiality differ markedly between classical and Rawlsian liberalism resulting in different problems. Classical liberalism overemphasizes interest-pluralism to the detriment of substantive value-pluralism. As I mentioned earlier, classical liberalism approaches the idea of general interests by aggregating or bundling private interests. Joshua Cohen explains that this "aggregative conception of democracy institutionalizes a principle requiring equal consideration for the interests of each member."[39] But he criticizes the aggregative conception for failing to give adequate weight to value-pluralism. He contends that a person's private beliefs are given short shrift:

> this conception fails to take seriously the stringency or weight of the demands placed on the person by her reasonable moral or religious convictions. . . . It is precisely this stringency that compels reasons of especially great magnitude for overriding those demands. But such considerations about the relative stringency of demands are absent from the aggregative conception.[40]

Cohen's reference to "reasons of especially great magnitude" refers to a second approach to identifying common interests which calls upon the force of practical reason. Cohen clearly sees the use of reason as a preferable approach to that of simply aggregating interests. His conviction demonstrates a similarity between his conception of deliberative democracy, which I discuss later, and Rawls's liberal conception of public reason. Like deliberative democracy, Rawls's theory of political liberalism views "the legitimation of political power and the examination of the justice of institutions to be a public process, open to all citizens to partake in."[41] Each theory stresses the importance of public reason, but their approaches are quite different. Political liberalism relies upon a conception of practical reason that severs identity- from value-pluralism too sharply.

In *A Theory of Justice* and *Political Liberalism*, Rawls aims to establish means through which the principles of justice for a well-ordered society can be chosen and realized. His theory of justice attempts to protect the fundamental equality of persons through a system of fair social cooperation among groups adhering to a plurality of reasonable doctrines. Rawls refers to individuals as moral, free, equal, and rational persons whose natures are best realized under conditions of justice chosen by parties to the "original position." This initial choice situation, a tool for social contract theorists, provides conditions for the selection of fairness principles that will best allow each person to pursue his/her own goods without disallowing others similar pursuits.

Rawls's original position is intended to represent an objective, general standpoint where parties can agree upon the principles of justice for the basic structures of democratic society. Within the original position, a "veil of ignorance" hides from us our "particular attachments and interests," along with our inclinations, aspirations, and conceptions of the good; the veil conceals anything that is irrelevant from the standpoint of justice.[42] Behind the veil of ignorance, the only relevant feature of persons is their possession of moral powers.[43] A lack of information about irrelevant differences (which include race, sex, class, religion, and other private affiliations) allows parties to share a symmetrical position from which they decide principles about the fair distribution of social goods. In the original position: ". . . equals in all relevant respects are to be represented equally. . . . [Hence,] citizens, viewed as free and equal persons, when represented equally in the original position, are represented fairly."[44]

Rawls's intention with the original position is to set up a situation in which persons can imagine what fair social institutions might look like. He finds it necessary to hide the particularities of their social positions so that they will be unable to protect interests gained from privilege rather than fairness. For example, since my socio-economic status is merely an "historical accident," it should not be considered relevant to moral deliberation. If I do not know whether I am rich or poor, I am more likely to create tax laws that will be fair to persons from either group. Based on reason, parties to the original position bargain until consensus is reached regarding principles of social justice.

Use of the original position has opened Rawls's theory of justice to attack from communitarians, feminists, and others. Critics charge that parties to the original position cannot possibly represent real human beings because they are disembodied and disembedded from social practices. In addition, they assert that this initial choice situation presents a monological model of moral deliberation which is based upon an impossible universality.[45] In *Political Liberalism*, Rawls responds to the charge of universality by simply stating that his political conception of justice is freestanding, implying no metaphysical or epistemological doctrine.[46] But Rawls presents an additional argument in defense of the original position. He says one cannot find a metaphysical conception of the self within his original position because it is not intended to represent real human beings. Rawls insists that it is wrongheaded to use the original position to interpret his views on the nature of the self because it is meant as a "device of representation."

The original position is a thought device in which "parties" make moral determinations. Parties are not the same as citizens. Citizens are persons; parties are "rational agents of construction, mere artificial personages, inhabiting our device of representation."[47] Parties do not suggest metaphysical or ontological assertions about human beings because they are hypothetical. They are simulations, role players pretending to be persons, intended to maximize the chances for fairness and for consensus in moral deliberations about justice.

Yet, Rawls's simple assertion that parties are "pretend" does not negate the model of moral deliberation presented by his original position. Parties deliberate in isolation, behind a veil of ignorance, bargaining through proxy about fair principles until consensus among them is reached. Benhabib contends that this monological model of moral reasoning is based upon faulty Kantian presuppositions. She explains:

> Kant's error was to assume that I, as a pure rational agent reasoning for myself, could reach a conclusion that would be acceptable for all at all times and places. In Kantian moral theory, moral agents are like geometricians in different rooms who, reasoning alone for themselves, all arrive at the same solution to a problem.[48]

Rawls's parties are moral agents who reason like Kantian geometricians. Thus, the original position, even as a device of representation, presents a strong commentary about the nature of moral reasoning.[49] Moral agents are able to reach reasonable decisions, and agree on these decisions independent of each other, devoid of social context or knowledge of situational particularities. In this view, morality, and reason itself, transcend social context. Persons may be socially situated, but moral deliberation takes place objectively, outside of such contexts, in a place where persons are treated equally and fairly. The original position suggests that within social contexts persons may have differences, but as moral agents they step outside of themselves to adopt what Iris Marion Young calls an "unsituated moral point of view."[50]

Young criticizes this "view from nowhere" approach to impartiality for denying or repressing differences in at least three ways. First, because all situations are treated with the same "moral rules," the particularity of situations is denied. Second, the concrete particularities of persons, such as needs and feelings, are abstracted from the original position. And, third, the plurality of political subjects is reduced to a single moral unity.[51] In these ways, the liberal ideal of impartiality, like the ideal of absolute equality, functions to either exclude or assimilate differences in the formation of a universal identity-type for political subjects.

Both civic republicanism and liberalism exhibit exclusionary and assimilating tendencies. Whereas civic republicanism collapses distinctions between the right and the good, resulting in "ethical overload," liberalism retains the distinction too strictly. In the aggregative conception, processes for bundling interests fail to give serious attention to value pluralism. Rawls addresses this weakness with his reconstructive project of practical reason. But his conception of moral reasoning posits an objective standpoint inhabited by autonomous selves that rejects the very forms of plurality he is attempting to protect. An ideal of impartiality based upon rational agents who reason monologically denies plurality as the human condition.

The variety of ways in which models of democratic politics exclude and assimilate differences suggests that a viable model must make room for particularity. Many political theorists call upon the particular as a necessary corrective to universality. Adrienne Cavarero appeals to "concreteness, or to what Hannah Arendt called the factuality of the real."[52] Michael Walzer wants to defend immediacy and provide a "thick, pluralist, and democratic correction" to the "superagent" of objective, universalist conceptions of politics.[53] Susan James defends an idea of "citizenly independence" whereby "it is the job of a democratic polity to provide conditions in which each citizen can contribute to at least some political decisions in his or her own voice."[54] And Anne Phillips calls for a "politics of presence" to challenge political exclusion with "a more complex understanding of the relationship between ideas and experience."[55]

Appeals to concreteness, immediacy, and particularity require conceptions of equality and impartiality capable of acknowledging the specificities of plurality. Accordingly, equality might not be viewed as absolute, or *in spite of* differences, but as substantive and constituted *through* differences. Along similar lines, impartiality might be better viewed as a condition of outcomes than as an objective standpoint. In other words, difference seems to disallow persons from occupying impartial standpoints vis-à-vis reason. But differences might be represented within concrete processes intended to result in reasonable agreements that are equally in the interests of all. Such processes are at the heart of a deliberative theory of democracy to which I now turn.

IV. A Deliberative Conception of Democratic Politics

Much contemporary work on democracy and difference operates with notions of a more active and vigorous democracy that depends crucially on public debate. Rejecting both the false harmony that stamps out difference and the equally false essentialism that defines people through some single, authentic identity, many look to a democracy that maximizes citizen participation and requires us to engage and contest with one another.[56]

Section III discussed how plurality is undermined within both liberal and civic republican traditions as "difference" is excluded from politics through universality and neutrality or ethicopolitical consensus. This section describes a deliberative conception of democratic politics which draws upon Jurgen Habermas's discourse theory of ethics.[57] Discourse theory splits the difference between liberalism and civic republicanism in a number of ways that positively impact the status of plurality. The theory calls upon procedural conditions to establish democratic legitimacy. These conditions require the inclusion of all persons affected by a decision and manifest equality between them. In terms of its normative grounding, discourse theory relies on a conception of practical reason that effectively sustains plurality. This conception is *intersubjective* and *fallibilistic*, allowing for a delicate balance between mutual understanding and indeterminacy. In addition, a discourse theory of democracy is based upon a sociological model that *decenters* politics and invokes a *participatory* notion of political community.

Like any normative political theory, deliberative democracy seeks to outline the conditions under which legitimate political decisions are made by a polity. For deliberative democrats, collective decisions are legitimated through processes of reasoned deliberation among free and equal citizens. For democratic self-rule to be meaningful, decisions must be perceived to be in the interests of all affected parties. Thus, Joshua Cohen asserts that "proper" democratic politics involves three necessary conditions: 1) public deliberation focused on the common good; 2) manifest equality among citizens; and 3) "shap[ing] the identity and interests of citizens in ways that contribute to the formation of a public conception of common good."[58] I will address each of these conditions through a discussion of the role of generalizable interests and will-formation within discourse theory.

As the foregoing discussion indicated, the idea of common or generalizable interests is both a fundamental and contentious concept for any theory of democratic politics. Civic republicanism *a la* Rousseau tends to identify common interests in terms of a "general will" that emerges out of harmonious social situations with little conflict of interest. Classical liberalism, on the other hand, takes conflict for granted and adopts a more minimalist approach. Hope of identifying a singular general interest is forsaken for a principle of neutrality described as "not taking interest in each other's interest." Habermas's communicative ethics seeks to resolve the difficulties inherent to each of these approaches by "[*critically* regarding the concept of 'general interest'] in order to reveal the partiality and biases of interests claimed to be universal or general."[59]

Discourse theory's interpretation of the relationship between practical reason and democratic procedure offers a unique contribution to the concept of generalizable interests. In Habermas's words:

> Discourse theory invests the democratic process with normative connotations stronger than those found in the liberal model but weaker than those of the republican model. . . . In agreement with republicanism, it gives center stage to the process of political opinion- and will-formation, but without understanding the constitution as something secondary; rather it conceives the principles of the constitutional state as a consistent answer to the questions of how the demanding communicative forms of a democratic opinion- and will-formation can be institutionalized. Discourse theory has the success of deliberative politics depend not on a collectively acting citizenry but on the institutionalization of the corresponding procedures and conditions of communication.[60]

These "procedures and conditions" are drawn from an idea of *communicative reason*.

To begin, Habermas's discourse ethics asserts that practical reason relies on fundamental linguistic understanding which transcends cultural contexts. As in much pragmatist philosophy, truth claims are based upon the consent of a community of inquirers. Within this context, the "higher-level intersubjectivity" of unrestricted communication aimed at mutual understanding allows "fallible results [to] enjoy the presumption of being reasonable."[61] Due to its linguistic or communicative foundation, practical reason is universalizable, but not metaphysical or ahistorical. A decision agreed upon now within one community may be revisited by another community with a different result.

Because truth and validity depend upon the conditions under which consensus is reached, communicative reason is a procedural concept. Habermas's discourse ethics then provides procedures intended to disallow particularistic interests from skewing democratic communicative processes. Habermas explains:

> [According to a discourse-theoretic reading, d]emocratic procedure, which establishes a network of pragmatic considerations, compromises, and discourses of self-understanding and of justice, grounds the presumption that reasonable or fair results are obtained insofar as the flow of relevant information and its proper handling have not been obstructed. According to this view, practical reason no longer resides in universal human rights, or in the ethical substance of a specific community, but in the rules of discourse and forms of argumentation that borrow their normative content from the validity basis of action oriented to reaching understanding. In the final analysis, this normative content arises from the structure of linguistic communication and the communicative mode of sociation.[62]

Essentially, discourse ethics requires democratic deliberation as the only form of "action" that enables legitimate and rational decisions to emerge as participants reach understanding and agreement.[63]

Cohen provides an "ideal deliberative procedure" by which such agreement is sought. His ideal procedure is subject to four requirements. First, ideal deliberation is *free* in that: a) participants regard themselves as bound only by the result of their deliberation and by the preconditions for that deliberation; and b) participants suppose that they can act from the results given that the deliberative quality of the decision provides sufficient reason to comply with it. Second, deliberation is *reasoned* in that parties are required to state their reasons for advancing, supporting, or criticizing proposals. It is the expectation that reasons alone, not other sources of power, will decide the fate of proposals. "No force except that of the better argument is exercised."[64] Third, ideal deliberation involves parties that are both formally and substantively *equal*. Formal equality derives from rules that do not single out individuals. Substantive equality prevails because existing distributions of power and resources do not impact parties' chances to deliberate or their role in deliberation. Fourth, and finally, ideal deliberation aims toward a rationally motivated *consensus* by finding reasons that are persuasive to all parties. If consensual reasons are not forthcoming, then deliberation concludes with some form of majority rule.[65]

These four elements of public deliberation—deliberation that is free, reasoned, equal, and aimed toward consensus—provide the necessary conditions for undertaking democratic politics. Not only is deliberation about the common good, but reasoned argumentation takes place in such a manner that as participants persuade one another, their conceptions of the common good are actually formed and shaped. Within this ideal process of "will formation," participants are manifestly equal because only the force of the better argument prevails. Thus, discourse theory's conditions of legitimacy enable a specific democratic polity to identify the basis of their "unity in difference." A general will is created through persuasive reasoning, rather than by coercion, reliance on a "Divine Legislator," or aggregation of interests.

Although Rawls's concept of generalizable interests also derives from practical reason, deliberative democrats offer a few reasons to prefer their approach. First, they find deliberation more amenable to the challenges of plurality, including discrimination, within actual social contexts. Gutmann and Thompson, for instance, believe that real-life deliberations are preferable to the hypothetical devices offered in theories like Rawls's political liberalism. They contend:

> In some familiar theories of justice, moral claims are constructed as hypothetical agreements among individuals who are not accountable to anyone and who are assumed to be living in a just society. . . . Deliberative democracy, in contrast, admits reasons and principles that are suitable for actual societies, which all still suffer from discrimination and other kinds of injustice. Actual deliberation has an important advantage over hypothetical agreement: it encourages citizens to face up to their actual problems by listening to one another's moral claims rather than concluding (on the basis of only a thought experiment) that their fellow citizens *would* agree with them on all matters of justice if they were all living in an ideal society [emphasis in text].[66]

According to a model of deliberative democracy, citizens not only face actual problems and engage in actual decision-making processes, but they do so without restricting the agenda for debate or the spaces within which deliberation might take place. Any item which affects citizens can be brought to the table, including the conditions regulating deliberation, and a variety of institutions within civil society are viewed as appropriate for discussions based upon public reason.[67]

Second, others favor a deliberative ideal of impartiality because it allows for the concrete particularities of identity to remain part of the democratic process.[68] Because public reason is regarded "as a *process* of reasoning among citizens," as opposed to a *principle* regulating how citizens ought to reason about public matters, the inevitability of plurality is accounted for.[69] Insofar as deliberative procedures are institutionalized, then, they provide the possibility of "real participatory structures in which actual people, with their geographical, ethnic, gender, and occupational differences, [can] assert their perspectives on social issues within institutions that encourage the representation of their distinct voices."[70]

Third, advocates of the discourse model of deliberative democracy defend deliberation as a necessary, but not sufficient, condition for practical rationality. Benhabib argues that deliberative processes are essential to the rationality of collective decision making. Deliberation is necessary because it fosters information gathering, the formation of coherent sets of preferences, and the adoption of "enlarged mentalities." Deliberation provides participants with more relevant information than they possessed at the outset, as well as the unique and varied perspectives of other participants. Such exposure to conflicting views and opinions then forces participants to reflect upon the ordering of their own preferences and coherence results from this reflexive process. Finally, deliberative reasoning also forces participants to adopt an "enlarged mentality" as they think from the standpoint of all involved in the effort to persuade one another with publicly acceptable reasons.[71]

Finally, deliberative democrats call into question not only Rawls's account of practical reason, but also his sociological model. For Rawls, the public sphere is limited to the state and specific governmental organizations; civil society and its associations are designated as part of the private sphere. Thus, institutions such as nonfamilial organizations and associations are viewed as beyond the grasp of processes of public reasoning. Benhabib insists that Rawls's theory cannot sustain such a strict distinction between civil society and the public sphere. She argues that not only are many organizations within civil society public bodies subject to legal scrutiny but, additionally, such institutions and their members influence political processes in ways that transgress his public/private distinction.[72]

Within a discourse theory of democracy, on the other hand, civil society is part of the public sphere. Discourse theory takes for granted a sociological image of a complex, decentered society that includes two types of politics. The formal politics of organized political systems and legitimate procedures generates authoritative political rule. But this is only one component of society, or "just one action system among others."[73] Formal, institutionalized political processes are complemented by informal political networks within civil society that generate public opinion. Public opinion then influences the formal procedures of will-formation that ultimately generate "final and coercive political power."[74]

Thus, a discourse theory of democracy posits a public sphere that is composed of both formal political arenas and informal, unrestricted networks of opinion-formation within civil society. According to Benhabib, lines between the public and the private are not obliterated, but they are constantly subject to negotiation through interrelated processes of opinion- and will- formation. In her conception, public reason is not abstracted from the partiality of private associations, but rather interconnected with and drawn from their discussions:

> Civil society and its associations are not public in the sense of always allowing universal access to all, but they are public in the sense of being part of that anonymous public conversation in democracy. A deliberative model of democracy is much more interested than Rawls in what he calls "background cultural conditions," precisely because politics and political reason are always seen to emerge out of a cultural and social context.[75]

In addition to grounding public reason within specific contexts, deliberative democracy's image of a decentered society offers another advantage for plurality. The wide variety of public spaces within civil society makes room for a plethora of differences.

Unrestricted, informal networks of communication within civil society allow for all sorts of value-, interest-, or identity-based groups to formulate and share opinions on issues of concern. Such processes of opinion-formation within these "subaltern counterpublics"[76] then impact the views and preferences of other citizens as well as political officials participating in formal deliberative procedures. In this manner, the public sphere retains and encourages, rather than excluding or assimilating, plurality. In Benhabib's words:

> When conceived as an anonymous, plural, and multiple medium of communication and deliberation, the public sphere need not homogenize and repress difference. Heterogeneity, otherness, and difference can find expression in the multiple associations, networks, and citizens' forums, all of which constitute public life under late capitalism.[77]

In summary, any conception of democratic politics must address the challenges that plurality poses to governance by, for, and of the people.

Deliberative democracy accomplishes this by offering a proceduralized notion of popular sovereignty within processes of opinion- and will- formation that include all parties affected by a decision. The deliberative model is premised upon an image of a decentered society in which a formal political system is tied into informal networks of autonomous public spheres composing civil society. Formal processes of will-formation depend upon the higher-level intersubjectivity of communicative processes of reaching mutual understanding. These processes are intended to result in collective decisions regarding political matters—matters relevant to the entire society and in need of regulation.[78] Subaltern counterpublics within civil society have opportunities to influence the agenda of political matters by working up public opinion on particular issues through processes of reasoned, public deliberation.

Because of its dialogical conception of practical reason and its rich notion of the public sphere, deliberative democracy provides a more adequate response to the challenges of plurality than those provided by either civic republican or liberal theories. Deliberative democracy offers a model of political community capable of sustaining, rather than excluding or assimilating, plurality. As Cohen explains:

> If political community depends on sharing a comprehensive moral or religious view, or a substantive national identity defined in terms of such a view, then reasonable pluralism ruins the possibility of political community. But an alternative conception of political community connects the deliberative view to the value of community. In particular, by requiring justification on terms acceptable to others, deliberative democracy provides for a form of political autonomy: That all who are governed by collective decision—who are expected to govern their own conduct by those decisions—must find the bases of those decisions acceptable. And in this assurance of political autonomy, deliberative democracy achieves one important element of the ideal of community. Not because collective decisions crystallize a shared ethical outlook that informs all social life, nor because the collective good takes precedence over the liberties of members, but because the requirement of providing acceptable reasons for the exercise of political power to those who are governed by it . . . expresses the equal membership of all in the sovereign body responsible for authorizing the exercise of that power.[79]

Such a notion of political community resting upon the autonomy of equal members within shared processes of moral reasoning accommodates plurality in all of its forms. Value differences and conflict are assumed; that is why the force of reasoning is paramount. Identities remain concrete within actual processes of deliberation. And interests are not assumed to precede but, instead, arise from discussion with others. This is a model of a participatory, rather than integrative or exclusionary, community.

Participation takes the form of reasoned deliberation among fellow citizens. Citizens reason together both to identify solutions to common problems and to agree upon the very conditions under which they will deliberate. For deliberative democrats, these features of the theory make it the "most adequate conceptual and institutional model" for democratic politics. But, for a variety of discontents, the theory threatens not only plurality, but liberty.

Critiques of Deliberative Democracy

It is helpful to distinguish between conceptual and institutional critiques of deliberative democratic theory.[80] Conceptual critiques either reject the ideals that the theory espouses or find the theory inherently incapable of achieving its ideals. Institutional critiques are more concerned with implementation of the theory and its capacity to realize its ideals in practice. Two common conceptual critiques of deliberative democracy concern the emphasis on consensus and protection of basic rights. Frequent institutional concerns center around the realization of substantive equality within actual deliberative processes and Habermas's distinction between spheres of opinion- and will-formation. Below, I address each of these critiques in turn.

Deliberative democracy's ideal procedure aims to achieve consensus or a "moment of agreement." For many pluralists, the immediate question that comes to mind is: how is this ideal of consensus reconciled with a social condition of radical plurality? Within a theory that acknowledges value pluralism, conflicts of interest, and identity differences this inevitable "moment of agreement" seems problematic. How do values eventually become commensurate? How are conflicts eliminated? What happens to differences in the ideal procedure?

Deliberative democracy's response to these sorts of questions involves a few steps. First, the deliberative process itself is viewed as a process of "will formation" that shapes individual preferences through free and reasoned discourse. Interests are not pre-political, nor are they fixed within a specific ethicopolitical framework. Rather, interests are formed during deliberations under conditions that allow autonomous individuals to make free choices. Such a constructivist model of interest- or identity-formation avoids essentializing group characteristics or staticizing individual or group interests. Yet, the danger remains that if difference is merely constructed, it can be easily obliterated in the process of forming consensual political decisions.

At this point, deliberative theorists provide further reassurances that differences need not be permanently overcome in order to reach demo-

cratic agreements. Frank Michelman and Hannah Pitkin argue that disso-
lution of disagreement is not necessary. Rather, participants come to
"hold the same commitment in a new way."[81] This results from participants finding appropriately political reasons convincing and consistent
with their other partial commitments. Or, similarly, they view their commitments a bit differently in light of the enlarged mentality that they adopt
as they engage in public reasoning. This approach to consensus building
may actually encourage rather than hinder the expression of differences.
Emphases on intersubjective understanding and an enlarged mentality
point to the importance of including all perspectives in the decision-making process. Indeed, public reasons will not be persuasive to all participants unless they are able to address each and every point of view in
some way. [82]

Another reassurance that plurality and consensus are mutually compatible approaches consensus more as an ideal than as an absolute. In
this sense, consensus might be thought of as a "critical yardstick" with
which to measure decision-making procedures and assess the extent to
which they are attaining democratic legitimacy. Connolly maintains that:

> It is possible to construct a democratic theory appropriate to late-modern states
> that combines a critique of consent and consensus when they are *absent* with
> critical engagement with them when they are *present*.[emphases in text][83]

In accordance with this view, Connolly eschews general consensus in
favor of mobile constellations of majority assemblages "in which programs are supported for a variety of reasons."[84]

Connolly's endorsement of majority-based, versus consensus-based,
political outcomes introduces a third reassurance against the dangers of
consensus. Both Benhabib and Cohen defend majority rule as a legitimate outcome of reasoned deliberation.[85] Benhabib contends that:

> In many instances the majority rule is a fair and rational decision procedure, not
> because legitimacy resides in numbers but because if a majority of people are
> convinced at one point on the basis of reasons formulated as closely as possible
> as a result of a process of discursive deliberation that conclusion A is the right
> thing to do, then this conclusion can remain valid until challenged by good rea-
> sons by some other group.[86]

In addition to this presumptive claim to rationality, majority rule is also
invoked due to pragmatic constraints such as time. Here the defense of
majoritarianism stresses the regulative aspects of the discourse model
and its presumptions of fallibility and indeterminancy. Specific topics,
and norms themselves, are to be revisited in the event that any affected

individuals or minority groups are unfairly impacted by outcomes of the decision-making process. This is the provisional nature of deliberative democracy.

Skeptics concerned with basic liberties, however, do not find provisional protections of rights easy to swallow. They quickly point out that under majority rule, minority views are effectively silenced. If any topic can be put on the political agenda, and if the outcome can be achieved at the expense of minority points of view, what is left to protect the liberty of individuals or minority groups from tyranny of the majority?[87] In answering this question it is important to remember that Habermas's discourse theory of democracy does not reject the basic rights that liberals so highly value. Rather, Habermas conceives of the source of those rights in a different manner. Habermas does not follow Kant's "deduction of right" nor Rawls's "original position." Instead, discourse theory privileges "a discourse model of practical debate as being the appropriate forum for determining rights claims."[88]

Benhabib explains that what is distinctive about the discourse model is that while it presupposes principles of liberty, such as her two principles of equal moral respect and egalitarian reciprocity, the actual content and interpretation of the principles is a result of deliberation. She contends that such norms allow minorities or those who disagree to withhold assent and to challenge both the rules and the agenda of public debate. But the opportunity to challenge norms must be preceded by a willingness to abide by them:

> The deliberative theory of democracy transcends the traditional opposition of majoritarian politics vs. liberal guarantees of basic rights and liberties to the extent that the normative conditions of discourses, like basic rights and liberties, are to be viewed as rules of the game that can be contested within the game but only insofar as one first accepts to abide by them and play the game at all.[89]

Under legitimate conditions of deliberation, agreement is only reached through the "freely given assent of all concerned." Accordingly, Benhabib insists that such procedures of "recursive validation" protect against the consequences that liberals most fear: tyranny of the majority or an overly strict formulation of the conditions of consensus.[90]

Other skeptics of deliberative democracy are satisfied with the conceptual soundness of the theory but remain concerned about its viability in actual institutional settings. Their concerns are more pragmatic, revolving around the empirical question: how, in a pluralistic society marked by histories of oppression and inequality, are citizens to participate "equally" in ideal procedures of political decision making? This question implicates not only individual participation in the ideal procedure, but also Habermas's sociological distinction between spheres of opinion- and will-formation.

As discussed previously, democratic legitimacy is contingent upon the consent of free and equal participants in the deliberative processes. Cohen further stipulates that participants be *manifestly equal* in that they share both formal equality with respect to the rules and substantive equality with respect to power relations external to the political process. Within the deliberative procedure, individuals are equal in their ability to offer reasons to persuade others. This notion of equality appears to brush over intersections between plurality and reason giving, especially in terms of the discrimination and stereotyping that often accompany identity-pluralism.

Discourse theory insists that only reasons matter, not identity or social status. Yet, neither identity nor status can be clearly delineated from the quality of reasons one gives or the ways in which one's reasons are received by other interlocutors. Feminist theorists argue that gendered styles of communication, including interruptions, how authoritatively one speaks, and how often one speaks, bring gender domination into the discursive arena.[91] Similar points can be made regarding cultural forms of communication. If, for instance, Asian Americans are less likely to speak out in public settings, or if African American styles of expression are interpreted as emotional rather than rational, it will be difficult to ensure that substantive equality among participants has been achieved. The question then becomes: what are some procedures by which substantive equality may be sought in the face of pluralistic social positions and styles of communication?

The potential difficulties for realizing substantive equality within the deliberative process result in part from the infiltration of external social inequalities. Different styles of communication and perceptions about fellow participants may impact the quantity of and quality granted to any individual's reasons. One approach to equalizing discursive participation would be to eliminate social inequalities.[92] There are two problems with this approach. First, social inequalities will not be abolished with the wave of a hand. Ideal models may lessen inequalities over time, but meanwhile we still need to invoke idealized norms and procedures to get from here to there. Second, the presumption that eliminating social inequalities will also do away with variations in communication styles and other discursive differences is overly simplistic; it denies plurality as a human condition. As long as human beings occupy distinct social locations and unique perspectives—as long as we are "different" from one another—substantive equality will be a difficult ideal to achieve. Thus, specific procedures must be institutionalized to decrease the impact of plurality, whatever its source or manifestation, on the equality of discursive outcomes.

Social inequalities that are likely to impact an individual's participation in the deliberative process are often due to the individual's status as a member of certain social groups. Therefore, some recognition of the ways in which group membership impacts the process may be necessary for realizing the ideal of substantive equality between individuals. Benhabib's concept of the "concrete other" encourages recognition of "each and every rational being as an individual with a concrete history, identity, and affective-emotional constitution."[93] These concrete aspects of individual identity encourage attention to one's status within salient groups.

Explicitly acknowledging "concrete otherness" would allow differences, and the complex social relations in which they are embedded, to become manifest within the discourse procedure. As Young asserts:

> In open and accessible public spaces and forums, one should expect to encounter and hear from those who are different, whose social perspectives, experiences, and affiliations are different. To promote a politics of inclusion, then participatory democrats must promote the ideal of a heterogeneous public, in which persons stand forth with their differences acknowledged and respected, though perhaps not completely understood by others.[94]

Specific techniques abound for building the attentiveness of Young's "politics of inclusion" into the structure of deliberation. For example, group memberships could be represented through caucusing or special voting rights for minority constituencies. Moreover, various communication styles could be accounted for by structuring conversations so that each participant is granted an opportunity to share his/her position on an issue and ideas for alternative resolutions.

Liberals and deliberative democrats alike who are interested in protecting individual rights, however, are wary of recognizing groups within democratic politics. Critics of group representation warn that the "nature" of any given group will be prone to essentialization. Moreover, questions will arise as to who can best define or represent a group's interests; and individual's may be judged in terms of whether or not their identity authentically represents that of the group. In response to such worries, Phillips advocates a "politics of presence" that draws upon "the notion of multiple identities or multiple 'subject positions,' each of which is subject to political transformation and change."[95] She argues that such an understanding of difference need not entail essentialized identities nor undermine attention to value-, interest-, or identity-pluralism.

In order to realize a "politics of presence" within institutions, Phillips recommends that a broad diversity of "subject positions" be reflected in the organizational structure. Multiple positionalities should be reflected without privileging any voices as more authentic than others or seeking a unified point of view. At the same time, the boundaries surrounding these subject positions must remain flexible and fluid since it is impossible to determine in advance whether a broad spectrum of relevant differences is adequately reflected.[96] The important points to keep in mind here are that substantive equality is only achieved as an ideal condition to the extent that: a) participants acknowledge the ways in which very real differences and social inequalities penetrate an idealized discourse model; and b) participants enact measures, down to the most minute aspects of the deliberative process, to account for such infiltrations.

Finally, Habermas's delineation between formal and informal political spheres may also have undesirable consequences for disadvantaged individuals and groups in pluralistic societies. Recall that Habermas decenters politics by rejecting holistic sociological models in favor of a complex model in which the political system is only one among many other social and economic systems. Decentering acknowledges and encourages plurality and optimizes institutional spaces for marginal perspectives to flourish and gain recognition.

But, despite this decentered approach, Habermas retains fairly strict distinctions between a formal political system, a civil society of autonomous public spheres, and a private sphere. He maintains that only the formal system is subject to ideal processes of will-formation. The unregulated networks of communication that comprise multiple public spheres are responsible for opinion-formation. As public opinions coalesce and gain strength they pressure the formal political system to grant space on the legislative agenda through which collective, binding decisions are made.[97]

Fraser suggests that informal networks of opinion-formation are advantageous for marginalized groups as "subaltern counterpublics" or "parallel discursive arenas where members of subordinated social groups invent and circulate counterdiscourses to formulate oppositional interpretations of their identities, interests, and needs."[98] Habermas seems to grant this point by including Fraser's concept of "weak publics" in his portrayal of civil society and informal public spheres. He sees weak, informal publics as the appropriate arena for struggles over recognition of needs—struggles aimed toward formal recognition by the political system.[99]

Fraser refers to multiple or counterpublics as weak because they participate in the opinion-formation stage of the political process, but have no decision-making authority.[100] Without any regulation, however, it seems that such informal public struggles will be even more susceptible to preexisting relations of domination and subordination than formal deliberations under ideal conditions. In effect, without regulation it is difficult to imagine how marginalized groups will effectively supplement formal political discourse in the manner Habermas intends.

Habermas's characterization of the informal public sphere as better suited for "struggles over needs" seems to deny disenfranchised groups the very conditions necessary to be heard and impact the opinion-formation processes of others. If marginalized groups face specific hurdles as they participate in public conversations, it is unlikely that their concerns will be just as likely as others to gain recognition within unregulated networks of communication.

Moreover, a strict separation between the spheres of opinion- and will-formation unnecessarily circumscribes notions of citizenship, political participation, and collective decision making. In an unregulated environment, citizens are likely to lack necessary conditions, such as information and influence, which support the quality of the opinions formed. If the informal public sphere plays as important a role in supplementing the formal political system as Habermas maintains, then this impoverished ideal of opinion formation is a cause for concern. Public opinions that lack depth and sophistication will nevertheless gain recognition and order the legislative agenda, thereby lowering the quality of the entire political process. In addition, citizens not included in formal discursive processes are excluded from *substantive* participation and relegated to *supplemental* participation in democratic governance.

These problems could be addressed with Cohen's proposal that social institutions *mirror* the ideal deliberative procedure. Habermas considers this a sociologically naive view that denies the complexity of the modern world. His point is well taken, but he has overstated his case. Mirroring the discourse model, at the level of a regulative ideal, need not rely on a holistic conception of social systems. Rather, invoking deliberative ideals to oversee opinion formation might take on quite different forms and designs to serve a variety of institutional purposes. As with the ideal of consensus, democratic proceduralism might be called upon as a critical yardstick with which to assess fairness of institutions within civil society.

The regulative attempt is worthwhile because it grants opinion-formation its pivotal role in the political process and seeks to approximate the social equality that democratic politics calls for within all public institutions.

The differences inherent in a pluralistic society, combined with entrenched power relations whereby what is different is excluded from or subordinated within the political process, are difficult for any ideal political model to grapple with. A discourse model of deliberative democracy offers a great deal of promise for generating legitimate collective agreements within a pluralistic society. Its stumbling blocks are primarily issues of institutionalization: What kinds of procedures best ensure substantive equality between participants in deliberation? How are we to democratize public institutions of civil society without threatening their plurality? Deliberative democracy requires institutional designs and procedures capable of accommodating differences while shaping common interests. The final portion of this chapter explores the implications of charter schooling as one such design within the public sphere of education.

V. Deliberative Democratic Education
and Charter Schooling

Deliberative democracy provides us with a theory of democratic politics. At this point, I endeavor to translate this theory of politics into a theory of civic education.[101] Habermas contends that "according to discourse theory, the success of deliberative politics depends not on a collectively acting citizenry but on the institutionalization of the corresponding procedures and conditions of communication. . . ."[102] What corresponding procedures and conditions are appropriate for civic education?

Early in this study I introduced three central aspects of democratic education: distribution, governance, and civic education. Deliberative democratic theory offers a conceptual model that mediates between the public interests at stake in each of these aspects and the institutional structure of charter schools. In terms of distribution, charters' associational nature corresponds with discourse theory's sociological assumption of decentered, multiple publics of opinion- and will-formation. In terms of governance, deliberative democracy suggests formal procedures by which legitimate decisions might be reached within individual charters. In addition, the theory emphasizes informal networks through which public opinion is generated. Charter schools comprise a network of multiple, diverse sites through which opinions on broader educational issues are formed, influenced, and transmitted. Finally, in terms of civic education, deliberative democracy requires that public charter schools prepare future citizens to participate in reasoned deliberations. At the same time, charter schools provide local democratic associations within which adults and students can gain such capacities.

Distribution and governance are each components of civic, or political, education which, in turn, is a key element of "conscious social reproduction." According to Amy Gutmann: "Political education prepares citizens to participate in consciously reproducing their society, and conscious social reproduction is the ideal not only of democratic education but also of democratic politics . . . ."[103] Along with straightforward civics curriculum, distribution and governance are components of civic education because they strongly influence the preparation of future citizens. As Gutmann explains:

> A democratic theory of education focuses on what might be called "conscious social reproduction"—the ways in which citizens are or should be empowered to influence the education that in turn shapes the political values, attitudes, and modes of behavior of future citizens. Since the democratic ideal of education is that of conscious social reproduction, a democratic theory focuses on practices of deliberate instruction by individuals and on the educative influences of institutions designed at least partly for educational purposes.[104]

Along with deliberate practices of civics instruction, distribution and governance are components of civic education insofar as they exert "educative influence" on the political virtues, knowledge, and skills students gain.

Practices of and *for* Democratic Civic Participation

Gutmann's conception of "conscious social reproduction" operates on at least two levels. I will refer to the first level as the *practice of* and the second level as *practice for* democratic participation. First, *practices of* conscious social reproduction include distribution and governance. A democratic theory guides the ways in which citizens are to influence these practices by justifying answers to two questions: a) "[w]ho should share the authority to influence the way democratic citizens are to be educated?"[105] and b) how should decisions about public education be made? These questions primarily concern the governance of education. In terms of the *practice of* educational governance, deliberative democracy outlines procedures for arriving at collective decisions, including conditions for who participates. The theory also departs from a decentered sociological model and stresses multiple publics within the sphere of civil society.

Second, *practices for* conscious social reproduction deliberate practices of instruction and the educative influences of institutional designs.

Gutmann maintains that "political education prepares citizens to participate in consciously reproducing their society [through] the cultivation of
the virtues, knowledge, and skills necessary for political participation."[106]
At this second level, educative *practices for* democratic decision making
take place. Here, the institutional designs that accompany educational
governance and distribution exert educative influences on the types of
political virtues and capacities that students gain. So, deliberate instructional *practices for* civic participation, along with the influences exerted
by governance and distribution procedures, comprise the overall project
of civic education. In order to explore a deliberative democratic theory of
civic education, therefore, we must examine the implications of the deliberative model of politics for governance and distribution, as well as straightforward civics instruction.

Realizing Public Interests in *Practices of* Charter
School Governance and Distribution

Habermas's discourse theory refers to the political integration of complex
democratic societies through intersections of communicative power across
multiple, decentered publics. Formal political arenas of will-formation and
informal networks of opinion-formation integrate the influence of public
opinion and the communicative power of practical discourses with the
result of politically authoritative administrative power. Within this tax-
onomy of political organization it is unclear where schools fit in. As public
education is currently organized, decisions are made at multiple levels
ranging from federal and state governments to local school boards, administrative offices, and classrooms. Public schools are state-sponsored
institutions filled with public employees who must make decisions that
carry collective import. Schools also generate public opinion on issues as
students gain knowledge and as parents, professionals, and community
members debate educational policy.

The range of functions carried out by public schools suggest their organizational structure bridges Habermas's strict distinction between spheres
of will- and opinion-formation. And, in doing so, schools call into question whether this distinction is sustainable. Just as Benhabib challenges
both Rawls and Habermas for drawing "overly rigid boundaries" between
public and private spheres, Cohen and Fraser also suggest that the boundaries between spheres might usefully be thought of as more fluid and
porous. As I mentioned earlier, Cohen urges that formal procedures of
will-formation be invoked as a mirror for other social institutions within
civil society. This strategy addresses Fraser's concern that spheres of

opinion-formation are weak publics by strengthening their legitimacy conditions.

Deliberative democrats Gutmann and Thomas join Benhabib, Cohen, and Fraser in advocating the democratization of institutions within civil society. They contend that citizens should experience reasoned deliberation within institutions outside of government. Unless citizens reason together in institutions where they spend most of their time, they will not gain necessary capacities for deliberating effectively in formal political arenas. In addition to identifying the preparatory aspects of deliberation, Gutmann and Thompson also believe that it is important for all citizens, not just public officials, to take part in reasoned discourse. Discussions in multiple institutional settings are not only a "rehearsal for political action" but themselves "part of citizenship."[107]

This more porous approach to public life expands the role of deliberation across spheres of opinion- and will-formation. In doing so, it brings Habermas's conception of citizens as anonymous bearers of opinions a bit closer to a notion of citizens as face-to-face participants in shared political activity. The danger in this move is the specter of citizenship as a good, as evidenced in the participatory politics of Aristotle's Athens for example. Liberals, in particular, would likely warn that individual liberty is threatened by such an expanded notion of democratic citizenship.[108] But, as I have explained, the deliberative urge to democratize institutions within civil society should not be equated with the democratic *polis*. Cohen offers an argument for "associative democracy" that bases solidarity not upon a common conception of the good life, but on shared institutional participation surrounding issues of common concern. He rejects arguments that this form of solidarity is inherently exclusionary or factionalizing, or a threat to liberty.

Cohen's institutional strategy of associative democracy arises in response to deliberative democracy's need for a vibrant public sphere of not only political participation, but equal political participation. Cohen echoes Fraser's assertion that the "subaltern counterpublics" which arise in secondary associations are spaces where the needs and interests of marginalized groups can be articulated. He also echoes Gutmann and Thompson's emphasis on the importance of discourse within secondary associations for building public competence in deliberating about the common good. According to Cohen, each of these functions of secondary associations is necessary for a well-functioning democracy, but neither happens automatically:

> The right kinds of association do not naturally arise, either for the purposes of addressing problems of underrepresentation or for more functional tasks: there is, for example, no natural tendency for an emergence of secondary associations to correct for inequalities of political opportunity due to underlying economic inequalities or to ensure the regulatory competence needed to advance the common good.[109]

Thus, Cohen puts forward a strategy of associative democracy intended to encourage secondary associations capable of fulfilling the functions of representing previously underrepresented interests and advancing regulatory competence. His associative strategy is usefully applied to charter schools for addressing whether or not a particular school's mission: 1) reflects the right kind of association in terms of adequately balancing its mission against public interests in democratic regulation and, 2) promotes regulatory competence in future citizens.

Charter Schools as Associative Democracies
Associative democracy involves the "idea of a regulatory role for associations" (p. 111). Associations take on a regulatory role in cases where the state is limited in its capacity to advance the common good. Cohen asserts there are four such kinds of cases. The first case encounters the problem of state *monitoring* when the objects of regulation are too numerous, dispersed, or diverse. The second type of case confronts the *means* of achieving regulatory standards when the objects of regulation are too diverse or unstable for the government to specify just what standards are appropriate at particular sites. A third case arises surrounding the determination of standards, or *ends*, themselves. In this case, appropriate standards are best decided upon by local stakeholders or government officials in prolonged cooperation with non-government stakeholders. Finally, a fourth case entails the issue of *coordination*. Here the concern is a social problem with multiple causes and intersections with other problems which necessitate overlap between conventional policy domains (pp. 110–12).[110]

All four of Cohen's cases might apply to public education. Public schools are too numerous, dispersed, and diverse to be easily monitored by state or federal officials. They are also too diverse to be amenable to standardized means for achieving educational goals. In addition, many educators argue that appropriate standards can best be determined within local contexts. And few would disagree that the problems students bring to school are the product of multiple causes and intricately connected with other social problems. Only one of these cases is necessary to recommend that a regulatory role for associations may better serve common interests than a limited state role. In terms of public education, the possibility that all four cases may apply at different times and places strongly suggests that Cohen's associative strategy is worthy of consideration.

This being the case, charter schools provide an institutional model that closely reflects the strategy of associative democracy. Charters are autonomous public associations concerned with addressing common educational interests. Charter schools are public institutions, yet they are granted regulative relief from direct state control. The associative strategy would view charters as "arenas for public deliberation that lie outside conventional political arenas" (p. 112). Thus, this aspect of deliberative democratic theory provides a normative model for charter school governance. Conversely, charters offer an organizational model for the theory's institutionalization.

A question remains, however, surrounding the distribution of educational interests across charters as associative democracies. Cohen recognizes that his associative strategy encourages a governance role for groups that "may heighten the role of group affiliation in defining political identity" (p. 111). This would be a negative consequence of associations if groups were to become factionalized within the polity. But Cohen contends that instead of creating political solidarity *within* certain groups, associative democracy will construct "new bases of social solidarity *through* a process of defining and addressing common concerns" [emphases in text] (pp. 111–12). The issue of concern, rather than any particular social group, provides the basis for political cohesion:

> The solidarities characteristic of such efforts will be the bonds of people with common concerns . . . who treat one another as equal partners in addressing those shared concerns. In short, these efforts—which could have very wide scope—have the potential to create new "deliberative arenas" outside formal politics that might work as "*schools in deliberative democracy*" in a special way [emphases added]. Deliberative arenas established for such coordination bring together people with shared concrete concerns, very different identities, and considerable uncertainty about how to address their common aims. Successful cooperation within them, fostered by the antecedent common concerns of participants, should encourage a willingness to treat others with respect as equals, precisely because discussion in the arenas requires fashioning arguments acceptable to those others. Assuming fair conditions of discussion and an expectation that the result of deliberation will regulate subsequent action, the participants would tend to be more other-regarding in their outlook. The structure of discussion, aimed at solving problems rather than pressuring the state for solutions, would encourage

people to find terms to which others can agree. And that would plausibly drive argument and proposed action in directions that respect and advance more general interests. Moreover, pursuing discussion in the context of enduring differences among participants would incline parties to be more reflective in their definition of problems and proposed strategies for solutions; it would tend to free discussion from the preconceptions that commonly limit the consideration of options within more narrowly defined groups. (pp. 112–13)[111]

As deliberative arenas that arise within contexts of shared concerns, Cohen's associations are at once particularistic, pluralistic, and participatory. They are particularistic in that specific shared concerns bind members together. Yet, they are pluralistic in that people with "very different identities" come together to address these concerns. And they are participatory because members deliberate together in order to collectively solve their common problems.

Public charter schools, organized to address one or more of the four cases Cohen describes, have the potential to represent previously underrepresented interests in the educational sphere. In addition, they might act as arenas, and even "schools," of deliberative democracy outside of conventional political arenas. Thus, charters need not be anti-democratic, as critics fear, but may embody a more participatory, more deliberative form of democratic politics in the public educational sphere. I am not suggesting, however, that the main thrust of charter schools be democratic participation. Rather, I contend that charters provide the possibility of a proliferation of quite distinct schools within the public educational sphere. While most charter schools will not be concerned first and foremost with democratic governance nor civic education, public interests in each of these aspects of education require that charters at least meet some minimal requirements.

Deliberative democracy, and particularly Cohen's associative strategy, provide a normative model of democratic politics that can be used to assess the extent to which charter school policies and practices meet such minimal standards. The norms of deliberative democracy can be usefully drawn upon, for example, to assess whether: 1) the organization of charter schools under a specific policy balances a plurality of interests in public education; 2) the governance procedures of specific charter schools result in legitimate collective decisions; and 3) the curricular and pedagogical practices within specific charter schools promote "regulatory competence" in future citizens.

Cohen's associative strategy provides an institutional model of democratic politics that addresses both the governance and distribution of public education. His model provides a theoretical answer to the questions that undergird the legitimacy of *practices of* democratic participation in the public sphere of education: a) "[w]ho should share the authority to influence the way democratic citizens are to be educated?"[112] and b) how should decisions about education be made? The model of associative democracy combines the ideal procedure of decision making with a strategy for distributing decisions based upon shared concerns. Because charter schools are schools of choice that form around common missions, they provide an institutional correlate for the associative strategy.

Since charters already embody the structural features of the associative strategy its norms may be applied to individual schools in order to measure whether the school's mission reflects the "right kind of association." According to the strategy, charter schools are legitimate secondary associations insofar as they a) promote the organized representation of presently underrepresented interests in the public educational sphere; or b) can demonstrate greater competence than existing public authorities for advancing the common good (p. 110). Moreover, the strategy provides a normative model for assessing whether a specific charter school is adequately balancing its particularistic mission against public interests in democratic regulation (governance) and promoting regulatory competence in future citizens (civic education). As *arenas of* collective decision making, charter schools must account for who shares decision-making authority and the processes according to which democratic decisions are made within their schools. As *schools for* attaining democratic competence, charter schools must meet some minimal standards for preparing students for their roles as future citizens. In the remainder of this book, I focus my attention on this final issue—whether and how charter schools fulfill their public role as preparatory schools for civic participation.

Realizing Public Interests in Charters' *Practices for* Civic Participation

Distinguishing between *practices of* and *practices for* democratic participation delineates distinct objects toward which legitimacy claims are targeted. Within *practices of* democratic politics, collective decisions are the ends to be deemed legitimate or not. In the public sphere of education, educational issues of common concern are the target of collective decisions. Applied at the educative level of *practice for* democratic participation, the desired ends are the attainment of civic capacities. At this level, a unique set of considerations arises for how such practices are to be institutionalized and how their legitimacy is to be assessed.

Recall that *practice for* democratic participation entails educative influences as well as deliberative practices of instruction that impact civic education. Civic education, again, involves " . . . the cultivation of the virtues, knowledge, and skills necessary for political participation."[113] I refer to these necessary attributes of political participation as "civic capacities." It is important to recognize that *practices of* democratic participation in the sphere of education directly affect *practices for* citizenship in so far as they exert educative influences. Take, for example, the case of charter schools as associative democracies with autonomous regulatory roles. As associative democracies, charter schools are not only educational, but political, institutions. An entire range of stakeholders—from students and parents, to teachers and administrators, to board and community members—may participate in decision making processes within the school. One could argue, in the tradition of John Stuart Mill, Alexis de Tocqueville, John Dewey, and Amy Gutmann that a participatory, democratic environment is an ideal setting for cultivating virtues of democratic citizenship.[114]

A number of empirical and normative questions are raised by the potential educative influences of charter schools as participatory democratic communities. Empirically one might ask: Do students become more civic-minded, or do students develop a distinct sort of democratic character, if they are educated in a participatory environment? In terms of discourse theory, the specific thrust of this question is: Do students develop a greater sense of political agency and efficacy—a sense that what they say matters—as a result of democratic participation in school life? At the normative level, questions arise surrounding the extent to which various stakeholders are equal participants in democratic governance. Teachers, for instance, are professionals—do their views count more than those of parents or other community members? Students are not yet adults nor full citizens, what is their status within a preparatory democratic community?

A parallel set of issues comes to the fore in terms of the "deliberate practices of instruction" component of civic education. First, a deliberative theory of civic education must consider what civic capacities students will need in order to become effective citizens. Discourse theory's emphasis on participation stresses the virtues of political agency and efficacy; citizens need to have a sense that what they say matters. In addition, citizens clearly need skills in reasoned discourse. These skills are of the utmost importance because political outcomes will only be as reasonable as the arguments that were included in the decision-making process. Habermas stresses this point:

Deliberative politics acquires its legitimating force from the discursive structure of
an opinion- and will-formation that can fulfill its socially integrative function only
because citizens expect its results to have a reasonable quality. Hence the discursive level of public debates constitutes the most important variable.[115]

The key role that the quality of discourse plays in the deliberative model
bodes the centrality of civic education as preparation for democratic politics.[116] Capacities in reasoned deliberation are intimately connected with
the sufficiency condition of practical rationality. Outcomes may be legitimate if they result from legitimate procedures, but they will only be rational to the extent that reasonable arguments were invoked within the procedures.

Thus, deliberative theory suggests that future citizens must acquire
three essential capacities in order to participate in a democratic politics
that relies upon the force of reason to reach collective agreements that
are equally in the interests of all. These are the minimal requirements that
public charter schools must be held accountable to in terms of public
interests in civic education. First, students must gain skills in reasoned
deliberation, including capacities in practical reason as well as procedural
discourse. Second, students must gain a willingness to participate in collective deliberations according to background conditions such as mutual
respect and egalitarian reciprocity. Third, students must gain a sense of
political agency or efficacy; in other words, a sense that what they say
matters.

Next, deliberative theory might be asked to account for how students
are to gain these necessary capacities and predispositions. The educative
response to deliberative theory's acute need for citizens capable of engaging in reasoned discourse appears fairly straightforward—teach students
how to reason and they will be ready to participate in democratic politics.
Develop in students faculties of practical reason such as capacities for
intersubjectivity and reflexivity, skills in persuasive argumentation, and an
ability to discern relevant information. Add on a sense of political agency
and efficacy, and students will be ready for citizenship.

But implementing such educative *practices for* citizenship is not so
simple. The province of moral and practical reasoning, as well-known
philosopher of education Israel Scheffler points out, raises "very difficult
questions, theoretically as well as practically."[117] Theorists of moral and
civic education, as well as critical thinking, continually disagree about the
appropriate capacities to be learned and pedagogies with which to teach
them.[118] Fortunately, for a deliberative theory of political education the
important issue is not to determine a set of fixed or immutable categories

surrounding how to teach students to reason. Rather, it will be more illuminating to identify the appropriate conditions under which *practices for* civic education, and their accompanying outcomes, should be deemed legitimate.

If deliberative democratic politics hinges upon the institutionalization of corresponding procedures and conditions of communication, what are the corresponding procedures and conditions of civic education? And how might they be institutionalized? Benhabib suggests that answers to these questions are not forthcoming from within discourse theory:

> The procedural specifics of those special argumentation situations called "practical discourses" are not automatically transferable to a macroinstitutional level. . . . Nonetheless, the procedural constraints of the discourse model can act as test cases for critically evaluating the criteria of membership and the rules for agenda setting, and for the structuring of public discussions within and among institutions.[119]

Essentially, educators are left to determine how to best mirror Habermas's requirements of communication within deliberate *practices for* civic education. As educators seek to institutionalize the three requirements for deliberative democracy, the procedural constraints of discourse theory provide "critical yardsticks" for assessing the legitimacy of deliberate instructional practices. Deliberative theory's normative standards—including free and reasoned discourse, manifest equality among participants, and inclusion of all affected—provide tools with which educators can assess the extent to which their practices are fulfilling public interests in civic education.

Conclusion

Because charter schools are public educational institutions they require a normative theory of democratic politics capable of balancing distinct educational values against collective interests in the schooling of future citizens. The deliberative model of democratic politics claims itself the most adequate conceptual model for addressing the challenges of plurality in complex, democratic societies. This model requires a corresponding theory of political education, as well as institutions that can breathe life into its ideals. Charter schools provide such institutions; and deliberative democratic theory provides charters with a normative vision. A deliberative theory of political education offers charter schools an ideal procedure, as well as an associative strategy, to guide *practices of* governance and distribution. These practices, in turn, serve as educative influences as charters prepare students for their future roles as democratic citizens. The deliberative ideal also urges charters to engage in "deliberate practices of instruction" aimed at fostering students' capacities to reason, willingness to abide background conditions, and a sense of political agency and efficacy. Educators can draw upon the theory's legitimacy conditions as critical yardsticks with which to assess *practices for* democratic participation.

Conversely, charter schools offer a structural avenue for institutionalizing the theoretical constructs posited by deliberative democracy. It is likely that social conditions of plurality and inequality will complicate both the institutionalization of deliberative theory and the task of civic education. Feminist and critical theorists, among others, often warn that the exclusionary and privileging tendencies of normative theories manifest themselves within the concrete, day-to-day practices of institutional life. Thus, in the interests of exploring the viability of a deliberative theory of civic education in practice, the next section of this book provides a case study of one charter school whose mission is civic education. This charter school is not merely attempting to minimally satisfy public requirements surrounding civic education. Rather, Winthrop Academy Charter School is attempting to forge a model of an excellent public education with a civics emphasis as its central core.

The case study illustrates two areas of complexity surrounding how charter schools might pursue democratic requirements of civic education within the particular contexts of their own school communities. First, the case illuminates tensions in realizing the ideal deliberative model within concrete practices of civic education. And, second, the case study pays particular attention to identifying the ways in which challenges of plurality manifest themselves in *practices for* democratic participation. In illuminating these two areas of tension, the case study demonstrates how deliberative theory's ideals can serve as critical yardsticks for both assessing educational practice within charter schools and suggesting areas where charter policy can promote democratizing change.

Notes

1. For contemporary theoretical accounts of democratic legitimacy, see, for example, Seyla Benhabib, "Deliberative Rationality and Models of Democratic Legitimacy," *Constellations* 1, no. 1 (April 1994), 27; Seyla Benhabib, "Toward a Deliberative Model of Democratic Legitimacy," in *Democracy and Difference: Contesting the Boundaries of the Political*, ed. Seyla Benhabib (Princeton: Princeton University Press, 1996), 69; Joshua Cohen , "Deliberation and Democratic Legitimacy," in *The Good Polity: Normative Analysis of the State*, ed. Alan Hamlin and Philip Pettit (London: Blackwell, 1989), 17; Joshua Cohen, "Procedure and Substance in Deliberative Democracy," in *Democracy and Difference: Contesting the Boundaries of the Political*, ed. Seyla Benhabib (Princeton: Princeton University Press, 1996), 95; Amy Gutmann, "Democracy, Philosophy, and Justification," in *Democracy and Difference: Contesting the Boundaries of the Political*, ed. Seyla Benhabib (Princeton: Princeton University Press, 1996), 344; and Amy Gutmann and Dennis Thompson, *Democracy and Disagreement* (Cambridge, MA: The Belknap Press of Harvard University Press, 1996), 13.

2. Robert A. Dahl, *Dilemmas of Pluralist Democracy: Autonomy vs. Control* (New Haven: Yale University Press, 1982), 2.

3. See Dahl, *Dilemmas of Pluralist Democracy.*

4. Jane Mansbridge, for example, describes early American towns such as Dedham, Massachusetts as tightly-knit communities where interests largely converged and governance was often by a town meeting. She characterizes such towns as "unitary democracies" and notes that their unitary nature was sometimes supported through exclusionary practices regarding who could live in the town. Jane Mansbridge, *Beyond Adversary Democracy* (Chicago: University of Chicago Press, 1983), 130–31.

5. Robert N. Bellah et al., *Habits of the Heart: Individualism and Commitment in American Life*, (Berkeley and Los Angeles: University of California Press, 1985), 83.

6. John W. Chapman and Ian Shapiro, eds., *Democratic Community: NOMOS XXXV* (New York: New York University Press, 1993), 3.

7. Arthur Schlesinger Jr., *The Disuniting of America: Reflections on a Multicultural Society* (Knoxville: Whittle Direct Books, 1991).

8. Charles Taylor, *Multiculturalism and "The Politics of Recognition"*, ed. Amy Gutmann (Princeton: Princeton University Press, 1992).

9. Seyla Benhabib, "The Democratic Moment and the Problem of Difference," in *Democracy and Difference: Contesting the Boundaries of the Political*, ed. Seyla Benhabib (Princeton: Princeton University Press, 1996), 6.

10.   See, for instance, Bellah et al., *Habits of the Heart* and Richard Pratte, *The Civic Imperative: Examining the Need for Civic Education* (New York: Teachers College Press, 1988).

11.   Seyla Benhabib, *Situating the Self: Gender, Community and Postmodernism in Contemporary Ethics* (New York: Routledge, 1992), 82. See chapter 3 for her complete discussion of participatory versus integrative communities.

12.   See, for example, Kenneth A. Strike, "The Moral Role of Schooling in a Liberal Democratic Society," in *Review of Research in Education* 17 (1991): 413–83. Strike discusses liberal misgivings of both civic republican and strong democratic models of public community.

13.   Benhabib, *Situating the Self*, 81.

14.   This view is not unique to discourse theorists, rather it is similar to that of other political theorists who emphasize democratic participation. Bernard Crick, for instance, once stated that "Diverse groups hold together because they practice politics—not because they agree about 'fundamentals' . . ." See Bernard Crick, *In Defence of Politics* (Chicago: University of Chicago Press, 1962), 24. Alexis de Tocqueville also stressed the integrative force of democratic participation. He argued that participation encourages interdependence, alleviates atomism, and weaves a social fabric in democratic societies. See Jan H. Blits, "Tocqueville on Democratic Education: The Problem of Public Passivity" *Educational Theory* 47, no. 1 (Winter 1997): 24.

15.   Benhabib, "The Democratic Moment and the Problem of Difference," 5.

16.   This schema is very similar to Michael Walzer's notion of the "divided self." He asserts that selves are divided in three ways: 1) among interests and roles such as citizen, parent, worker, teacher or student; 2) among identities such as family, nation, religion, gender, and political commitments; and 3) among ideals, principles and values. Michael Walzer, *Thick and Thin: Moral Argument at Home and Abroad* (Notre Dame: University of Notre Dame Press, 1994), 85.

17.   See John Rawls, *Political Liberalism* (New York: Columbia University Press, 1993), 4 and Cohen, "Procedure and Substance in Deliberative Democracy," 96. Bellah et al. describe this type of pluralism as "differences based on morally intelligible commitments," 287. Anne Phillips refers to it as the "politics of ideas" in "Dealing with Difference: A Politics of Ideas or a Politics of Presence?" in *Democracy and Difference: Contesting the Boundaries of the Political*, ed. Seyla Benhabib (Princeton: Princeton University Press, 1996), 139–52.

18.   I would include in this category Bellah et al.'s description of "patently unfair" differences, 287; Phillips's "politics of presence" in "Dealing with Difference: A Politics of Ideas or a Politics of Presence?"; William Connelly's "dominant constellation of identities" in *The Ethos of Pluralization* (Minneapolis: University of Minnesota Press, 1995), xiv; and Deborah Rhode's concept of "difference as disadvantage" in "The Politics of Paradigms: Gender Difference and Gender Disadvantage," in *Beyond Equality and Difference: Citizenship, Feminist Politics*

and Female Subjectivity, eds. Gisela Bock and Susan James (New York: Routledge, 1992), 149–63.

19. Hannah Arendt, The Human Condition (Chicago: University of Chicago Press, 1958), 8.

20. Connolly, 104.

21. Dahl, 5.

22. Rawls's "fact of reasonable pluralism" is difficult to characterize. He rejects broad metaphysical claims in favor of a context-specific political liberalism suggesting that his "fact" would be restricted to a descriptive commentary on life in complex, modern societies. But, he poses his fundamental question of toleration based upon the "fact of reasonable pluralism as the inevitable outcome of free institutions" hinting at something deeper. Rawls, Political Liberalism, 4.

23. Connolly, xx–xxi.

24. This argument refers specifically to a communitarian reading of civic republicanism and is drawn largely from Jurgen Habermas, "Three Normative Models of Democracy," in Democracy and Difference: Contesting the Boundaries of the Political, ed. Seyla Benhabib (Princeton: Princeton University Press, 1996), 21–30 and Jurgen Habermas, Between Facts and Norms (Cambridge: MIT Press, 1996), particularly Chapter 7 "Deliberative Politics: A Procedural Concept of Democracy."

25. Habermas, "Three Normative Models of Democracy," 23–24.

26. Nel Noddings uses this term and makes similar points in her essay "On Community," Educational Theory 46, no. 3 (1996): 245–67.

27. This concept is drawn from Kenneth Baynes, "Liberal Neutrality, Pluralism, and Deliberative Politics," Praxis International 12 (1992): 63.

28. John Rawls, A Theory of Justice (Cambridge, MA: Harvard University Press, 1971).

29. See John Rawls, "Justice as Fairness: Political not Metaphysical," Philosophy and Public Affairs 14, no. 3 (1985) and Rawls, Political Liberalism.

30. For further discussion of these concerns see Benhabib, Situating the Self, especially 95–104.

31. Iris Marion Young makes these arguments and includes other categories of "difference" such as race and ethnicity in Justice and the Politics of Difference (Princeton: Princeton University Press, 1990).

32. Phillips, 139–40.

33. Susan James, "The Good-Enough Citizen: Female Citizenship and Independence" in Beyond Equality and Difference: Citizenship, Feminist Politics and Femal

Subjectivity, eds. Gisela Bock and Susan James (New York: Routledge, 1992), 51.

34. Benhabib argues that Young's radical critique of impartiality is incompatible with her call for a heterogeneous, civil public sphere in "Toward a Deliberative Model of Democratic Legitimacy," 82.

35. Phillips, 140.

36. Ibid., 141.

37. Adriana Cavarero, "Equality and Sexual Difference: Amnesia in Political Thought," in *Beyond Equality and Difference: Citizenship, Feminist Politics and Female Subjectivity*, eds. Gisela Bock and Susan James (New York: Routledge, 1992), 36.

38. Ibid., 37.

39. Cohen, "Deliberation and Democratic Legitimacy," 98.

40. Ibid., 98–99.

41. Benhabib, "Toward a Deliberative Model of Democratic Legitimacy," 74.

42. Rawls, *A Theory of Justice*, 516–17; 18.

43. Rawls, *Political Liberalism*, 79.

44. Ibid., 79–80.

45. See William Kymlicka, *Liberalism, Community, and Culture* (New York: Oxford University Press, 1989) for a discussion of five communitarian arguments against a liberal conception of the self, including the positions of Michael Sandel and Charles Taylor.

46. Rawls, *Political Liberalism*, 10–11.

47. Ibid., 106.

48. Benhabib, *Situating the Self*, 163.

49. In addition, I would contend that Rawls is not able to maintain the distinction between real selves and parties to the original position. He claims: "Both autonomy and objectivity are characterized in a consistent way by reference to the original position. *The idea of the initial situation is central to the whole theory and other basic notions are defined in terms of it*" [emphasis added]. Rawls, *Theory of Justice*, 516. This characterization of autonomy, then, applies to persons, not merely parties and provides grounds for applying my critique to his view of selves as reasoning agents. Rawls also argues that "the ideas of society and person" within his theory of political liberalism are ideas of practical reason that are "as basic as the ideas of judgment and inference, and the principles of practical reason." Rawls, *Political Liberalism*, 110. Nevertheless, Rawls does suggest an approach to public reasoning which stresses an "overlapping consensus" and is accordingly more dialogical than the approach to reasoning implied by

the original position. Thus, I do not intend this critique as aimed at his entire conception of moral reasoning, but rather those particular aspects which follow from the assumptions behind the original position and its veil of ignorance.

50.   Young, *Justice and the Politics of Difference*, 104.

51.   Ibid., 100.

52.   Cavarero, 38.

53.   Walzer, 90–92.

54.   James, 50.

55.   Phillips, 141.

56.   Ibid., 143.

57.   When I use the phrase "deliberative democracy" I am referring primarily to a discourse theory of deliberative democracy as articulated by Jurgen Habermas with which Seyla Benhabib, Joshua Cohen, and Iris Marion Young affiliate themselves. Amy Gutmann and Dennis Thompson clearly wish to separate themselves from the discourse theorists whom they see as undervaluing basic rights such as liberty and opportunity. Gutmann and Thompson are concerned to both respect principles of liberty and opportunity and subject these principles, as well as deliberation itself, to ongoing, reflexive deliberation. They criticize Habermas for giving deliberation priority over liberty and opportunity. And they criticize Benhabib for advocating an approach to democratic legitimacy with "too little moral content." Yet I would assert that Gutmann and Thompson's defense of respecting basic principles while simultaneously subjecting them to deliberation is wholly akin to Benhabib's assertion that "basic rights and liberties are to be viewed as rules of the game that can be contested within the game but only insofar as one first accepts to abide by them and play the game at all." See Gutmann and Thompson, *Democracy and Disagreement*, 17–18; 366n16 and Benhabib, "Toward a Deliberative Model of Democratic Legitimacy," 80. For further elaboration of these theorists approaches to deliberative democaracy see also Benhabib, "Deliberative Rationality and Models of Democratic Legitimacy;" Benhabib, *Situating the Self*; Cohen, "Deliberation and Democratic Legitimacy;" Cohen, "Procedure and Substance in Deliberative Democracy;" Gutmann, "Democracy, Philosophy, and Justification;" Young, *Justice and the Politics of Difference*; and Young, "Communication and the Other."

58.   Cohen, "Deliberation and Democratic Legitimacy," 19.

59.   Seyla Benhabib, *Critique, Norm, and Utopia: A Study of the Foundations of Critical Theory* (New York: Columbia University Press, 1986), 311–12.

60.   Habermas, *Between Facts and Norms*, 27.

61.   Ibid., 299; 301.

62.   Ibid., 296–97.

63. For detailed discussions of the relationship between discourse ethics and rationality, see Seyla Benhabib, "Deliberative Rationality and Models of Democratic Legitimacy," 26–52 and Benhabib, "Toward a Deliberative Model of Democratic Legitimacy," 67–94.

64. Cohen, "Deliberation and Democratic Legitimacy," 22.

65. Ibid., 22–23. Habermas and Benhabib both state their agreement with this formulation of the ideal procedure. Although Habermas criticizes Cohen for applying the procedure to a holistic conception of society and Benhabib adds some of her own features including the right to question the agenda and the right to raise arguments about the rules of discourse. See Habermas, *Between Facts and Norms*, 305 and Benhabib, "Toward a Deliberative Model of Democratic Legitimacy," 70.

66. Gutmann and Thompson, 16.

67. Benhabib, "Toward a Deliberative Model of Democratic Legitimacy," 75 and Gutmann and Thompson, 359.

68. I am referring here to Young and Benhabib, among others. Young draws on Benhabib's critique of Habermas's vacillation between the impartiality of the "generalized other" versus a more located standpoint of "concrete other." See Benhabib, *Situating the Self* and Young, *Justice and the Politics of Difference*, 106.

69. Benhabib, "Toward a Deliberative Model of Democratic Legitimacy," 75.

70. Young, *Justice and the Politics of Difference*, 116.

71. Benhabib, "Toward a Deliberative Model of Democratic Legitimacy," 71–72. Benhabib acknowledges Bernard Manin's "On Legitimacy and Political Deliberation," *Political Theory* 15, no. 3 (August 1987): 338–68, in the discussion of deliberation imparting information. She also notes that the idea of an "enlarged mentality" is drawn from Hannah Arendt, following Kant. Benhabib's claims surrounding the formation of coherent preferences and an enlarged mentality are similar to four aspects of justice as a process—reconciliation, reciprocity, recognition, and judgment—offered by Jane Flax, "Beyond Equality: Gender, Justice and Difference," in *Beyond Equality and Difference: Citizenship, Feminist Politics and Female Subjectivity*, eds. Gisela Bock and Susan James (New York: Routledge, 1992), 205–06.

72. Benhabib, "Toward a Deliberative Model of Democratic Legitimacy," 75–76. It is important to note that Benhabib disagrees note only with Rawls, but also with Habermas as to the appropriate demarcations between civil society and private/public spheres. She accuses Habermas of drawing "overly rigid boundaries"— such as "between matters of justice and those of the good life, public interests versus private needs, privately held values and publicly shared norms"—that reflect a stricter understanding of the public/private split than the views she espouses. Benhabib, *Situating the Self*, 111–12. The following discussion presents primarily her view on how discourse theory can conceive of public/private

demarcations more flexibly without jeopardizing basic liberties such as individual autonomy.

73. Habermas, *Between Facts and Norms*, 30.

74. Benhabib, "Toward a Deliberative Model of Democratic Legitimacy," 76.

75. Ibid., 76.

76. This term was coined by Nancy Fraser, "Rethinking the Public Sphere: A Contribution to the Critique of Actually Existing Democracy," in *Habermas and the Public Sphere*, ed. Craig Calhoun (Cambridge, MA: MIT Press, 1992), 83–84.

77. Benhabib, "Toward a Deliberative Model of Democratic Legitimacy," 84.

78. Habermas, *Between Facts and Norms*, 299.

79. Cohen, "Procedure and Substance in Deliberative Democracy," 102.

80. Benhabib, "Toward a Deliberative Model of Democratic Legitimacy," 81 offers such a distinction in response to specifically feminist concerns. I have adapted and broadened her categories to make room for criticisms that emanate from other quarters.

81. Frank Michelman, "Law's Republic," *Yale Law Journal* 97 (1988): 1527.

82. Jane Mansbridge concluded from her study of New England town meetings that consensual processes can elicit more perspectives than majority rule. "If, in order to make a decision satisfy everyone, everyone is encouraged to speak, the final decision will incorporate a more thorough assessment of each member's needs." Mansbridge, *Beyond Adversary Democracy*, 172.

83. Connolly, 102. Connolly is drawing upon a comment Michel Foucault made in an interview when he was asked about Arendt's and Habermas's concept of political power as "acting in concert" versus power as domination. In response, Foucault stressed the idea of critical, rather than regulatory, principles and urged us to be against nonconsensuality versus for consensuality. It is this sentiment that I wish to capture with the idea of a "critical yardstick," which I have borrowed from Benhabib, *Situating the Self*, 48.

84. Connolly, 95.

85. Cohen, "Procedure and Substance in Deliberative Democracy," 100 and Benhabib, "Toward a Deliberative Model of Democratic Legitimacy," 72.

86. Benhabib, "Toward a Deliberative Model of Democratic Legitimacy," 72.

87. Mansbridge, for example, concluded from her study of town meetings that consensus-based processes include specific costs for minorities. "In a consensual system, the minority is, in a sense, eliminated. After it agrees to go along, it leaves no trace. Its objections go unrecorded. Indeed, if those in the minority are intimidated, cannot give their reasons convincingly, or do not care enough to make a

scene, they may never voice their objections. Mansbridge, *Beyond Adversary Democracy*, 170.

88. Benhabib, "Toward a Deliberative Model of Democratic Legitimacy," 78.

89. Ibid., 80.

90. Ibid., 78–80.

91. See Nancy Fraser, 119; Jane Mansbridge, "Feminism and Democracy," *The American Prospect* 1 (1990); and Young, *Justice and the Politics of Difference*.

92. Fraser, 121 advocates such an approach.

93. Benhabib, *Situating the Self*, 159.

94. Young, *Justice and the Politics of Difference*, 119.

95. Phillips, 142.

96. Ibid., 145–46.

97. Habermas, *Between Facts and Norms*, Chapters 7 & 8.

98. Fraser, 122–23.

99. Habermas, *Between Facts and Norms*, 314.

100. Fraser, 134.

101. I employ the phrase "civic education" broadly to indicate what some authors, including Michael Oakeshott and Amy Gutmann, refer to as "political education." Any approach to the political aspects of education contains assumptions about politics and political activity. According to Oakeshott, "[our thoughts on political education] might be supposed to spring from our understanding of political activity and the kind of knowledge it involves." Michael Oakeshott, *Rationalism in Politics and Other Essays* (Indianapolis: Liberty Press, 1991), 45. In the case of deliberative democracy, we have a well-developed conception of political activity that says virtually nothing about political education. I hope to begin to fill in this gap.

102. Habermas, *Between Facts and Norms*, 298.

103. Amy Gutmann, *Democratic Education*, (Princeton: Princeton University Press, 1987), 287.

104. Gutmann, *Democratic Education*, 14. Gutmann also distinguishes "conscious social reproduction" from "political socialization" which she identifies as an unintended or unconscious process which can take place without members of the polity "consciously shaping its future" through education, 15.

105. Ibid., 3.

106. Ibid., 287.

107. Gutmann and Thompson, 359.

108. See, for example, Strike, 422; 474.

109. Cohen, "Procedure and Substance in Deliberative Democracy," 110. Subsequent
     page references in the text are to this essay. For further elucidation of Cohen's
     model of associative democracy, see Joshua Cohen and Joel Rogers, "Secondary
     Associations and Democratic Governance," *Politics and Society* 20 (1992); 393–
     473 and Erik Olin Wright, ed., *Associations and Democracy* (London: Verso,
     1995).

110. Each of these four cases addresses conditions under which *public* interests are
     best served by a form of non-state regulation. In the case of charter schools,
     particular schools also may arise out of a desire to promote largely *private* inter-
     ests, for example, interests in cultural transmission. Nevertheless, such private
     interests must be balanced against public interests in the distribution and gover-
     nance of schools and in providing civic education. Thus, Cohen's four conditions
     exemplify how such public interests may be fulfilled by providing particularistic
     charter schools with regulatory responsibility.

111. Similar to the way in which Cohen's associative strategy decentralizes political
     power, Jan Blits argues that Tocqueville believed that strong associations decen-
     tralize public opinion: "They break up the imposing massiveness of democratic
     society as a whole, replacing unity and sameness with plurality and diversity. Just
     as local governments and voluntary associations in democracies serve to mediate
     between the individual and the centralized state, so they also serve to mediate
     between the individual and the mass society." Blits, 29.

112. Gutmann, *Democratic Education*, 3.

113. Ibid., 287. Gutmann refers to these processes as "political education."

114. See, for example, Blits, 23–24; Gutmann, *Democratic Education*, 283–84; and
     John Dewey, Democracy and Education (New York: The Free Press, 1966/1916),
     especially chapter 2.

115. Habermas, *Between Facts and Norms*, 304.

116. Gutmann and Thompson echo this sentiment. They argue that education is the
     "single most important institution outside the government" in making democracy
     more deliberative. In addition, practice for deliberative democracy will require
     "significant changes in traditional civic education." Gutmann and Thompson,
     349.

117. Israel Scheffler, "Moral Education and the Democratic Ideal," in *Reason and
     Teaching*, ed. Israel Scheffler (Indianapolis and New York: The Bobbs-Merrill
     Company, 1973), 140.

118. Where Scheffler, for instance, stresses the quality of reasonableness, Patricia White
     emphasizes the importance of "democratic dispositions" such as hope, confi-
     dence, courage, self-respect, and honesty, among others. For discussion of

particular democratic virtues, see Blits, "Tocqueville on Democratic Education: The Problem of Public Passivity"; Gutmann, *Democratic Education;* Oakeshott, *Rationalism in Politics and Other Essays;* Pratte, *The Civic Imperative: Examining the Need for Civic Education;* Scheffler, "Moral Education and the Democratic Ideal"; and Patricia White, *Civic Virtues and Public Schooling: Educating Citizens for a Democratic Society* (New York: Teachers College Press, 1996).

119.   Benhabib, "Toward a Deliberative Model of Democratic Legitimacy," 70.s

PART TWO

INSTITUTIONALIZING DELIBERATIVE DEMOCRACY THROUGH CHARTER SCHOOLING

Chapter 3

Chartering *Practices for* Democratic Participation

I. Pursuing a Critical Interpretive Ethnography of Winthrop Academy

This segment of my investigation into charter schooling begins to step out of the realm of theory and into the concrete halls of school life. A case study of Winthrop Academy Charter School explores how the ideals of participatory democratic community become meaningful in everyday practice. The case study is intended to demonstrate how deliberate democratic principles can be used as critical yardsticks in two ways. First, the principles can be applied to the research process itself to inform the role of the researcher and the methodology for the study. Second, the principles can be applied to assessing whether public interests are being fulfilled within specific charter school practices. In addition, the case enriches our understandings of how deliberative democratic theory might be institutionalized in public charter schools in ways that maximize their democratic potential. Before describing Winthrop Academy and its experiences with civic education, I discuss the methodological orientation of the case study within the context of deliberative democratic theory.

Recall that the overall aim of this book is to explore the democratic potential of charter schools to cultivate strong educative communities that represent a variety of particular interests while simultaneously holding themselves accountable to shared public interests. Essentially, I am investigating how charter schools might both embody and prepare students for membership within pluralistic, participatory democratic associations that foster a sense of community. With this overarching goal in mind, I undertook a two-pronged agenda at the outset of the last chapter. First, I offered a theoretical framework to provide a normative vision for how public charter schools might best balance public and private interests in a pluralistic, democratic society. I turned to deliberative democracy as a procedural model for legitimately representing interests. This normative model insists that charters abide by democratic principles of equality, inclusion, and participation within public deliberations.

Second, I translated this theoretical model into civic educational aims and applied it to charter schooling. I delineated two aspects of public charter schools—*practices of* and *practices for* democratic decision making—that the deliberative model can be usefully applied to. At the empirical level, I will now turn to how this utopian task is approximated and complicated within the life of one charter school. A case study examines the concrete practices with which Winthrop Academy attempts to achieve its mission of civic education. The findings from the case will inform both the theoretical framework and charter school policy and practice.

Any project of empirical research faces the task of orienting itself in relation to existing epistemological, ontological, and normative frameworks. For me, this task was simultaneously simplified and constrained by the theoretical framework laid out in the previous chapter. Simplified because Habermasian critical social theory combines normative and empirical dimensions. The theory, therefore, does not merely prescribe how the world should look tomorrow, but self-consciously bases these claims on careful attention to how people actually make sense of and negotiate today's world. It proceeds from the assumption that philosophy is of limited value if not empirically grounded in everyday social relations among individuals. As Seyla Benhabib puts it:

> Even when we cannot take for granted that historical progress itself will guarantee the normative ideals in the name of which social actors struggle, a normative theory which cannot show how the "ought" and the "is" are to be *mediated* is useless from a critical standpoint. The task of critical social theory is not to develop Kantian imperatives, but to show the potential for rationality and emancipation implicit in the present [emphasis in text].[1]

From the outset, the empirical component of my case study was driven by precisely this question of mediation. I sought to inform critical social theory by testing some of its empirical claims and to identify promising ways of institutionalizing its utopian dimensions. In other words, I hoped empirical research would facilitate tangible processes of reconciliation between the "ought" and the "is" and at the same time make use of what "is" to refine our conceptions of the "ought." Because of its amenability to and even insistence on empirical analysis, critical social theory would be strengthened by my research. Conversely, the theory's rich commentary on questions of truth and value suggested specific approaches to empirical analysis.

Yet, what seemed straightforward at first glance became increasingly entangled in contradictions upon closer examination of Habermas's work and academic jargon surrounding research within the critical theory tradition. While Habermas's theory aspires to mediate between the "ought" and the "is,"[2] no systematic methodological account of empirical research grows directly out of his critical social theory. In addition, what is referred to as critical research within qualitative social science in general, and the field of educational research in particular, draws from a variety of sources that are not always logically compatible. Thus, I drew upon certain aspects of Habermas's theory of communicative action, as well as insights from postmodernism and interpretivism, to meld a viable brand of critical inquiry that I call "critical interpretivism." Now, I will introduce the case study where I applied this research orientation and talk more specifically about the methodologies I employed.[3]

II. Introducing The Study

Before there were any classrooms, any teachers, or any students, there was an idea for a school. And this idea came to be called Winthrop Academy. On Friday of the first week of school at Winthrop Academy, all 65 students gathered in the Common Room for their first weekly Town Meeting. The principal, Beth Taft, asked where the name came from. One student stood up and said "Some political guy make a quote."[4] Another student arose and proudly said "Governor John Winthrop." "Who was which governor of this state?" Ms. Taft asked. Someone responded, "the first" and Ms. Taft went on to explain "he came in 1630 with a boat of [some of the first settlers to Massachusetts]."

Although students, and most of the faculty, were just beginning to formulate what these references to John Winthrop meant for them and their school, other members of the community had already articulated their particular understandings. Winthrop Academy's co-founders, Beth Taft and Cathleen (Cathy) Eichler, had a fairly clear idea of how the name John Winthrop and visions of life in America that his name evokes connected with the type of public charter school they hoped to create. Or at least they did a good job of convincing the state Department of Education and 65 families and students that they had not only a clear idea, but an idea worthy of investing in and pursuing. According to their mission statement, written for the school's original charter:

Winthrop Academy is dedicated to rekindling the passion for democracy, the commitment to public service, the respect for hard work, and the hunger for learning in urban youth. This will be the mission of Winthrop Academy Charter School, a 7th-12th grade school in urban Eaton, whose focus will be **Civic Education**. This mission will inform our curriculum, our pedagogy, our attitudes, and our management structure, and guide our efforts to teach students to be thoughtful and active citizens.

America's founders knew that the preservation of democracy required education. For Thomas Jefferson, education was the "bulwark of a free people against tyranny." And James Madison wrote that without education, popular government is "but a Prologue to a farce or a tragedy, or, perhaps both." Our public schools were created to make democratic citizens.

Today, this mission is increasingly urgent. Many of our students are unconcerned with what is happening in the world, much less in their city. Many of our students do not see the point of voting, and are reluctant to claim the United States as their country. We cannot afford to be indifferent to the civic attitudes and allegiances of our citizens. The habits of tolerance, of thoughtful debate, of community involvement necessary for a democracy to flourish are not innate. They must be taught, exercised, and owned. The time has come for a new Winthrop Academy, a school which prepares students to understand, practice and embrace the principles and habits of democracy.[5]

As its founders envisioned it, Winthrop Academy aspired to become not only a model for public schooling, but for democratic public life in America.

Because of its focus on democratic civic education, Winthrop Academy provided me with an optimal setting for exploring how a charter school balances a particularistic mission, which sets it apart from other public schools, with public interests in democratic organization, governance, and *practices for* citizenship.

In light of my interest in the question "how are deliberative democratic ideals institutionalized in one charter school's *practices for* citizenship?" I would like to clarify why Winthrop Academy was an especially appropriate place to locate the case study research for this book and how I went about the research. Then I will offer a more thorough introduction of Winthrop Academy, its members, and its vision.

Focus of the Study and Methodology

I selected Winthrop Academy as a "critical" or "ideal-typical" case through a process commonly referred to as purposeful sampling.[6] In straightforward terms, that means that I chose Winthrop Academy because I felt that the process of institutionalizing democratic ideals within a charter school would be exemplified there as well or better than at any other charter school. Research methodologists describe a critical case as one that can be characterized by the statement: "If it happens there, it will happen anywhere."[7] Winthrop Academy is one of the few charter schools that I am aware of in the nation with a civic education mission. As such, I thought it reasonable to assume that Winthrop Academy would be as or more likely than any other charter to manifest the challenges and complexities of inculcating students with civic capacities through educative *practices for* democratic citizenship. I want to make clear that although I invoke the norms of deliberative democracy, Winthrop Academy does not profess to be a test case for Habermas's theory of discourse ethics. Nevertheless, it does offer striking parallels.

Winthrop Academy is a charter school with a democratic civic mission and a diverse population within a highly complex, pluralistic city. As part of its civic education mission and its New England legacy, the school has hosted a weekly Town Meeting from its inception. According to faculty's descriptions of Town Meeting, it was envisioned as something quite similar to the formal democratic spaces of Habermas's discourse model of deliberative democracy. This made it an ideal forum for examining how the legitimacy conditions of deliberative democracy translate into legitimacy conditions for civic education. Hence, from an early point in the research, my case study of Winthrop Academy was not intended as a full school ethnography, but as an in-depth investigation of *practices for* democratic decision making, especially within curricular practices such as weekly Town Meetings.[8]

In keeping with a critical interpretive orientation to meaning and understanding, I approached the case study research at three distinct levels. First, I focused on how members of the Winthrop Academy community interpreted democratic ideals and attempted to make them manifest within the institutional structure of Town Meeting. Second, I looked for Town Meeting processes or practices that seemed to either foster or complicate the realization of democratic ideals. And, third, I tried to identify ways in which Winthrop Academy's interpretations of these ideals both drew from and were constrained by broader social contexts. These three levels of analysis respectively reflected 1) attention to participant's internal perspectives, 2) face-to-face processes of meaning making, and 3) broader social contexts. Taken together these multiple layers of analysis comprise the backbone of an interpretive orientation.[9] In addition to approaching each layer with a critical analysis, I added a fourth level of reflection on the role of critical ethnographic research by asking: In what ways might my critical orientation and my presence as a researcher challenge local meanings and/or encourage democratic social action?

In addition to selecting Winthrop Academy as a critical case for investigating *practices for* citizenship, I approached the school as a sort of pilot case for identifying issues surrounding *practices of* governance and distribution. As I have mentioned in previous chapters, charter schools raise unique challenges to deliberative theory's ideals of equality and inclusion. First, charters, like all schools, grapple with hierarchical relationships between students and teachers. Their educative purpose also leads to tensions between professionals as "experts," parents, and community members. Each of these groups has varying stakes in decisions and specific roles *vis-à-vis* students which complicate any straightforward notion of "equal" status as decision makers. Second, because of charters' unique missions, individual schools may include certain students and exclude others. To the extent that charters are associations formed around common interests, people who do not share those interests will be left out. Thus, I kept issues of equality and inclusion in mind during my time at Winthrop Academy in order to flag particular manifestations which came to the fore in this setting.

I informed each strand of inquiry through multiple avenues of data collection including participant observation of a range of school events (including classes, Town Meetings, faculty meetings, and special events, among others), interviews with faculty and students, student surveys, and document review. Data were collected over a two-year period from September 1995 to June 1997. During this time I attended, observed, and/ or participated in school events at least once per week, if not more often. I was generally at the school for at least three hours per week.

In sum, this case study represents an attempt to democratize educational research, public charter schools, and discourse surrounding education reform. The ethnographic description provided in the following sections is intended to capture Winthrop Academy's experiences with democratic civic education from multiple perspectives of members of the school community. These multiplistic experiences are interrogated in terms of broader social contexts and theoretical frameworks which dialectically inform the institutionalization of democratic ideals. Needless to say, these are lofty aims but I also look for utopian successes in small examples. I consider this case study successful to the extent that it: 1) adequately captures Winthrop Academy's internal experiences and thus helps the school's members to further understand their culture and practices, 2) spurs members of the Winthrop Academy community to pursue democratic social transformation in light of these enriched understandings, and

3) provides research consumers with a deeper understanding of democratic theory as well as meaningful interpretations of civic education to accommodate into their own experiences with the democratic aspects of public education.[10] I see my role as providing a critical mirror that reflects *Winthrop's Academy's* experiences and encourages reflexive processes whereby readers make their own contextualized decisions surrounding whether the school's practices fulfill public interests, what democratizing changes might be appropriate, and how such change might be undertaken.

The School
In September, 1995 Winthrop Academy opened as a public charter high school with 65 ninth- and tenth-grade students and eight rooms on the 2nd floor of a multi-use building in central Eaton. In its second year, the school added a few more classrooms on the 1st and 2nd floors, and expanded its student body to 98 students. The students represent a cross-section of the city's population. In terms of ethnicity, during the first year students were 48 percent African American, 6 percent Asian, 17 percent Hispanic, and 29 percent White.[11]

Most of the Asian students are of Chinese and Vietnamese descent. Many of the students labeled African American for demographic purposes are of Cape Verdean descent. Eaton boasts a significant Cape Verdean population, as compared to other American cities, due in large part to a shipping route that existed earlier in this century between Eaton and the Cape Verdean Islands, located off the coast of South Africa. Many of these students are first-generation Americans and speak their native language as well as English. The Hispanic students claim Puerto Rican as well as various other Latino roots and speak Spanish as their first language. Quite a few of the white students are Irish-American. Most of the students are from working-class families around the city of Eaton. Students commute to Winthrop Academy from their homes in the city proper as well as outlying neighborhoods and townships. Most students are able to use public transportation to get to school.

Each year all of Winthrop Academy's students arrive at the school through a lottery-based admissions process. The process begins with a recruitment effort characterized by printed flyers and brochures, faculty visits to area middle schools, and word-of-mouth. After parents and students learn of Winthrop Academy they must attend one mandatory admissions session, in order to learn about the school's mission and aspirations, and fill out an application. Each student who completes these necessary steps is then placed into a random lottery selection. A local city judge blindly draws names out of a hat and, based upon availability, each student is assigned a slot either as an admitted member of the school or as a potential student on the waiting list. Students on the waiting list move up only as admitted students choose to decline their place or leave Winthrop Academy.[12]

Throughout the admissions process Winthrop Academy faculty stress the ways in which their school is unlike other public schools. They believe that one of the greatest strengths of charter schools is their aspirations toward specific missions. As opposed to traditional public schools, Winthrop Academy is not trying to match the needs and interests of all students in a one-size-fits-all fashion. Rather, the faculty is interested in attracting parents and students who share their vision (see table 3.1).

Winthrop Academy faculty are passionate about their vision; passionate enough to found a brand new school that they manage themselves and predict will be "a national model of teacher-driven reform."[13] And, so far, parents and students are flocking to the school. Each academic year there is a waiting list of students who cannot attend because there are no more seats available. But these parents and students do not seem to be choosing Winthrop Academy primarily for its civic mission. Instead, students explain that they have come to the school because it offers a "new opportunity." It is small, so there are "not that many people to fight," and "instead of thirty kids, fifteen or sixteen to one teacher." It is racially balanced and "open to anyone." And it emphasizes excellence. Kerry, a white female student, remembers selecting Winthrop Academy because "I liked how they were so pushy in the beginning about how good they wanted the education to be, pushing toward that." Daniel, an African-American male student, looked forward to being "in a learning environment to actually do something where I'm not a statistic, where I make a difference in my life and in what goes on in school."[14]

Despite the variety of reasons that students and families have for choosing Winthrop Academy, the vision of preparation for democratic citizenship is central to the school's sense of identity and its practices. This is nowhere more evident than in the weekly practice of Town Meeting. In the remainder of this section I describe what goes on in the weekly Town Meetings. Then, section III draws upon faculty members' perspectives in order to gain insight into the school's civic education curriculum.

Table 3.1 Winthrop Academy's Vision

Our Vision

Winthrop Academy prepares students to exercise their rights and responsibilities as American citizens. We foster in Eaton youth a curiosity for life-long learning, the habits of hard work and a commitment to public service. Winthrop Academy emphasizes the responsibility of educated citizens to question, to act, and to avoid complacency.

To nurture curiosity in our students we make accessible to them the best of human thought and endeavor. We teach the traditions and important documents of our democracy and encourage students to advance and build on those traditions. We seek to ensure that our own conclusions are never our students' starting points, but rather, that their skills and questions are honed so that they can go forward and imagine, ask, wonder, and contribute in ways we cannot yet know.

We strive to make our classes, our assessment strategies, and the experiences we offer students as authentic as possible—preparing them to meet the challenges and standards of the real world. To make learning authentic for our students, our school must be a learning organization with mechanisms to take and use feedback. We learn from our successes and failures. We maintain intimate learning environments with classes averaging 18 students. The process of establishing and building Winthrop Academy is not a distraction from the Winthrop Academy education; it is integral to it.

It is the responsibility of parents, teachers and the community to work together to nurture the potential of every student. Students are active partners in their learning and ultimately responsible for their own educations. At Winthrop Academy we seek to connect our teaching to students' experiences and to teach them with a faculty that is representative of their backgrounds. In order to fulfill our civics mission, we believe our faculty should reflect Eaton's diversity.

Hard work is important for all members of the Winthrop Academy community. It means that we teach students to value effort as an essential but not sole component of excellence, and that there are standards to which we must all hold ourselves accountable. Hard work also means that students deserve the experience of accomplishing things they thought they couldn't do. And most importantly it means that Winthrop Academy students **earn** their diplomas for what they know and can do, and that they are prepared to succeed in college.

For teachers, hard work means that we practice what we demand of students.

Within all this hard work, we remember to be joyful.

To promote public service, we make the City of Eaton an extended classroom. Its institutions, neighborhoods, and citizens are important resources accessible to students. Our students learn to value their whole city.

Winthrop Academy graduates citizens who will vote.

As a **public** charter school, Winthrop Academy does not ignore the crisis in public education. We disseminate what we learn, and are open to observers. We seek to balance our duties to our own students with our commitment to sustained change in public education.[15]

Town Meeting

On a typical Friday morning at Winthrop Academy Charter School the minutes between 11:45 and 11:55 are hectic ones. At 11:45 third period classes end and 11:55 marks the beginning of the weekly Town Meeting. During these ten minutes all of the school's 98 high school students file into the large Common Room at the end of the corridor. Visitors, looking both slightly puzzled and expectant, hurriedly sign their names in the guest book and look over their copies of the "Town Meeting Visitor Guidelines." I help a student volunteer set up the video camera to tape the upcoming meeting. The faculty moderator, Max Simon, quietly consults with other faculty members to review the agenda. And throughout these preparations, 98 students find seats and then gossip with their neighbors, poke their neighbors, or avoid their neighbors—depending on the nature of their relationships. Eventually, usually at about 11:57, Mr. Simon steps up to the podium and quickly gives the gavel two raps on the podium's top. The crowd quiets down.

After the room is completely silent, Mr. Simon begins with words similar to these that he used on a particular Friday in the late fall of 1996. "Ladies and gentlemen." He pauses. "This is our time to remember it's far easier to act than to think, to talk trash rather than do good, to put down rather than pull up, to talk and talk and talk rather than say one thing well. It is time for Town Meeting. Listen to each other and teach each other as we struggle not only with academics, but with how we act with fellow members of our community."[16]

Mr. Simon—a 6'4" science teacher known for his strict sense of discipline, dry wit, and tendency toward theatrics—begins each Town Meeting with this sort of invocation. He urges students to keep in mind the "proper decorum" for conduct during this time, and indeed, during all of their time as members of the Winthrop Academy community. He also reminds students that if they fail to abide by this proper decorum, they will be asked to leave Town Meeting and will have to discuss their actions with him afterward. So far, over the course of the 1996-97 academic year, no student has been asked to leave.

Winthrop Academy's members—faculty and students alike—have participated in a Town Meeting each Friday afternoon since the school opened its doors on September 6, 1995. Each week's nearly hour-long Town Meeting (meetings are scheduled to last fifty minutes) is intended to serve two purposes within the school. First, Town Meeting is a forum in which students practice democracy. Second, Town Meeting provides a place for the school to build a sense of community. These two intersecting goals reflect Winthrop Academy's civic education mission. The school strives to prepare and graduate "independent, resourceful, and responsible citizens prepared to advance community, culture, and commerce."[17]

Town Meeting fulfills each of its dual functions—providing a forum for practicing democracy and for building community—through intersecting segments of its structure and agenda. Each Town Meeting begins with Mr. Simon, the moderator, reminding students of faculty's expectations for appropriate *ways of being* within Town Meeting.

> Max Simon: Ladies and Gentlemen. Today during Town Meeting we'll cover a lot of stuff. . . . .If democracy is to really work, each voice is to really be heard. It doesn't matter what religion you are, how much money you have, what neighborhood you live in. Even if you're a billionaire, Ross Perot. I get one vote, as a citizen, no one is more important. We are a school based on civic responsibility; no one will compromise the voice of anyone else. If you do, either you don't believe that or haven't learned that. Those who don't want to give respect to those who are speaking, . . . whether it's an adult, fellow student, or guest, we will ask you to meet us after school and you will get a research project. You may have noticed that those who disrespect those who are speaking are those who rarely speak. Those who are down low try to keep others from rising. That's why we made this school, so those with opportunities before them will have nothing to compromise their potential, they'll have all resources to go ahead. You're lucky to live in a society that gives you that right, [unlike] other societies, you can choose all that. [We're trying to prepare you to] make the decisions you can make by giving you the best education paid for by taxpayers from this city. If you refuse to do a project, you will get detention. If you don't have enough respect to get up in front of those you were disrespecting, then [you do not receive] a lesson but a punishment. We don't want to punish you. We want you to respect yourself first, then those around you. With self respect, you say things the right way and intelligently.[18]

Following such a reminder, Mr. Simon briefly outlines the agenda for the day, often pointing to the easel at the side of the podium where the day's main topic for debate is posted. Next, he asks for a formal motion to open Town Meeting. In the tradition of Robert's Rules of Order, a student stands, says "Mr. Moderator my name is [x], and I make a motion to open Town Meeting," and sits back down. Then, another student stands, says "Mr. Moderator my name is [y] and I second that motion." A bit tongue-in-cheek, Mr. Simon says "All those in favor of opening Town Meeting shout 'Aye,'" and a burst of "ayes" erupts around the room. Then, again tongue-in-cheek, Mr. Simon says, lowering his voice, "all those opposed to opening Town Meeting whisper 'Nay.'" Inevitably a group of students shouts "Nay." Grinning, Mr. Simon announces, "the 'Ayes' have it."

Before beginning the debate segment of Town Meeting, a few more things happen. First, Mr. Simon welcomes any visitors—and there are almost always between two and seven visitors—by reading their names from the guest book. Next, faculty members recap the week's attendance and make announcements to the school body.

Max Simon (Science Teacher, White): One absence only this week, same as for the past three weeks. {Listed students who owed time for being late. Announced Science homework.} [19]

    We had in-school suspensions this week only Monday and Tuesday. That's a vast improvement.

    Please be conscious that school ends at 4:00. If no teacher wants to see you, you have the privilege to leave at 3:30. If you're done, either get to work or please go home. That's not because we don't love you dearly, or we don't want you to be here, but you can't be hanging out in the hallway because teachers are seeing students and academic probation starts. So stay all day [to work], but you can't hang out at the lockers. Stay all you want to work, you know the school's open until 7 [p.m.], but work, go to the gym, not just lockers.

    Plan ahead, carry a bag with all of your stuff for the morning so you don't have to go to your locker between each class. Everybody's hanging out at the lockers having a good time. That's not what we're about. We're about taking care of business. If you can't take care of business, you can't become someone hanging out in the hallway. If hanging out was all it took to take care of business, all those people hanging out on corners in front of pizza parlors would be millionaires and presidents. It's not an exaggeration, it's the truth. The reason we get after you is because we know what's good for you and we're trying to show that to you and teach it to you and let you understand what you've got to do to take care of business. Keep that in mind, planning ahead.

Shaka Reid (History Teacher, African American): My Advisory is working on getting there on time.[20] {He thanked a few students for meeting about a Teen Center partnership with the YMCA.} Anybody interested in being part of that conversation see me after Town Meeting; there's a meeting on Monday. Good week teaching; keep it up.

Cathleen Eichler (School Founder and Humanities Teacher, White): We had a few tardies this week. {Reminder of homework due.}

Sam Asher (Math Teacher, White): I am delighted to welcome Natasha back to school. {Listed students who owed math Problems Of the Week (POWs).}

Dipan Patel (Science Teacher, White):   Remember that labs are due. I
    need to see {listed certain students} before you leave today.

Harry Chase (Humanities Teacher, White):   I would like to point out that
    2 days absent counts as 2 absences. We have had 3 people deathly
    ill this week and out of school and 2 tardies besides. There is an
    essay due for the *Scarlet Letter* and questions on *Julius Caesar*.

Jerard Navarro (Spanish Teacher, Hispanic):   All of my advisees were
    here all week, no absences. They keep making me proud.

Frank Nardelli (Humanities Teacher, White):   After this meeting I shall be
    holding court in Room 4. It behooves all students who owe work to
    see me today.

Liz Richardson (Gym Teacher and Basketball Coach, African America):
    Scrimmage canceled today.

Heather Freeman (Swimming Teacher and Academic Probation Coordi-
    nator, White):   In swimming there seems to be a virus going around;
    people are forgetting swim caps. Remember, this affects your grade.
    I would like to announce the three most improved swimmers of
    week: {listed students}.

Brenda Schank (Director of Programs, White):   There is a volunteer from
    last year willing to take one or two students to Dartmouth College
    in New Hampshire. See me if you are interested. Thanks for those
    of you who let me know about your internship requests; this spells
    the difference between an internship you're interested in and one
    you're not that excited about.

Pat Tinkler (Teacher's Aid, Hispanic):   The Drama Club is taking care of
    show business. We need more girls; see me or Mr. Navarro.

Joshua Ross (Math Teacher, Hispanic):   Tomorrow we start preparing for
    SAT from 10 a.m.–12 p.m. I've posted missing homework lists in
    the room, go look after this meeting.

Beth Taft (School Founder and Principal, White):   I'd like to welcome a
    new student, Taneesha Black, she'll be starting here on Monday
    morning. You'll also have a chance to meet some other new stu-
    dents on Monday morning.

After the announcements are completed, a faculty member, student,
or group of students paves the way into the formal debate segment of
Town Meeting by leading an "Inspirational Moment." Shaka Reid has
read from James Baldwin and played original songs on his guitar, Sam
Asher has read from Junot Diaz's recent book *Drown*, Max Simon has
recounted stories from his coaching days with "Teach for America" in
Louisiana, and a student has played an acoustic guitar version of "Stairway

to Heaven." Following the inspirational moment, generally fifteen to twenty minutes into the fifty-minute Town Meeting, the topic for debate is introduced. Town Meeting topics take many forms (see tables 3.2 and 3.3). One form of Town Meeting topics structures discussion as a feedback session for students to give input to faculty for consideration. Such topics range from the school lunch to student failure in academic courses. For instance, on May 10, 1996 faculty posed the following question to

Table 3.2 Winthrop Academy's Town Meeting Topics for 1995–96

Date	Topic	Action
September 8, 1995	Introduction of Town Meeting Terminology	
September 15, 1995	Nominations for Judicial Hearing Board	Students Nominated
September 22, 1995	Elections for Judicial Hearing Board	2 Students Elected
September 29, 1995	Resolved: Winthrop Academy should institute a Cal Ripken Perfect Attendance Award	Approved
October 6, 1995	Student Clubs	
October 13, 1995	Outsider Speaker: Eaton Police Department	
October 20, 1995	Student Committee Introduces School Pledge	Revisions Recommended
November 3, 1995	Debate and Suggestions on Winthrop Academy Pledge	Revisions Recommended
November 17, 1995	Students submit a petition requesting extra time between gym and Spanish classes	5 minutes added between classes
November 22, 1995	Thanksgiving Celebration	
December 1, 1995	1. Resolved: Winthrop Academy supports President Clinton's decision to send U.S. troops to Bosnia 2. Winthrop Academy Pledge	1. Debate postponed 2. Approved pledge
December 8, 1995	1. Debate on Bosnia resolution 2. Cross-the-Line Exercise	1. Vote split 29 for/29 against sending troops
December 11, 1995	Monday morning meeting	Voted against (32 /25) sending U.S. troops to Bosnia
December 15, 1995	1. Feedback on letter to President Clinton 2. Two students take the Winthrop Academy Pledge	1. Letter endorsed with revisions

Continued on next page

Table 3.2 Continued

Date	Topic	Action
January 5, 1996	1. Preparation for Internships 2. School Mascot Name	2. Voted in favor of two team names; faculty selected "Blue Storm"
January 12, 1996	Martin Luther King, Jr. Day Celebration	
January 26, 1996	What can the Winthrop Academy community do to ensure that more people do their homework?	Meeting adjourned early due to student disruption
February 3, 1996	Preparation for Internships	
February 9, 1996	Internship Progress Reports	
March 1, 1996	Resolved: Winthrop Academy should have a shorter school day.	Debate postponed
March 5, 1996	Emergency meeting regarding noise in the YMCA lobby during lunch.	Students vote to have their YMCA privileges revoked if they violate YMCA policy.
March 15, 1996	Resolved: Winthrop Academy should have a shorter school day.	Endorsed with 51 in favor/5 opposed
March 22, 1996	What are some topics we can suggest to the YMCA to add to the gym program?	Meeting adjourned early due to student disruption
March 29, 1996	Gym Day Awards	
April 12, 1996	Faculty demonstrate expectations for student dress with a fashion show.	
April 26, 1996	Preparation for June Jury Assessments	
May 3, 1996	1. Resolved: Students should be able to earn back points for Gym Day. 2. Civics Issue regarding 1st Amendment guarantees of free speech	1. Recommended to gym teachers that students earn points 2. Debate postponed
May 10, 1996	1. Civics Issue regarding 1st Amendment guarantees of free speech 2. We have had two months of the Perfect Homework list, how are we doing?	1. Vote that punishment of hate speech in a school is a violation of free speech (27/16) 2. Faculty promise policy change in light of student feedback
May 17, 1996	1. Preparation for New York City trip. 2. Outside Speaker: Office of Jury Commission	
May 24, 1996	Outside Speaker: Legal Defense Office	
June 7, 1996	Volunteer Recognition and Gym Day Awards	
June 21, 1996	End-of-Year Awards and Celebration	

Table 3.3 Winthrop Academy's Town Meeting Topics for 1996–97

Date	Topic	Action
September 6, 1996	Reviewed "Town Meeting Guidelines"	
September 13, 1996	Resolved: Winthrop Academy should endorse a Presidential candidate.	Debate postponed 1. Voted against en-
September 20, 1996	1. Resolved: Winthrop Academy should endorse a Presidential candidate. 2. Resolved: The children of illegal aliens should be denied public education.	dorsing a candidate 2. Debate postponed
September 27, 1996	Immigration Policy	No Vote
October 4, 1996	Resolved: A citizen of Winthrop Academy who witnesses another citizen violating our handbook must report it.	Debate postponed
October 11, 1996	Winthrop Academy Handbook Violations	Debate postponed
October 18, 1996	Winthrop Academy Handbook Violations	Opposed 52/36/6 abstain
October 25, 1996	How can we bring student's GPAs up?	
November 1, 1996	Improving Academic Performance	
November 8, 1996	Pres. Clinton's and Senator Kerry's term agendas	
November 15, 1996	California Proposition 209	Debate postponed
November 22, 1996	California Proposition 209	Opposed 45/6
December 6, 1996	1. Nominations for Judicial Hearing Board. 2. Resolved: Winthrop Academy students should have an alternative to shirts, i.e. pins.	1. Eight nominees; two elected the next week 2. Approved
December 13, 1996	1. What are some alternatives to Winthrop Academy shirts? 2. GED requirement for all high school seniors	
December 20, 1996	Holiday Celebration	
January 10, 1997	Martin Luther King, Jr. Day Celebration	
January 17, 1997	Dr. Assisted Suicide should be legalized	
January 24, 1997	1. Internship Preparation 2. Resolved: Dr. Assisted Suicide should be legalized	2. Voted Against
January 31, 1997	Internship Preparation	
February 7, 1997	Internship Progress Reports	
February 14, 1997	Internship Final Reports	

Continues on next page

Table 3.3 Continued

Date	Topic	Action
February 28, 1997	Outside Speaker: Suffolk County District Attorney	
March 7, 1997	Resolved: The U.S. government should fund research on cloning human beings?	Debate postponed
March 14, 1997	Resolved: The U.S. government should fund research on cloning human beings?	Voted Against
March 21, 1997	What does it mean to be a citizen at Winthrop Academy?	
April 4, 1997	Outside Speaker: Transit Authority Officer	
April 11, 1997	Preparation for Interdisiplinary "Leonardo" Week	
April 18, 1997	Presentations from "Leonardo" Teams	
May 9, 1997	In-School Suspension Policy	Debate Postponed
May 16, 1997	In-School Suspension Policy	Debate Postponed
May 23, 1997	School Uniforms	Debate Postponed
May 30, 1997	Ways of Being	Debate Postponed
June 6, 1997	Outside Speaker: Judge	
June 13, 1997	Juries	
June 20, 1997	End-of-Year Awards and Celebration	

students: "We have had two months of the Perfect Homework list, how are we doing?" Since March, 1996 faculty had been implementing a policy whereby students who completed all of their assigned homework on a given week earned the privilege of leaving school half-an-hour early the following week. Frustrated and confused by the particularities of the policy, some students informed Ms. Taft, the principal, that they wanted to bring the issue before Town Meeting. In light of the points brought out in the Town Meeting discussion, faculty promised to review and revise the policy.

A second form of topics structures Town Meeting as a decision-making session. In this case, Town Meeting members are faced with a resolution that must be debated and voted on. Some of the resolutions concern issues of school policy; others engage issues of local, national, or international significance. In both cases, Town Meeting members must keep in mind their jurisdiction over the issue. As the school's *Town Meeting Guidelines* handbook explains:

The jurisdiction of **Town Meeting** is:
* school policy—rules, regulations, rights and privileges of our school
* recommendations—requests for action from other authorities, e.g. from our Board of Trustees of the school, the U.S. Congress, the office of the Mayor of Eaton. **Town Meeting** has the power to make the recommendations in the name of the school.
* resolutions—the sentiment (how we think of an issue)
  (Jurisdiction is the legal power, the right, or the authority to hear and to determine a cause. In other words, the jurisdiction of Town Meeting of Winthrop Academy is the policy or set of decisions which the members have the power to make, to change, and to carry out. Town Meeting currently has direct authority over some matters of school policy and has the power to make recommendations and resolutions, in the name of the school, on matters which touch upon the mission of Winthrop Academy.)[21]

Town Meeting members endorse resolutions that either regulate or recommend action regarding school policy or, in cases of wider-reaching issues, recommend action to a distinct governmental entity. One of the weightier school policies that students tackled in Town Meeting was the issue of shortening the school day. In the spring of 1996, a fairly large group of students and teachers felt that the scheduled 8:30 a.m. to 3:46 p.m. school day was too long. On March 1, 1996, the issue was brought before Town Meeting for debate. The resolution read: "Winthrop Academy should have a shorter school day." Due to the quantity of speakers wishing to address the resolution, debate was postponed until the next Town Meeting. On March 15, 1996, Town Meeting concluded debate and endorsed the resolution with 51 members voting in favor and 5 voting against.[22]

A small group of students then brought the resolution before the school's Board of Trustees on March 21, 1996. Even though Cathy Eichler—one the school's founders, a Humanities teacher and a Board member—was vehemently opposed to the resolution and voted against it in Town Meeting, she urged the Board to follow Town Meeting's recommended action.

Cathy Eichler: We've asked young people to make [large changes. They have shown] extraordinary growth and investment. I am proud. They have come to us with this respect. We pride ourselves on keeping a watchful but open mind within this practical, strategic experiment. This comes at good time of the year with our first group. Let's see what this change produces. If it produces the desired result, students will be more focused on academic work. I say it is wrong to move to a shorter day. Still, I am committed long term to keeping young people occupied in this educational endeavor. I am also very committed and proud of the way faculty,

students, and administrators got together. We had two days of debate in Town
Meeting. This showed the mettle of school. I urge the Board to vote on this.[23]

The Board voted unanimously in favor of the recommendation and faculty shortened Winthrop Academy's school day to end thirty minutes
earlier at 3:16 p.m. The following week, the faculty announced to students the change in school policy with a stipulation: students with perfect
homework had the privilege of leaving at 3:16; all others had to stay until
3:46. I will return to the implications of faculty's decision when I discuss
student's perceptions of Town Meeting later in the next chapter.

Town Meeting has also endorsed or rejected resolutions on local, national, and world politics. The first issue of broad political significance
brought before Town Meeting concerned President Clinton's decision to
send U.S. troops to Bosnia. In December, 1995, after an emotional debate and tied vote, Town Meeting voted against sending troops to Bosnia.
A letter was drafted and sent to President Clinton indicating Winthrop
Academy's disagreement with his decision. Other issues for debate have
included First Amendment protection of hate speech, research on cloning
human beings, doctor-assisted suicide, immigration policy, and California's
Proposition 209.

A third type of Town Meeting topic structures the meeting as an information session or educational event. These types of Town Meetings are
similar to assemblies with guest speakers from around the city of Eaton.
Others are opportunities for students to gain necessary information on
upcoming school activities such as the two-week internships that take
place every February or the structure of final juried assessments at the
end of each school year.

A fourth, and final, type of Town Meeting topic structures the meeting
as a time for the community to reflect and celebrate. During each of its
two years in session, Winthrop Academy Town Meetings have featured
readings and reflections to commemorate Thanksgiving, the December
holidays, and Martin Luther King, Jr. Day. Town Meeting has also hosted
awards ceremonies for student's sporting events, volunteer recognition,
and academic recognition at the end of the school year.

Town Meeting's weekly structure, along with the various forms that
topics take, reinforce each of the forum's dual purposes—to practice democracy and to build community. As students debate and vote on resolutions, as students participate in setting school policy or recommend action to other bodies, and as students become more informed about their
city, their country, and their world, they practice the skills and attributes

of democratic citizenship. Similarly, as the school gathers together, celebrates together, and participates in decision making together, a sense of community takes shape.

Yet the community building aspects of Town Meeting are not only celebratory, or participatory, they are also regulatory. Town Meeting members are expected to follow a specific protocol for participation. For example, a member must be recognized by the moderator, stand, and state his or her name in order to speak. In addition, specific students are sometimes required by faculty to step up to the podium and make a public apology to the body for violating one of the norms of the school community. Similarly, the Moderator frequently reminds students of behavioral expectations and directs whether or not actions are appropriate. And all faculty members use the time allotted for announcements to stress school policies that students are expected to follow.

When these types of things happen, specific forms of regulation are taking place. This type of regulatory atmosphere reflects Winthrop Academy's educative mission. The faculty are not attempting to build a purely democratic community within the school. Rather, they aspire to build an educative community within which students gain skills and attitudes fundamental to democratic citizenship. Although Town Meeting is intended to facilitate these civic aims, it is but one aspect of the school's academic program and wide-reaching educative efforts.

In addition to Town Meeting, there is another key place where the aims of safety, learning, and civics intersect, and that takes the form of a school uniform. Winthrop Academy requires all students to wear a shirt bearing the school's logo. According to the school handbook, the shirts are to be worn "as a symbol of school pride and as a part of maintaining a safe school environment."[24] Faculty also view the shirts as a symbol of membership within the school community. Cathy Eichler recently explained to the school's Board of Trustees why the shirts are especially significant for her:

> Cathy Eichler: We are a public school open by lottery to everyone; how do we make our message clear? Many people are attracted for many reasons other than our mission. It is hard to be clear to people that we want to educate students to be citizens, not consumers. One way is that the families and students who are here are folks who knew we required uniforms and decided it was worth it, even if it was a compromise. [A uniform is] one way a public school can have a community of people who are like-minded at least about that; identified with our community and educational environment.[25]

Mrs. Eichler made this statement to the Board because of a Town Meeting vote in January 1997 resolving that " Winthrop Academy students should have an alternative to shirts, such as pins." Shirts have been a contentious issue at Winthrop Academy since the first Town Meeting on September 8, 1995, when a female student stood and said "a lot of us have discussed in advisory that we don't like wearing shirts when teachers don't have to." Her statement was followed by cheering from many students in the audience. Since then, the topic has come up in various ways in many Town Meetings—ranging from Ms. Taft, as the principal and Town Meeting moderator, proclaiming the issue "non-negotiable" in September 1995 to the Board of Trustees recommending in January 1997 that faculty and students form a joint commission and return to the Board with recommendations for action.

The many manifestations that the "shirt issue" has taken during Winthrop Academy's two-year life demonstrates tensions between the school's dual missions of providing a learning environment for academic excellence as well as a forum for practicing democratic participation. Whereas most faculty see the shirts as an integral element of a safe and serious learning environment, and most parents seem willing to go along with this contention, many students see the shirts as infringements on individual liberty and freedom of expression. Accordingly, students immediately made use of the Town Meeting forum to identify the shirt issue as something of concern to them. And faculty were faced with questions surrounding students' authority over agenda items within Town Meeting and the jurisdiction of Town Meeting in terms of school policy. To what extent would students practicing democracy within Town Meeting correlate with students participating in decision making at Winthrop Academy? In order to understand the particular nuances of the tensions surrounding this question, it is important to have a sense of the relationship between Winthrop Academy's emphasis on civics and other components of its educational mission.

III. Civic Education at Winthrop Academy

Winthrop Academy's "Academic Promise" to students for a high school education includes the following curricular elements: English (4 credits), History (3 credits) , Science (3 credits), Math (4 credits), Second Language (Conversancy), Public Service, Physical Education (4 credits), Technology, The Arts, and Town Meeting.[26] The school is very committed to the idea that students will *earn* their diplomas, even if this means that it may take them more than four years to finish high school. Earning credit for one's first-year English course, for instance, means that a student must demonstrate that she knows how to write one well-developed paragraph, among other requirements. This student will not earn credit simply for attending English class or earning passing grades throughout the year; she must demonstrate certain competencies upon completion of the course.

In English, students read Homer's *The Odyssey* and Shakespeare's *The Tempest* during their first year. They deliver oratory readings to their classmates and practice literary and textual analysis. During the second year, they read *The Crucible, Macbeth,* and *Red Badge of Courage,* among other works. They are expected to graduate "knowing how to write a well-organized and interesting essay in standard English, to read with understanding, and to speak effectively."

Winthrop Academy's History curriculum emphasizes an historical exploration of American democracy beginning with roots in Ancient Greece. During their first year, students learn about Athens, Sparta, and Rome. As sophomores, they begin the study of primary American documents including the Declaration of Independence and the Constitution. Students make frequent class speeches on current events topics of their own choosing. Students are expected to graduate "knowing how to defend their views on historical and contemporary issues, and to analyze and appreciate important American documents."

First-year science students study Earth Science and then move on to Biology in the second year. In 9th grade, students are introduced to the periodic table and lab experimentation. At the end of the year they design their own planet using appropriate computer software. In 10th grade, the study of biology and life sciences includes a strong emphasis on genetics. Students combine lab experimentation with opinion essays on science topics in the news. Students are expected to graduate "able to understand scientific aspects of civic problems, and to design, perform, and analyze scientific experiments."

At Winthrop Academy students encounter a Math curriculum that combines algebra, geometry, and a bit of trigonometry during each year of study. Students learn basic math skills as they are needed within a problem-solving approach to mathematical thinking. In the first-year course, they are also encouraged to write and talk about their mathematical thinking as they work through problems and face stumbling blocks. Students are expected to graduate "able to use and apply algebra." In future years, students who begin Winthrop Academy as 7th graders will be expected to study calculus by their junior or senior years.[27]

All Winthrop Academy students must be conversant in a second language in order to graduate. Spanish is the only language currently offered as a formal course. Students who are already fluent in Spanish apply their skills to the cultural study of Spain and hone their written skills. In addition, "students reading far below grade level in English and/or requiring academic support will postpone their second language requirement."

Physical Education at Winthrop Academy includes a swimming requirement and a YMCA pass to its fitness club. Many students swim for the first time as a result of this requirement. The Physical Education program also includes activities ranging from basketball to aerobics to weight training. Students can use their YMCA passes to make use of all fitness facilities after school hours.

Technology is incorporated across the disciplines at Winthrop Academy. Students must use word processing programs to prepare many of their assignments for History and English. The Spanish class makes use of listening and speaking language software. Spreadsheets and graphics programs, along with other scientific software, are incorporated into the math and science curricula.

In terms of the Arts, " Winthrop Academy works with Eaton's cultural institutions and local artists to make the arts an integral part of the Winthrop Academy experience." Students travel to local museums to view exhibits or for a brief lecture during Humanities class. Students also frequent the theater, walk around the city focusing on architecture, and participate in a music mentoring program with a local school of music.

Public Service takes many forms at Winthrop Academy. During public service sessions (one-period per week), students participate in a range of activities including: recycling cans and paper from the school, reading to children in the YMCA's day care program, hosting an all-day public service event where students helped clean up the local zoo grounds, collecting food for the homeless, visiting elementary schools, and conducting exit polls following the 1996 Presidential election. In addition, students have participated in two-week internships at work sites around the city of Eaton each February.

Combined with public service, Town Meeting is one of the key places where Winthrop Academy's civic mission is made explicit. A recent, working draft of the formal civics curriculum, discussed by faculty on March 14, 1997, clarifies the purposes of Town Meeting as well as its connections to the broader civics mission (see table 3.4). The civics mission encompasses three major components: 1) Participation in the culture, commerce, and communities of Eaton; 2) Practicing civic engagement and civil interaction; and 3) Learning about and experiencing how the city works. I focus my analysis of Winthrop Academy's experiences with

Table 3.4 Winthrop Academy's Civics Curriculum

DRAFT—March, 1997

Winthrop Academy graduates democratic citizens prepared to advance community, commerce, and culture. To advance this mission, civics at Winthrop Academy has 3 components:

1) Participation in the culture, commerce & communities of Eaton.
   a. Students <u>visit cultural institutions</u> of Eaton, and attend cultural events, performances, and exhibits.
   b. Students <u>perform public service</u> in Eaton.
   c. Students <u>perform 2 week internships</u> during their first three years at Winthrop Academy, participating in the cultural and/or commercial and/or community life of Eaton.

2) Practicing civic engagement and civil interaction.
   a. Students participate in a weekly school Town Meeting which prepares them to think about the issues of our day, to express their views and to tolerate and understand views different from their own.
   b. Students are taught to speak effectively in public and are expected to deliver speeches of various increasing lengths at the end of each year at Winthrop Academy, culminating in a 10-15 minutes speech before the entire school community.
   c. Students are taught to practice and maintain ways of being conducive to a civic school community. Students earn a citizenship grade based on their exhibition of these ways of being. This grade is determined by their advisor.

3) Learning about and experiencing how the city works.
   a. Students take a series of civic modules—quarter long 2x a week courses, culminating in an independent City Project, which is a senior's authentic contribution to a civic issue. Modules would begin as hands-on Eaton classes culminating in an "I know my city badge." An issues module would precede the senior year, preparing students to frame their own issue for the City Project. The senior internship would be connected to this City Project.

---

the second objective—practicing civic engagement and civil interaction—and its relationship to the skills and predispositions required for deliberative democracy.[28]

The Civics Mission
Despite the apparent clarity of the three civic objectives listed above, Winthrop Academy's faculty continue to struggle with just what each objective entails as well as how these objectives are to be attained. Faculty

members are struggling to define and clarify how their civic mission fits with the rest of the academic curriculum and their vision for a school culture. This struggle emanates from a few sources. First, a civics emphasis is the vision of the school's founders, but is not necessarily shared in the same way or to the same degree by the other faculty members. Second, because the founders are committed to building a democratic process among faculty and creating an organizational structure and culture that will survive long after they are gone, the civic "mission" is evolving to include the perspectives of the growing faculty. And, third, the school is in the midst of its initial years and is just building a formal curriculum. Hence, faculty are working to translate an overarching civics mission into concrete curricular objectives.

Many facets of the struggle to clarify the civics curriculum are apparent in the following conversation from a Monday night planning meeting at Max Simon's home. This meeting took place in December 1996, well into the school's second year of operation. But it was one of the first occasions for core faculty members who joined the school in its second year—Harry Chase (Humanities/English), Dipan Patel (Science), and Jerard Navarro (Spanish)—to discuss the civics mission with previous faculty members. The conversation that took place over the course of this meeting nicely illuminates a variety of ways in which Winthrop Academy faculty interpret the civics mission. The discussion began as Harry Chase wondered about the ordering of the literature curriculum and how this related to the civics mission. Referring to the current practice of tying literature in with the chronology of the history curriculum, for example teaching the *Scarlet Letter* to correspond chronologically to where Shaka Reid is in the American history curriculum, Dr. Chase asked, "What is the civics package in this? Because I would not choose to limit myself to teaching American literature in the sophomore year."

Following this question, there was some discussion about how the civics emphasis is too general to be tangible for teachers in each subject area.

Cathy Eichler: It's also too general for the kids. If you stopped them in the hall, they wouldn't know what we're talking about [in terms of civics].

Beth Taft: One way to think about the civics strand is to think about how to engage kids in their community. Perhaps freshman year we could offer a City of Eaton course; then senior year they would have the City Project with the civics aspect.

> I suspect if we don't do it that way [with some concrete courses, even if only offered on a quarterly basis], it's never going to be quite clear the role it plays in the school.

Cathy Eichler: The concern with civics is the enormous amount of catch-up we need to do with general knowledge. One way to assure that the basics get covered is to do it chronologically.

This comment sparked a discussion of the lack of basic skills and low general knowledge level among the students. For instance, a full 75 percent of students come to Winthrop Academy reading below grade level. This concern with general knowledge and basic skills, in turn, raised the issue of bringing in students as 7th and 8th graders and hopes that such problems with basic skills could be addressed during the junior high years. As faculty began to ponder when the first class of 7th or 8th graders might be admitted, Sheridan Neill, the school's Director of Operations, interceded "this is a discussion group, not a decision group [because not everyone from the school is here]." He then turned the focus back to the civics mission.

Sheridan Neill: I don't understand the relationship of civics to the rest of the subjects. I see the standard as something like "to know your city and feel free within it" and the goal as "to become a citizen." [How does this relate to the subject areas?]

Dipan Patel: It relates to genetics [in a number of ways], for example, [a student] asking me "when am I ever going to need to know this?" and me discussing the ethical questions [of choosing your baby's eye color, etc.]. This is going to go way beyond the abortion debate.

Jerard Navarro: Or using the time in Advisory to explain the curriculum itself. Every subject can add something. The question is how much or how little our subject can add to the civics program. But, there must be some specific courses, such as basic knowledge about the political system that [students otherwise] ignore absolutely.

Beth Taft: It's also about the way we get kids to ask questions like "so what?" or "what follows from knowing this?" Responsibility comes from knowledge and the connection to decisions we make in the world.

Brenda Schank: Civics—is it a subversive mission or is it something we use to attract students?

Cathy Eichler:	I was fooled [by parents' and students' willingness to attend Winthrop Academy regardless of their connection to the mission]. We knew what we meant—what it means to be a citizen of this country in the last quarter of the twentieth century. I was fooled at the total malaise of kids, families, and guidance counselors.
Sheridan Neill:	Even as a staff member, I don't feel like I have any connection to it [the civic mission].
Beth Taft:	It seems to me you can approach civics through three prongs: intellectual, in the community, and Town Meeting. The intellectual has to do with our academics, for example, the importance of being able to read well and critically; the community aspect is reflected in our service component; and Town Meeting is sort of the anchor. I wouldn't underestimate the extent to which insisting on a rigorous academic program for all, not just those who test well, is itself a civics mission.
Sheridan Neill:	Is it a separate thing or what ties us all together? Or is what ties us all together simply our interest in kids and learning?
Cathy Eichler:	That's about building a community, not civics.
Dipan Patel:	But building our community is civics; taking responsibility for one's community.
Harry Chase:	There's a difference between civics and culture.
Cathy Eichler:	And "communal"—civility can be part of either, [what I'm referring to is encouraging voting and involvement in public life].
Dipan Patel:	But that's beyond our purview.
Cathy Eichler:	Is it? You don't have the power to educate democrats?
Harry Chase:	I don't see my job as educating democrats. A good education is something irrespective of the form of government; it has to do with a level of thinking and rationality. . . . Which is subsumed to the other: educating the person or the form of government?

Thus far, this conversation among faculty demonstrates that as they seek to build a common understanding of the civics mission, a variety of different perspectives emerge, and sometimes clash. One area of difference surrounds individual faculty members' commitment to a civics mission. One person says "Even as a staff member, I don't feel like I have any connection to [the civic mission]." Another says "I don't see my job as educating democrats." Yet no mention is made of rejecting or altogether changing the school's emphasis on civics. This may be because faculty members were hired realizing the founders' vision for the school.

Even as many faculty members take the civics mission for granted, and attempt to build common understandings around it, many of them seem attracted to Winthrop Academy primarily because of opportunities for creating a unique type of learning environment. This leads to tensions surrounding what it means to provide a "good education" versus a "civic education." Harry Chase is prompted to ask "Which is subsumed to the other: educating the person or the form of government?" and Sheridan Neill wonders ". . . is what ties us all together simply our interest in kids and learning?" For Beth Taft, these aims are reconciled insofar as "insisting on a rigorous academic program for all, not just those who test well, is itself a civics mission." Yet for other faculty members this relationship does not appear so straightforward. They continue to struggle not only with prioritizing a "good education" versus a "civic education," but with defining what a civic education should entail and how it relates to particular subject areas.

At this juncture of the meeting individual faculty members began to present curriculum from their specific subject areas. First, Jerard Navarro presented the Spanish curriculum. Following his presentation, Max Simon began a discussion of the Science curriculum. In the course of this science-related conversation, he remarked "Civics also has to do with how fairness, justice, and equity are carried out through our classes and how we treat each other in the hallways." His suggestion adds yet another element to civic education—civil interaction with fellow citizens.

Next, Sam Asher began discussing the math curriculum. He talked about math as including a bit of algebra, geometry, and trigonometry each year for three years, and perhaps offering calculus in fourth year. He stressed the importance of process and having students control the direction of the class for themselves, hopefully relying on him as teacher only to answer occasional questions. Within this context, the conversation turned to the importance of argumentation as an aspect of mathematics and of citizenship.

Sam Asher: The most important criterion is to make a convincing argument and what that really means, in the final analysis, is that you present a clear, complete, convincing argument because you've covered all the angles; not because we said so, but because you determined it.

Beth Taft: {to the whole group} Is there something, any one subject where that's not what you want them to do? Are there similar ways to measure it?

Dipan Patel: The language of argument has similar aspects.

Beth Taft: Wouldn't you say it's one aspect of being a citizen?

{Others murmur and nod in agreement} Might there be a way to take that notion—these questions—that could underlie what we do?

Brenda Schank: Isn't that the core questions?

Brenda Schank is referring here to a set of Core Questions that the faculty drafted at the beginning on the 1996–97 academic year. These questions are posted on the wall in each classroom, in the Common Room, and in the Computer Room. They are intended to reflect a basic impulse underlying Winthrop Academy's academic mission and common to all of its activities.

Core Questions

*What are your assumptions?

*What is your evidence?

How do you know?

*How do you connect with . . .?

*What if the situation were different?

*Why does this matter?

What follows from this?

Beth Taft responds to Brenda Schank's inquiry, "I don't think we're using them."

Jerard Navarro: I see a common process in all of our classes as engaging our kids in a process of rational thinking.

Beth Taft: I'm not convinced that the kids know that. Maybe this simple phrase, "clear, complete, and convincing" [exemplifies] the rigor that's the same thing across the disciplines. The civic glue is not so much the content, but the critical, rigorous thinking.

Dipan Patel: The questions on the wall, verbatim, may not be what I'm trying to convey [in my day-to-day teaching], but the concept is.

Beth Taft: We need to give kids access to the concept of a certain
                  kind of rigorous thinking.
Brenda Schank: Why is that civic?
Beth Taft: Because it's only in a democracy where it requires that
                  citizens question.
Harry Chase {and others}: "That's not true." "No."
Beth Taft: OK, the survival of democracy [requires that citizens
                  question].

{Other people make noises that sound like disagreement.}

Sam Asher: [Wait, let's not get caught up in that, the important thing
                  is identifying] a common way of thinking in the meta-
                  sense. God knows Town Meeting needs it. We cannot be
                  too explicit. I have one or two students who can say back
                  to me what we're trying to accomplish.
Harry Chase: It's not about teaching a mode of thinking. You teach
                  reasoning—reasoning is public thought, thought exposed;
                  it's presentation of thought, not thought itself because
                  we don't know anything about that.
Sam Asher: Yes we do.
Harry Chase: That's not true.
Beth Taft: Sam said "argument."
Sam Asher: I'm trying to give them tools and structures they can use
                  in their thinking.
Dipan Patel: This seems like a semantic distinction between reason-
                  ing and thinking.
Cathy Eichler: I'm trying to teach them to describe their thinking and
                  identify reasoning that's appropriate to the subject.
Harry Chase: It has to do with education as decentering versus their
                  ego-centered world. We teach them the hoary problem
                  of the other mind. Externalization. They have to be able
                  to step outside themselves, to see what other people see.
                  Perspective. That's really what reason is—seeing a thought
                  as someone else would see it and presenting it that way.
                  We're teaching reasoning—conventions for reason that
                  we accept.
Beth Taft: To end, I would ask us to think about, for our time in
                  January, could you say that the standard is: "Can you
                  make an argument that's clear, complete and convinc-
                  ing?" Then we'd spell that out in each area.[29]

Again, the concluding portions of this conversation demonstrate distinct ideas surrounding what curricular objectives Winthrop Academy's civic mission entails. While Max Simon stresses "how we treat each other in the hallways," others debate the role of reasoning and how to teach it. Faculty also struggle to determine whether a civics mission requires its own particular subject matter, such as "basic knowledge about the political system" and the city of Eaton, or a "common way of thinking" or "language of argument" that pervades the entire Winthrop Academy curriculum. Or perhaps all of these elements.

Although faculty struggle to agree upon a set of Core Questions, or a common standard such as presenting an argument that is "clear, complete, and convincing," their effort to articulate such shared norms brings to light how civic objectives permeate their curriculum. Beth Taft suggests that a commitment to "critical, rigorous thinking" may be the "civic glue" that binds the curriculum. Students are expected to gain reasoning skills within courses ranging from English Literature to Math. Faculty member's particular interpretations of just what reasoning means and requires pedagogically suggest that various skills will be learned in various settings. Approaches to "critical, rigorous thinking" look different in different courses, but express many elements of reasoned argumentation that are highly valued by deliberative democrats.

For example, Sam Asher encourages students to believe a mathematical argument "not because we said so, but because you determined it." His emphasis on evaluating the quality of the argument, not the status of the speaker, encourages students to understand that the "force of the better argument prevails." Then, as they step into Harry Chase's Literature class where "reasoning is public thought," students are expected "to be able to step outside of themselves, to see what other people see." Here, students may begin to gain familiarity with achieving the "enlarged mentality" that enables mutual understanding.

Thus, despite the differences and tensions in their perspectives as they attempt to build an explicit civics curriculum, faculty's particular understandings often complement one another. Interviews with faculty members also indicate that they share some strong agreement surrounding the sort of educational environment they believe is appropriate for future democratic citizens. For example, faculty distinguish between "democratic education" versus "education for democracy" and between students as "future" versus "potential" equals within the school community. And each of these distinctions has ramifications for their approach to civic education, particularly within Town Meeting.

Education for Democracy[30]

Winthrop Academy faculty are not aspiring to create a "democratic school." Sam Asher explains, "I don't think that Winthrop Academy purports to be a pure democracy. It's a partial democracy. It would be irresponsible of us to make it a pure democracy." Running a school as a pure democracy would be paramount to abdicating their responsibility as teachers and as adults. "Education *for* democracy," on the other hand, emphasizes that students need to learn some things in order to become democratic citizens, and that teachers play an integral role in facilitating students' development into autonomous, self-legislating human beings. Beth Taft clarifies what she sees as the distinction between "democratic education" and "education for democracy":

> It has to do with how you understand democracy and the balance between freedom and discipline or order. [Education for democracy includes] honing one's powers of discrimination, not like racial discrimination but the ability to make distinctions, and supporting one's views. Preparing for democracy requires a balance within a school between permissiveness and discipline.
>
> These are unfinished citizens and we've got to get them ready. They'll be empowered by learning certain things like how to participate in reasoned discourse by supplying evidence for their arguments, whether its scientific or mathematical or an English essay.
>
> A democratic education where everybody's voice counts takes the education piece out of it. If students run the place, educators abdicate their responsibility to mold citizens and care about the quality of their opinions. At Winthrop Academy, we make a big deal of differences between a child and an adult. . . . If we were all equals we wouldn't make this distinction so directly. For instance, decorum—how to speak, looking people in the eye, shaking hands.
>
> We are about the education of young people whose place in the world we ultimately expect to be equal to ours. If we lived in a society with strict classes or stations, that sense would be different. I'd direct you to a section of our mission statement on this point which states that teachers' conclusions should not be students' starting points; we provide them with access to information that informed our conclusions. We're not dictatorial, but that doesn't say we're equals. Then, there is nothing to teach you. We're a community of educators and students, educating precisely because of students' potential to be equals with potentially a lot to teach us.

So "education for democracy" is akin to a finishing process for unfinished citizens. It has to do with teaching students how to participate in reasoned discourse—by supplying evidence, exercising powers of discrimination regarding the quality of opinions, and supporting one's own views. It has to do with proper decorum—how one speaks to and treats fellow human beings. And it has to do with access to information in order to form one's own conclusions.

Students as Potential Equals

Within Winthrop Academy's "education for democracy," an unequal relationship between students and teachers is explicitly acknowledged and defended by faculty.

> Max Simon: Students as equals—never, impossible. The student/teacher relationship is never equal, not if I can grade you. Eventually you can surpass me, become my teacher.
>
> For kids this age, the objective is not to be treated as equals, but to achieve adult responsibility. So they have the power to do that. They have the power to leave early, to earn open campus. There never should be exceptions. That's what taxes or employment is—you do x and y, you get z. I see them as potential adults and equal as fellow citizens.
>
> The teacher/student relationship is not a hierarchy in that one is more important than the other, it's just a type of relationship. It's a two-way street. Certainly I learn from them everyday. But the nature of the pedagogical construct can't be "I don't want to do this."

Shaka Reid also sees the pedagogical relationship as a two-way street with teachers learning from their students, but with teachers as "first among equals."

> Shaka Reid: I think there are arenas, some more comfortable than others, in terms of equality. . . . teachers and kids are not equal. In any environment there is a hierarchy of equality. In my class, I'm first among equals. My role is to teach, that can be very directive. Yet, I do learn. So, my primary role is to teach, but I do learn; and their primary responsibility is to learn, but they do teach. The percentages vary.

Teachers need to act as "first among equals" in order to look out for kids' interests and to help them gain the internal resources for making choices later in life. At Winthrop Academy, teachers provide the structure and discipline that a "democratic school" might not. If all decisions were made through majority rule, students would always outnumber teachers. Because students are still kids, their preferences today are not necessarily in keeping with their best interests in developing social skills that will be required of them tomorrow by various socio-cultural institutions. If students do not develop these skills at this point in their lives, access to certain institutions may be unavailable to them as adults. Sam Asher feels that this is particularly true for kids from the inner-city—kids who are marginalized in terms of race and class—who are seldom exposed to the "culture of power" that drives many of America's social and economic institutions.

> Sam Asher: There's a difference between adults and kids. Kids don't vote. Adults should look out for the kids' interests. Especially these kids need structure because it may be missing in other places; they need power. I don't think it's families that are lacking, it's social institutions like their neighborhoods.
>
> Structure and power toward what ends? Have you read Lisa Delpit's stuff? {I nod.} Delpit talks about how kids don't know that "culture [of power]"—how to talk, dress, interact.[31] There are certain moves you make in society that get you power. Some kids grow up with it. Our kids, kids here in the city, we're raising generations of kids who don't have access to that power. I want them to have structure so that at least they'll have the choice to buy into that or not. Our job is to teach them that.
>
> If Winthrop Academy were a pure democracy, they'd win every time: there are 65 of them and however many of us. What I try to do in my class is show that there's power in being able to work well with others, in helping someone, in leading the class. There are responsible ways for kids to feel powerful and smart. I'd like for kids to come out with an ingrained sense of structure that's part of them. It reminds me of a photography teacher who told me that you have to learn all of the rules, then break them. This applies to kids too. Internal structure lets you be effective. We take for granted the way we work and get things done, but that has to be taught explicitly. . . . Kids need to learn how to think and how to discipline themselves.

For Sam Asher, part of the responsibility that comes with being a public school teacher is providing students with access to the "cultural capital" that will allow them to negotiate mainstream institutions.

Rules of the Game

Internal structure, an ability to follow rules, and a sense of discipline are necessary capacities for making the kinds of choices available to democratic citizens. They are the types of capacities that distinguish between an adult and a child, between coercion and democratic social interaction.

> Max Simon: A rehearsed and practiced attitude. Discipline. There's a difference between a cop using intimidation and fear to maintain order, threats, violent posturing, versus a cop as a member of a community outlining what is acceptable through sincere interaction. Respect for authority, interaction, people uphold law. Do we intimidate and threaten? Or clearly outline what is expected, then cement actions by being uniform and carrying them out in Town Meeting and throughout the school?

Yet in a democracy, citizens not only uphold laws, they make laws. For democratic citizens, being law-abiding is different from being intimidated or threatened because one has consented to participate in processes whereby laws are made. For students who are not yet citizens, the process of learning to be law-abiding does not necessarily coincide with participation in law-making. Students need to commit to some of the background rules, such as respect for others, before they can fully participate in the "game" of democracy.

> Max Simon: I firmly believe that it's a balance between including students in the process around empowerment and remembering that they are still teeny boppers. In order to effectively empower them, give them their voice, a great deal of work must be put into consistency of what is acceptable, why it's acceptable, and the consequences of performing an action that's not acceptable.

As students gain a sense of the rules—of what is acceptable—they earn their place as adults and as equals within the democratic community. Adults act according to what is acceptable without external coercion or authoritarian inducements.

> Shaka Reid: I'm fostering equality by asking them to be more like me as an adult, to help me create a common space and agenda, versus following rules and directives. I'm trying to move them toward being an adult, rather than just relying on authoritarian strategies toward non-adults, by creating common times for one-to-one interaction.
>
> Acting like an adult also has to do with how we speak to each other. Students will say to me "how is this possible?" "This can't be right." It's hard for me to effectively respond when you get angry and ask all of these questions. At that moment, I'm going to shut off discourse because you're reverting, it breaks down to the teacher/student relationship.
>
> It's like in basketball, if the referee's not calling fouls, the game digresses. This is a good analogy for school and obeying rules and refereeing action. We can have great discourse with you respecting me and vice versa.

Effective democratic discourse requires respect for rules and respect for persons. Within "education for democracy," faculty act as both instructors and as referees—they both teach students the rules and call foul when the rules are broken. Through this educative process, students are expected to gain internal structure, discipline, a rehearsed and practiced attitude. With these attributes, they will be capable of making choices and acting like democratic citizens. After these capacities have been achieved, as Sam Asher's photography analogy suggests, rules might be challenged. But students cannot break rules before they've learned to play the game of democratic citizenship.

In order to effectively participate in the game of democracy, students must learn to play by the rules. But like any game, participation entails much more than simply knowledge of the rules. Participation as a citizen in the Winthrop Academy community entails both know how of the skills and attributes required within the game as well as a sense of agency.

Know How

Winthrop Academy faculty hope that students will learn how to participate effectively within the school community, and then will take this knowledge with them as they participate in other civic communities. Faculty identify the need to teach both civic engagement and civil interaction and assert that students lack these sorts of capacities as they enter the school. According to Max Simon, students come to the school with the "misconception that they have no impact. [They have an attitude that] 'you're going to do what you're going to do anyway.'"[32] In addition, many students engage in social behaviors that complicate building a safe, let alone a civil, community. Students swear at one another, "throw down" and threaten one another, sometimes fight, and sometimes steal from other members of the school community.

For Winthrop Academy faculty, such attitudes and behaviors are antithetical to democratic habits of mind. Democratic citizens need to know how to do certain things. They need to know how to express their views through reasoned argumentation. And they need to know how to treat their fellow citizens with respect. Faculty believe that as students learn to do these things, they will gain a sense that they can make a difference, along with a sense of civic pride and responsibility.

Having a Say

A large component of civic participation at Winthrop Academy centers around having a say in the school community. Faculty emphasize teaching students to express their views and to speak effectively in public (see table 3.4). They stress that students need to learn how to speak and how to listen. And faculty place a great deal of import on the quality of student speech. As Mr. Simon reminds students in Town Meeting ". . . it's far easier . . . to talk and talk and talk than to say one thing well." A civic education must prepare future citizens with the requisite skills to make quality contributions. According to Beth Taft,

> This has to do with the difference between democratic education and education for democracy—preparing people to make quality contributions. Fourteen and fifteen year olds aren't there yet; they need to learn skills such as how to reason, how to speak, and how to offer an argument.

Effective speech has a certain structure; it is orderly and efficient "with a beginning, middle, and end." It includes "a thesis statement, data to support it, and conclusions."[33] And having a say entails more than simply speaking effectively. Having a say means knowing how to participate in a "civilized exchange of ideas" where one entertains opposing views.[34] Finally, having a say also entails certain capacities such as confidence in public speaking, the courage to speak, and understanding that one's voice is important.

Ways of Being

Some aspects of having a say within a civic community, such as tolerance for diverse points of view, closely intersect with ways of being conducive to democratic social interaction. Faculty's emphasis on ways of being has to do with fostering a "sense of decorum . . . a 'gentleman'/'gentlewoman' code . . . that helps students know how to act with one another." A good citizen is characterized as someone who is responsible, respectful, active, resourceful, and informed, among other things.

During Winthrop Academy's first year, the faculty reinforced their expectations for appropriate ways of being with a graded Citizenship Report (see table 3.5). These Citizenship Reports were completed by a student's Advisor. The reports evaluated qualities including excellence, community, integrity, accountability, respectfulness, preparedness and promptness, and cleanliness. Combined with capacities for having a say, these various ways of being comprise an integral part of "know[ing] how to be a practicing member of a democracy while upholding the ideals of democracy." Yet it is interesting to note that the report did not include an evaluation of aspects of citizenship such as tolerance for opposing viewpoints or capacities in reasoned argumentation.

In part due to these limitations, and because some faculty were troubled by the idea of assigning a grade to these sorts of attributes, the Citizenship Report was not used during the early part of the school's second year. As faculty continued to struggle with the pedagogical challenge of how to cultivate democratic "ways of being" in students over the second year, they returned to the idea of the Citizenship Report. Dissatisfied with its original form, they decided to bring the topic to Town Meeting for students' feedback. On March 21, 1997, Town Meeting discussed the question "What does it mean to be a citizen at Winthrop Academy?" and debated the merits of faculty assigning students a grade for citizenship. This debate and some of its implications for education for democracy are discussed in the next chapter.

Table 3.5 Winthrop Academy's Citizenship Report

CITIZENSHIP REPORT

Student: Advisor:

1	2	3	4	5
Not At All	Infrequently	Sometimes	Almost Always	Always

_____ Represents Winthrop Academy by displaying the
     qualities of excellence, community, integrity,
     resourcefulness, and accountability.
_____ Gets to class prepared and on time.
_____ Wears Winthrop Academy shirt.
_____ Does not chew gum during school hours.
_____ Does not wear hat during school hours.
_____ Keeps the school clean.
_____ Helps others who need help.
_____ Attends school.   Missed 0 days = 5, missed 1 day = 4, missed
                                2 days = 3, missed 3 days = 2, missed 4 or
                                more days = 1.
_____ Does not cut class.   Cut 0 classes = 5, cut 1 class = 4, cut 2 classes
                                = 3, cut 3 classes = 2, cut 4 or more
                                classes = 1.
_____ Uses respectful language.

CITIZENSHIP GRADE _____

Know how, then, includes knowing how to "have a say" within reasoned democratic deliberations as well as knowing how to conduct oneself according to "ways of being" conducive to democratic civil interaction. According to faculty, students must know how to do these things before they will begin to gain a sense of agency.

Agency
Once students know how to have a say and know how to conduct themselves within a civic community, once they have the tools to undertake civic action, they will begin to see that their participation matters. Without these tools, students feel disenfranchised and disempowered.

> Max Simon: It's complex, a culture of disbelief in our system and a belief that they have no power in the system. It's ingrained in the factory model of high schools with a billion students; no one knows them. Then it's the same at the State University. The potential is there, with things like . . . Town Meeting, but they don't know.

Knowledge of how to act lays the groundwork for effective action. In other words, "you have to know how to play the game before your desire to win [makes a difference]." And the best way to learn how to play the game is to practice.

In sum, Winthrop Academy faculty are interested in providing an education for democracy to students who are potential equals as future citizens. Within an ideal democratic community, all citizens have an equal say and exhibit ways of being conducive to civil interaction. Yet Winthrop Academy does not profess itself to be a democratic community. Rather, faculty stress their educative mission; they aim to prepare students for democracy by inculcating certain skills and attributes necessary for effective civic participation. Education for democracy requires that students practice democratic capacities, not that they participate in democratic decision making.

Winthrop Academy's theory of education for democracy both closely parallels and sometimes diverges from the emphases of deliberative democratic theory. As chapter 2 outlined, deliberative democratic theory suggests at least three requirements for civic education: 1) Students must gain skills in reasoned deliberation. 2) Students must gain a willingness to respect background conditions such as mutual respect and egalitarian reciprocity. 3) Students must gain a sense of agency or a sense that what they say matters. First, in terms of skills in reasoned deliberation, Winthrop Academy stresses reasoned argumentation, public speaking, and democratic proceduralism. Faculty differ a bit from deliberative democrats, however, in that they place a greater emphasis on voting than on achieving mutual understanding and consensus. In addition, their attention to public service and membership within civic communities goes beyond the participationist ethic of deliberative democracy. Where deliberative democrats would be satisfied with all members of a civic community being assured of *having a say*, Winthrop Academy aspires to instill a service ethic within its students.

Second, in terms of a willingness to abide by background conditions such as mutual respect and egalitarian reciprocity, Winthrop Academy faculty speak about rules of the game in a way that sounds much like Seyla Benhabib's position. She contends that ". . . the normative conditions of discourses, like basic rights and liberties, are to be viewed as rules of the game that can be contested within the game but only insofar as one first accepts to abide by them and play the game at all."[35] Similarly, faculty believe that students must first learn the background rules and how to play the game before they actually can participate in democratic deliberation.

Third, in terms of students gaining a sense of agency or a belief that what they say matters, faculty contend that "know how" precedes agency. Students will not gain a sense that their participation makes a difference until they have mastered the requisite skills of participation. Thus, Winthrop Academy faculty place a strong emphasis on the skills or "know how" component of civic education. Both a willingness to play by the rules and a sense of agency follow from the acquisition and effective utilization of such skills. And skills come with practice. The next chapter explores students' perspectives on Town Meeting as a forum for such practice. Students' perspectives inform how faculty's intended civic educational objectives are being fostered or hindered as they implement what Amy Gutmann refers to as "deliberate practices of instruction" through Town Meeting.

Notes

1. Seyla Benhabib, *Critique, Norm, and Utopia: A Study of the Foundations of Critical Theory* (New York: Columbia University Press, 1986), 225.

2. Benhabib notes that the extent to which Habermas is any more successful than other critical theorists in this endeavor of mediation is unresolved, ibid.

3. This case study is based upon life at Winthrop Academy Charter School in Eaton, Massachusetts from August, 1995 through June, 1997. The name of the school, the city where it is located, and the names of all faculty members and students are pseudonyms in order to protect the identity of the research site and participants. The Methodological Appendix (appendix C) provides a much fuller account of my critical interpretive orientation to the case study research and how I attempted to put it into practice. After outlining the theoretical orientation to the research I describe in close detail my role as a participant-observer, sampling for interviews and surveys, quantity of data collected, approaches to analysis, and quality criteria.

4. In this quotation—"Some political guy make a quote"—the verb "make" is not grammatically correct; it should be "made." One way to address this would be to insert a [sic] within the quote directly after the mistake. I have chosen not to employ this option. Throughout my ethnographic case study of Winthrop Academy I draw upon student speech that does not conform to standard, grammatically-correct English. I do not wish to repeatedly distract from the students' words by pointing out these divergences from standard usage. Moreover, I believe that representing the students' words as they were actually spoken or written will give the reader a more accurate picture of students' usage of mainstream English. In the case of quotations, the reader can assume that apparent mistakes are not typos nor grammatical errors on my part. Rather, I have chosen to represent student speech in the text as it was presented to me.

5. Beth Taft and Cathleen Eichler, "Winthrop Academy Charter School Application" (submitted to the Massachusetts Executive Office of Education, Boston, MA, February, 1994), 1.

6. Margaret D. Le Compte and Judith Preissle, *Ethnography and Qualitative Design in Educational Research*, 2nd ed. (San Diego: Academic Press, 1993), 77 and Michael Q. Patton, *Qualitative Evaluation and Research Methods*, 2nd ed. (Newbury Park, CA: Sage Publications, 1990), 174.

7. Patton, 174.

8. I approach Town Meeting as a curricular practice because it is included by faculty as a primary aspect of their "formal" or "official" civics curriculum. According to Philip Jackson's curriculum typology there are at least four levels of curricular enactment. First, there is the formal or official curriculum that a school explicitly

announces. Second, there is the "enacted" or "delivered" curriculum which entails what is taught. Third, there is the "experienced" or "received" curriculum which represents what students grasp. And, fourth, there is the "null" curriculum of that which is not offered or "the curriculum that might have been." See Philip W. Jackson, "Conceptions of Curriculum and Curriculum Specialists," in *Handbook of Research on Curriculum*, ed. Philip W. Jackson (New York: Macmillan Publishing Company, 1992), 9. I subscribe to a broad definition of curriculum that encompasses each of these four levels. Accordingly, my analysis of Town Meeting as a curricular practice includes formal curriculum documents, observation of the delivered curriculum within Town Meeting, interviews with students to inform their perceptions of the experienced curriculum, and attention to what aspects of civic education might have been but were not included in Town Meeting practices.

9. These three levels of meaning are drawn from the work of Reba Page and Fred Erickson. See, in particular, Frederick Erickson, "Qualitative Methods," in *Research in Teaching and Learning, Volume 2*, Frederick Erickson and Robert L. Linn (New York: Macmillan Publishing, 1990), 82–83; Reba Neukom Page, *Lower Track Classrooms: A Curricular and Cultural Perspective* (New York: Teachers College Press, 1991), 11–12; and Reba Page and Linda Valli, eds. *Curriculum Differentiation: Interpretive Studies in U.S. Secondary Schools* (Albany: SUNY Press, 1990), 4–5.

10. These three criteria of success are meant to reflect three quality criteria—credibility, catalytic validity, and generalizability—which are discussed in much greater detail in appendix C.

11. As I stated earlier, my case study research covered the two-year period including academic years 1995–96 and 1996–97. Despite the lag time, much of my description of the school is written in the present tense for readability purposes. With the addition of over thirty students in the school's second year, the breakdown by ethnicity changed to 5 percent Asian, 59 percent African American, 9 percent Hispanic, and 27 percent White.

12. For the 1997–98 school year Winthrop Academy had a waiting list of approximately 100 students. Of Winthrop Academy's original 65 students, 13 had left to attend other schools as of June 1997. Other students were accepted off of the waiting list to fill these slots.

13. *Winthrop Academy Charter School* Admissions Flier, Summer, 1995.

14. These students' comments are from interviews conducted in February and March of 1996. I did not interview any parents, so references to parents' motives in choosing Winthrop Academy are based on the perceptions of students and faculty members.

15. *Winthrop Academy Charter School Handbook 1996–97*, 2–3.

16. Winthrop Academy Town Meeting, January 24, 1997. In this introductory section, segments drawn from specific Town Meeting transcripts are intended to represent the tone and content of a typical Town Meeting.

17. *Winthrop Academy Charter School Handbook.*

18. Winthrop Academy Town Meeting, May 10, 1996.

19. This transcript is from Winthrop Academy Town Meeting, December 6, 1996. The racial categories that I have used to label the faculty are the same as those required by the Commonwealth of Massachusetts for the racial identification of students: African American, Asian, Hispanic, or White. I assigned these categories to each faculty member; they did not label themselves. These categories brush over the ethnic identifications of faculty members, for instance, Mr. Nardelli's tendency to speak in Italian or Mrs. Eichler's references to her Irish American heritage. The categories also disguise the ethnic or national identity of teachers such as Mr. Ross, who is Peruvian, or Mr. Navarro, who is from Spain. Nevertheless, I employ these categories because they are the same as those assigned to students, so they allow for a comparison between the racial composition of the faculty and student bodies.

    When drawing from my observational record of Town Meeting or interviews with faculty and students I use a couple of different symbols. [ ] around text symbolizes wording approximate to but not necessarily verbatim that used by the speaker. { } around text signifies my description of events rather than the actual speech of the participants.

20. At Winthrop Academy students are members of Advisory Groups, which are similar to homerooms. Students begin the school day in Advisory, hence prompting Mr. Reid's references to students "working on getting there on time." Students also meet with this group to complete Public Service projects and other group tasks. Advisory groups are intended to provide students with a sense of a close-knit group, or a team spirit, within the larger school community. In addition, the Advisor provides an essential link between the school, the student, and the family. Advisors call home to keep parents updated on students' progress or any problems and are involved with any decisions that the school must make about an individual student.

21. *Winthrop Academy Town Meeting Guidelines*, drafted August, 1996, 3.

22. Since this debate took place during the school's first year there were only 66 students (versus 98 in the second year) and, with staff, the total Town Meeting membership equaled approximately 75 members.

23. Winthrop Academy Board of Trustees Meeting, March 21, 1996.

24. *Winthrop Academy Charter School Handbook 1996–97*, 18.

25. Winthrop Academy Board of Trustees Meeting, March 4, 1997.

26. Specific components of this "Academic Promise" are articulated in the *Winthrop Academy Charter School Handbook 1996–97*. Subsequent quotations regarding academic expectations refer to this document.

27. Winthrop Academy's charter with the state of Massachusetts sets out a plan to begin admitting 7th grade students during the school's fourth year of operation.

The following year these students will be 8th graders, another 7th grade class will be admitted and Winthrop Academy will be a 7th–12th grade secondary school.

28. My decision to focus upon Winthrop Academy's civic objective of "practicing civic engagement and civil interaction," particularly within the context of Town Meeting, results in other key aspects of their civic mission being downplayed within the case study. For instance, their emphasis on public service and its connection to civic involvement and active citizenship is not developed. My focus on the procedural context of Town Meeting reflects deliberative democratic theory's preoccupation with a specific form of civic participation—reasoned deliberation. A plethora of questions that I did not take up in this study surrounds service as a form of participation within civil society, and the sorts of democratic virtues students might gain from performing public service as an aspect of civic education.

29. This transcript is from a conversation among faculty during an informal dinner meeting on Monday, December 16, 1996.

30. Unless otherwise noted, the quotes from faculty in this and the following sections are from interviews conducted in April 1996.

31. Sam Asher is referring to educator Lisa Delpit's work surrounding a "culture of power" and how cultural differences impact access to that power, particularly in terms of the teacher/student relationship and various approaches to the teaching of writing. See, for example, Lisa Delpit, "The Silenced Dialogue: Power and Pedagogy in Educating Other People's Children," in *Beyond Silenced Voices: Class, Race, and Gender in United States Schools*, eds. Lois Weis and Michelle Fine (Albany: SUNY Press, 1993), 119–39.

32. Interview with Max Simon conducted November 2, 1995.

33. Ibid.

34. Interview with Cathy Eichler conducted November 3, 1995.

35. Seyla Benhabib, "Toward a Deliberative Model of Democratic Legitimacy," in *Democracy and Difference: Contesting the Boundaries of the Political*, ed. Seyla Benhabib (Princeton: Princeton University Press, 1996), 80.

Chapter 4

Town Meeting as a Forum for Practice

I. Participation in Town Meeting

This chapter aims to illustrate the complexities of institutionalizing deliberative democratic ideals within concrete civic educational practices at Winthrop Academy. The chapter illuminates how the faculty's civic educational objectives are both fostered and hindered as students *practice for* future democratic participation in the context of Town Meeting. Following this chapter, the book concludes with a discussion of how Winthrop Academy's experiences reflect and challenge the ideals of deliberative democratic theory. The final chapter demonstrates how deliberative democracy's normative ideals can be employed as critical yardsticks for assessing curricular *practices for* democratic citizenship and offers suggestions for minimizing hindrances to equal and inclusive civic education, particularly in the context of charter school reform.

Town Meeting is a forum for students to practice democracy—students practice civic engagement by *having a say* and practice civil interaction by exhibiting appropriate *ways of being*. As the civics curriculum states, "Students participate in a weekly school Town Meeting which prepares them to think about the issues of our day, to express their views and to tolerate and understand views different from their own" (see table 3.4). In Town Meeting faculty expect students to speak in order to articulate their own points of view, to listen in order to hear and understand the views of others, to make public presentations at a podium in the front of the room, and to engage in the use of parliamentary procedure. In these ways, Town Meeting's objectives closely mirror the procedural formality of deliberative democracy's "ideal speech situation."

In Town Meeting students are expected not only to practice democracy's requisite skills, but faculty hope they will gain an appreciation for its processes and its commitments. According to Cathy Eichler,

> The goal of Town Meeting is for students to develop a profound respect for and patience with the democratic process. At this [small] level, they're speaking, honing their skills, and learning the historical significance and necessity of the Town Meeting process. Democracy is messy and inefficient, but it's the best we have. You tell me another way.
>
> The goal is for Town Meeting to provide a bridge, not internal direction for the school, that's the role of faculty and the Board of Trustees. We want students to be able to transfer what they learn into where they are going to be when they leave Winthrop Academy. What will their politics be? Will they vote?[1]

Town Meeting is also a place for members of Winthrop Academy to build a sense of community. The meeting is a ritual within each week's busy schedule and already an integral part of Winthrop Academy's tradition. The Common Room, where Town Meeting takes place, provides a space in which the entire school population can "gather in one room to gain a sense of belonging to something shared in common." It is "a place where we come together, sit down, and be together," a place to work toward "confirmation, not separation," and a place where "students gain an identity as part of Winthrop Academy and learn things they can apply in other settings." In sum, Town Meeting is "a metaphor for society and community."[2]

In many respects, Winthrop Academy's Town Meeting is living up to its intended purposes. Virtually all of the students feel like they are members of a community at Winthrop Academy. And many of them feel that their voices are heard and that they participate in decision making within the school.[3] Students report that they "have a say" in their school community primarily through Town Meeting. In this forum, Daniel says, students feel they can express their views and "let the school community know what we feel and what we want to say." Kerry adds, "if there is something [we] want to discuss throughout all of the school, [we] can bring it up."[4]

Students have sent letters to the White House, letters to the editors of local papers, and letters to local organizations that have hosted them during their two-week internships. Students have challenged and changed school policy. Students have effectively used the Town Meeting process to shorten the school day and successfully petitioned the faculty to add time between swimming and Spanish classes (for students to change their clothes).

Yet faculty are not satisfied that their intended objectives are being fully achieved. In addition to struggling with *what* their civic mission is and what a civic education entails, faculty also are struggling with *how* students learn to act like democratic citizens. As Beth Taft puts it:

> We've never said to kids that they're equal here. There's a distinction between the role of teachers and the roles of kids. The question then becomes: *how do you prepare kids for democracy without being explicitly democratic?* And that raises the role of Town Meeting. . . . *The question raised for me is: Can you get students to buy into practicing democracy if they don't have full power in the school? And what does it mean to practice?* In Town Meeting, students vote, they share equality among themselves. As they get better at persuading, they'll be more likely to effect what we do. [emphases added]

Faculty are frustrated with a couple of things. First, as Harry Chase observed in a March 1997 Faculty Meeting, ". . . part of the problem [with Town Meeting] is that a few speak . . . and the rest are spectators." Dr. Chase's observation is born out by students' own perceptions of their participation in Town Meeting. While almost all students report that they vote in Town Meeting, only fifty-three percent have voiced an opinion, and less than half report that they have placed an item on the agenda, made a motion, or given a speech.

Most Town Meeting debates are dominated by the presence of a few students who participate in "legitimate" ways—they voice opinions and make speeches at the podium, they listen while others speak, they make motions, and they vote. The same students tend to speak multiple times while a great many others never, or rarely, rise to speak. Many spectators simply sit in their seats much of the time, occasionally raising a hand to vote or, in rare instances, rising out of their chairs to speak. Yet others expend most of their would-be civic energies grunting or coughing, laughing or clapping, trying to surreptitiously paint their nails or get their math homework done.

Second, faculty are frustrated by the behaviors of many of the student spectators in Town Meeting. Faculty refer to a phenomenon that they call "dissolving" where students dissolve into laughter, talking to one another, or cheering. Most faculty, and some students, view dissolving as a sign of disrespect which, in turn, accounts for low levels of student participation and precludes substantive debate. Insofar as students who dissolve are disrespecting the process and the speaker, they are discouraging others from participating in the process. According to Shaka Reid:

> Town Meeting is dominated by two types of people: those who are constructive and those who are not, then there are those in the middle. If everyone was

constructive, quiet kids might speak up more because the atmosphere was not threatening. There are parameters where you feel safe. Fifty-five kids don't say anything in Town Meeting. Three to five kids try to mess it up.

Dissolving behavior is also cited by teachers as evidence that students do not yet know how to debate or engage in ways of being appropriate for democratic participation. They see dissolving as evidence that students just do not know how to participate in democratic processes. As Beth Taft sees it:

> We put a tool out there for them to use before they learned to use the tool. They need to feel like it's an appropriate place or . . . they'll act out or inappropriately, they'll prefer uncivilized disobedience. Town Meeting as a tool is an organized way of making themselves heard, but it doesn't give them the authority to change things. Yet, the better they are at putting their views out, the more likely they will make a difference.

For Ms. Taft, dissolving is a sign that students do not know how to effectively utilize the Town Meeting process. Another faculty interpretation of dissolving is that students see Town Meeting more as a traditional class than as a forum within which they have the power to pursue their own ends. Cathy Eichler expresses this view:

> I see [dissolving] as a measure of them not having bought into Town Meeting as theirs. It's during the school day, and at the end of the day, their exit time. I argued against Friday afternoon for Town Meeting. But others saw it as the culmination of the week. I don't know if we've been successful. Those things make it seem like a class.

Whatever the causes of most students acting as "spectators" and exhibiting "dissolving" behaviors, these two phenomena are problematic for the aim of "education for democracy." To the extent that acquiring democratic skills and predispositions requires practice, not all students are practicing. Thus, faculty's intended objectives are being achieved by only a small percentage of the student body. In addition, the existence of "spectators" and "dissolving" raises the possibility that certain students are being excluded or marginalized from practicing civic participation.

Disproportionate participation in *practices for* civic participation is particularly problematic due to the crucial role education plays in preparing future citizens who are manifest equals within democratic processes, because they are similarly capable of offering quality contributions to the argument at hand. Within democratic deliberations, all participants may not speak and this is not a problem if all relevant views are aired. When students are *practicing for* democratic deliberations, however, the standard for inclusion of all relevant speakers must be set a bit higher. All students need to practice in order to gain skills in persuasive argumentation. Moreover, because the rationality of democratic outcomes is contingent upon the quality of the deliberations, all students need practice determining whether or not a particular argument is relevant.

The unintended outcomes of "spectators" and "dissolving" raise the question for faculty of how to engage more students in practicing skills of reasoned argumentation, as opposed to hooting and hollering, and respectful ways of being, as opposed to "dissing" their peers. According to Beth Taft:

> Part of why Town Meeting hasn't necessarily worked is because we haven't given them the tool and they haven't learned how to use it. You need to learn now to use a system effectively. They haven't yet seen the power of the tool. *How do you teach them to practice?* We've said, here's a forum—that presumes they have the ability, desire, and interest to change things. That reflects our hope, our expectation for them to be fully engaged. They need to learn how to find things to talk about. That's the paradox, it's an empty tool [if there's nothing they're interested in engaging]. We're offering a process, but that doesn't mean it's going to work. It should be not because I'm telling you, but because [you] want to. I shouldn't have to sit down each week and guide them toward what they want to talk about. But over time it will be something they want, some kids already see the power and could use it. [emphases added]

In order to better understand how to teach students to practice, it is useful to consider what sorts of dynamics spur spectatorship and dissolving behavior among students as opposed to participation in reasoned debate. Discussions with students illuminate a variety of barriers that hinder the achievement of faculty's intended outcomes of practicing for future democratic participation. Some barriers are posed by fellow students, some by faculty's words and actions, and others by students' reactions to the topic at hand. Taken together, these barriers form a complex web of hurdles that result in many more students remaining spectators than actively participating within weekly Town Meetings.

I'm Nervous and Scared[5]
Many students are nervous and shy about speaking in Town Meeting, especially at the podium in the front of the room. One cause of their nervousness is a fear of being laughed at. When I ask one student, Thi, why he doesn't speak much in Town Meeting, he explains:

Thi: Well, when you try to get up there and say something it's pretty hard for you to say what you have to say because they have students who sit down there and laugh at you if you say something wrong, they think it's funny and they're just pushing all that pressure at you, so that's why. . . . *I'm nervous and scared.*

Thi's nervousness may be due in part to discomfort with cultural styles of communication different from those of his home culture. Thi is of Vietnamese descent and Asian cultural styles of communication are characteristically less directive, and less inclined to large public presentations, than communication styles within the Anglo tradition that is reflected in Town Meeting's parliamentary procedures. Indeed, Winthrop Academy's Asian students rarely speak during Town Meeting.

But nerves and fear are not simply due to cultural differences. Debbie, a white student, expresses a similar concern:

Debbie: I say "oh, my God" because everyone's going to sit there and laugh at me.
Stacy Smith: Why do you think people will laugh?
Debbie: I don't know, I'm sure they wouldn't, but I just have this big fear that someone's going to come and jump at me if I get up.

Another African American student is afraid that she will be the one doing the laughing. She says that speaking does not make her nervous, yet she doesn't feel comfortable planning or giving a speech.

Natasha: . . . it's like if I do say something, if I hear her, if I'm planning on doing it, I've got to do it before I hear anybody else or I'll be saying what they said all over in my own words.
Stacy Smith: You're worried that you're going to repeat what's already been said?
Natasha: OK, there could be five speakers right? And if I hear what they say first, you know some of my input is from each of them, some of the same things that I agree with, and it's gonna be all the same thing over that somebody already said.
Stacy Smith: You'd feel it was repetitious. But what if you planned out a speech before the meeting?
Natasha: I wouldn't.
Stacy Smith: Why?

Natasha: I don't know, because I don't think I should go up there.
              And plus I'd be too silly and I'd start laughing and then I'll
              be getting kicked out.
Stacy Smith: Are you nervous, is that why?
Natasha: No, I just be laughing. It's just like, when I see [another
              student], she be like, and she be sitting there, and I be like
              "oh, no." It cracks me up.

Like Thi and Debbie, Natasha appears apprehensive about the reactions of fellow students—they will laugh while she is at the podium and, in turn, cause her to laugh. But Natasha's comments also indicate that she is apprehensive about the reaction of the moderator or other faculty members. She says, "I'll be getting kicked out."

As moderator, Mr. Simon attempts to instruct students in the proper use of parliamentary procedure. For instance, he occasionally asks students to repeat a motion they have just made if they fail to say the words correctly. If a student says "I motion to open Town Meeting," Mr. Simon might respond, "now think about that, is that really what you want to say?" Or he might ask for a student to "properly" open Town Meeting. Such clarifications are intended to teach students the proper grammar of parliamentary procedure. They should say "I *make* a motion to open Town Meeting." But, some students may be scared off by these tactics—afraid of being embarrassed in front of their fellow students by making a mistake.

Referring to a recent change of moderator from Ms. Taft to Mr. Simon, Mark says ". . .now it doesn't matter what we think, Mr. Simon, if you say one thing he'll point you out and put you out in front of everybody. He treats us like criminals." Kareem hypothesizes that students with low self-esteem would have trouble being "put . . . out in front of everybody."

Kareem: He disrespects, I've seen him pretty much, like not out and out
          call someone stupid, but I've seen him pretty much make com-
          ments which are kind of toward that suggestion. He'll say there's
          a difference between being smart and acting smart and stuff like
          that and that's not really the best thing to say to someone,
          especially someone who has low self-esteem. Like, one time he
          tried to say something like that to me and it didn't bother me
          because I know I'm smart, I already know. But if that had been
          someone else, they probably would have felt like "oh, well, I'm
          stupid."

Kareem's explanation raises the possibility that some students choose not to actively participate in Town Meeting in order to avoid being pointed out by Mr. Simon.

Other students, in contrast, find comfort in the strict proceduralism of Mr. Simon' moderation style. Stella, a white student, explains:

> . . . that's what we need, we need some structure . . . it makes it run smoother and more people get to say what they want and have everyone else hear it than just talking to each other and you don't really know what other people think. Because the structure of it helps if it's really working, but if it's out of control, then it's just a waste of time.

Another white student, Megan, adds "once Mr. Simon has control, then anyone who wants to speak is heard."

When I asked students who do not participate much in Town Meeting why this is, the primary reasons they offered were shyness, nervousness, and fear of being laughed at. These fears may be due to a variety of factors—cultural styles of communication, self-consciousness in front of one's peers, and worries about a negative reaction from the moderator. Some students said that in order to feel comfortable getting up and speaking, they would need to feel respected by the other students. According to many of these students, Mr. Simon's moderation style provides structure within which they feel respected; because there is no laughter from other students, they can be heard. In this case, the role of the moderator functions to reinforce the intended purposes of Town Meeting's parliamentary procedure—to include all speakers who desire to be heard on the issue at hand and to keep discussion impersonal and orderly.[6]

A few other students, however, articulated that they feel disrespected by Mr. Simon's words and actions. For them, the sense of structure he imposes paints them as criminals or as stupid. In this case, Mr. Simon's use of the role of moderator to instruct students on proper grammar or to regulate students' behavior is in conflict with the intended purposes of parliamentary procedure. Rather than including participants within orderly debate, his moderation style discourages some speakers from sharing their perspectives with other Town Meeting members.

They'll Sweat You Out

Some students also feel that it is not worthwhile to subject themselves to negative reactions from their peers. After overcoming their nervousness about speaking to the crowd, they still have to face the fallout from peers who disagree with them. These students feel that if their peers disagree with them, they are not going to change their minds no matter what is said.

Stacy Smith: How about in Town Meeting—when you do get up and speak, do you feel like people listen? Do you feel like it ever changes their mind or that it impacts how they vote when it comes to a vote?

Camara: Well, if you're agreeing with them, then they'll listen, but if you're disagreeing, they'll be like "aaagghh," jumping and screaming.

Derrick: *They'll sweat you out.*

Camara: Exactly. "I don't care, I've already got my mind set on this."

Stacy Smith: So you don't feel like you often change somebody's mind or change their vote?

Camara: No.

Stacy Smith: How about you Deidre?

Deidre: I agree with her. Sometimes if you're talking about something that's real serious to you, they don't take it as serious as you do and they just be like "I don't care, I don't want to hear this" or something stupid like that.

Sensing that their peers "don't care" or "don't want to hear this," students may have little impetus to overcome their nervousness of speaking at the podium. Students not only face the risk of having students laugh just because a fellow student is speaking, or especially if the speaker makes a mistake, but they risk the negative responses of peers who are "just pushing all that pressure at you," especially if they disagree.

I Just Don't Have Anything to Say

Students are not all or always nervous and scared. Thi explains "sometimes I just don't have anything to say." Sometimes students find that they have nothing to say if the topic of debate "just [isn't] interesting" or if they "haven't really felt strongly about anything." Similarly, students tend to choose not to participate if they do not feel like the topic is important.

Mark: If the topic is on gym day, no one is going to speak about that anyway.

Stacy Smith: Why is that? Why wouldn't you speak about gym day?

Kareem:	Because it's not really that important.
Mark:	Because it doesn't really affect us, we don't care how it is, we're missing a day of school.
Stacy Smith:	So you're happy about that?
Mark:	Yeah.

The example of the "Gym Day" topic raises an interesting set of questions surrounding students' role in selecting the Town Meeting agenda. "Gym Day" is an event that Winthrop Academy students have participated in a couple of times where they spend the better part of the school day competing against other Advisory Group teams through various sports activities. The "Gym Day" topic was chosen by a group of students who met with principal Beth Taft over a Thursday lunch meeting to discuss possible topics for the following day's Town Meeting. Ms. Taft instituted these Thursday lunch meetings in late February, 1996 in response to feedback from students that "Town Meeting is not addressing what's on our minds." A small group of students identified "Gym Day" as a topic for discussion in Town Meeting because one student in particular was concerned that her Advisory Group would not be able to participate in this event. Some students in her Advisory had been neglecting to swim during swim class, and by doing so, they were forfeiting the entire group's opportunity to participate in the Gym Day event.

A group of students selected the "Gym Day" topic, but many other students felt that it was "stupid" or "not that important." This example suggests that informal processes for involving students in setting Town Meeting's agenda do not necessarily ensure that all students will feel the topic is an important one. In cases such as the Bosnia debate, for instance, students had no say in selecting the topic yet thought it was quite important and engaged in a lively debate. The Bosnia topic, in fact, was proposed by Ms. Taft and was responded to with skepticism by a couple of faculty members who felt that students weren't ready to engage in substantive debate. Ms. Taft urged, "let's try it." Students debated the issue in two Town Meetings and outvoted the faculty (who were largely for sending troops to Bosnia). A letter stating that Winthrop Academy was opposed to sending troops was sent to President Clinton.

Some students are quite comfortable with faculty assigning the Town Meeting topic in this manner. Skeptical of his own abilities to identify an important topic, Thi prefers for the agenda to be decided for him rather than to have a voice in its creation.

Thi: . . . it's hard to find a topic and if they can find one for us, for me, this is for me, because I can't really find a topic to talk about and if they just give me a topic then it's easier to stick to that.

It seems that students' perceptions of how important a Town Meeting topic is drives their participation more than the extent to which they have participated in selecting the topic. Yet, if they feel that an issue is important and they do not get a chance to debate it in Town Meeting, they become frustrated. Thus, there is a tension between the sense of agency that comes with having a say in identifying topics and the fact that many students do not yet know how to select important topics.

That's Not up for Discussion

Students sometimes perceive that faculty do not allow important topics to come up for debate within Town Meeting. Kareem senses that ". . . with things that affect us, they either say 'well *this item's not up for discussion* or I'll talk about this later on.'" Questions of whether or not an agenda item is up for discussion arose surrounding the shirt issue within the school's very first Town Meeting. As I mentioned in the last chapter, the shirt issue illuminates key tensions between Town Meeting as a forum for *practice* versus a forum for *participation* within faculty's mission of education for democracy. The unfolding of the shirt issue brings to light difficulties surrounding agenda setting, jurisdiction, and democratic proceduralism that are unique to civic educational practices.

On Friday, September 8, 1995, Winthrop Academy participated in its first Town Meeting and faculty were intent on conveying to students what types of things could happen in Town Meeting as well as the proper procedures to follow within this forum. After Ms. Taft, the moderator, introduced the idea of Town Meeting and made several announcements, she asked students for additional announcements and made a distinction between announcements and matters for discussion. Ms. Taft indicated that matters for discussion were items to be addressed within the debate segment of Town Meeting. She then asked for student announcements. A white female student raised her hand, stood and said "a lot of us have discussed in Advisory that we don't like wearing shirts when teachers don't have to." Her statement was followed by cheering from many other students. Ms. Taft responded "Town Meeting is not a place to yell out {in response to the cheering}. This is an issue to bring out in Town Meeting."

Later within the meeting, Cathy Eichler led a discussion with students of the important terms and formal procedures for Town Meeting. In the midst of this discussion, Mrs. Eichler mentioned that an issue like who wears the Winthrop Academy shirts is controversial and, therefore, a matter for discussion during Town Meeting. Soon after, an African American male student stood and asked "why will discussion of shirts be controversial? It should be cut and dry." She responded by saying that the item already was controversial because she and he had already disagreed about it. Next, an African American female student rose and said "you shouldn't be able to just say who wears what." Mrs. Eichler, as moderator, called her out of order. She then went on to discuss important Town Meeting terminology. She explained that the procedural terms were inherited, not invented at Winthrop Academy, that New England was the home of Town Meeting, that every single member has a vote, and that Roberts' Rules of Order would provide the rules for discussion. After Town Meeting, Mrs. Eichler said to another faculty member "I didn't want to get into that issue of shirts today."

At the following Town Meeting, September 15, 1995, Ms. Taft inserted a "quick word regarding the agenda" after all other faculty had made their announcements.

Beth Taft: Town Meeting is an opportunity to practice democracy and share concerns beneficial for discussion as a community. Some issues are non-negotiable, for example, a shorter day or what to wear. These issues were presented from the outset and are part of the contract of being part of Winthrop Academy. For example, what to wear reflects the profession of being a student. There is also a profession of teachers and Winthrop Academy teachers dress according to such standards.

In the wake of this announcement some students made clicking noises, or "sucked their teeth," in disagreement and others raised their hands to be called upon. Ms. Taft did not call on any students. Instead, she went on to make another announcement regarding how students needed to identify themselves by name in order to place an item on the agenda.

These initial Town Meeting exchanges over the shirt issue demonstrate tensions between faculty and students as they began to construct "ways of being" for the Winthrop Academy community. Notice, students did not state their case as not wanting to wear shirts at all. Rather, they said "a lot of us have discussed in Advisory that we don't like wearing shirts *when teachers don't have to*" [emphases added]. Students wanted to know why faculty did not also wear shirts. The student impulse here could be interpreted as a desire to symbolically create a community of equals at Winthrop Academy. Yet, faculty were pursuing another agenda— "education for democracy," not a democratic education. Some students wanted to be similar to faculty; others wanted to express their individuality through their dress. Faculty wanted to clearly distinguish themselves, as professional educators, from students. Distinct clothing explicitly represented the unequal status between students and faculty.

As part of their mission of "education for democracy," faculty immediately began to teach and invoke formal democratic procedures such as Robert's Rules of Order. But because students were unfamiliar with these procedures they frequently violated them, albeit unconsciously. Therefore, the procedures may have looked to students like devices that were masked as neutral, but which simply reinforced faculty's position of authority over Town Meeting. For instance, when students aired the issue of shirts, the faculty moderators told students not to "yell out," called one student out of order, and finally informed students that the shirt issue was non-negotiable. Students also may have sensed that faculty were uncomfortable facing the shirt issue during the first Town Meeting and that faculty invoked the rules of parliamentary procedure in order to preclude rather than promote debate about the shirts. By deciding whether or not the shirt issue was a "matter for discussion," and by using the role of the moderator to silence student input, Winthrop Academy faculty exercised ultimate control over the first two Town Meetings. Such actions suggest that students' perceptions that faculty disallow discussion of "things that affect us" were probably born very early in the school's experiences. And these perceptions linger long after.

The shirt issue has arisen many times at Winthrop Academy, both in Town Meeting and in other school contexts, following the initial Town Meeting encounters between students and faculty. During Town Meeting faculty announcements throughout the school's first year, faculty chided students for not bringing their shirts to school, for not keeping their shirts clean, and for not wearing their shirts properly. But by the end the year, students still were not exhibiting the "ways of being" surrounding school uniforms that faculty expected. Students seemed to be "negotiating" this issue in some very specific ways—not wearing their shirts, wearing dirty shirts, writing on their shirts, taking off their shirts the instant the school day ended, and constantly asking whether they had to wear shirts at school-related events. In these ways, the shirt issue was constantly alive, and continued to be an undercurrent in teacher-student relations.

On March 22, 1996, Ms. Taft prepared students for a final announcement prior to the beginning of a Town Meeting debate:

Beth Taft: Listen closely. Some of you have appeared over the last week, the last several weeks, with things appearing on your Winthrop Academy shirts. I want to say clearly and definitively that a uniform is a uniform. It is not to be cut up, written on, ripped, or worn inside out, period.

A couple of weeks later, on April 12, 1996, the faculty even hosted a spoof fashion show during Town Meeting to humorously deliver familiar messages about the shirts. Mr. Simon began the show by announcing: "We are very proud to introduce a fashion show for you of our most esteemed faculty members showing examples that are no longer acceptable at Winthrop Academy. Although most of you know the rules by ear, you now shall also know the rules by sight." Faculty proceeded to demonstrate Winthrop Academy T-shirts hidden under flannel shirts, bulging over huge winter parkas, slung around the neck, and ended with their interpretation of "the stinkiest, raunchiest shirt I've ever seen." The show was greeted by delighted laughter, hooting, and applause from the student-filled audience.

A few months into Winthrop Academy's second year, in December of 1996, the shirt issue was brought before Town Meeting. The Student Advisory Council (SAC), a group of approximately ten students who applied and were selected by faculty to provide student leadership within the school, brought the following resolution before Town Meeting: "Winthrop Academy students should have an alternative to Winthrop Academy shirts, such as pins." Mr. Simon, as moderator, introduced the issue to the Town Meeting membership.

Max Simon: Ladies and Gentlemen. In order to include the student body in the decision making process of what topics are brought to Town Meeting, the Student Advisory Council held elections this week. We've got five topics we voted on, and the two close top ones were "all students should have a computer" and "Winthrop Academy students should have an alternative to Winthrop Academy shirts, such as pins."

Therefore, we are going to open the floor to hear proponent's and opponent's arguments to this resolution. OK, remember again we're arguing as if this has already been resolved, to see if this can be accepted. So, I make a motion to open the floor to debating this issue. One at a time please.

Jabran (SAC representative): Point of clarification. If the students actually do vote that this would go into effect, it would have to be taken to the Board of Trustees first for the Board to evaluate first. Just don't think that if we vote here that this is going to pass. I just wanted to put that out.

Max Simon: In other words we could make a resolution that we all paint our faces green, that doesn't mean we should do it. This is the step to making the recommendation to change policy. May I have now other points of clarification or arguments on this resolution.

Following the ensuing debate, during which six students spoke in favor of the resolution while one student and a few faculty members spoke against it, Town Meeting members voted overwhelmingly in favor of the resolution. A few weeks later, two students, both of whom serve on the SAC, presented the shirt issue and the resolution to the Board of Trustees and the Board recommended that faculty and students explore the issue further and return to them with more concrete recommendations.

In terms of students perceptions that Town Meeting does not address "things that affect us;" the shirt issue illustrates some interesting dynamics. Clearly, students feel that wearing shirts every day as a school uniform is an issue that affects them. They persistently raise the issue with faculty and "negotiate" or resist the wearing of shirts in a plethora of different ways. Yet, when the issue was formally placed on the Town Meeting agenda, only seven students spoke on the matter, a mere 7 percent of the student body. And when the resolution was presented to the Board of Trustees for formal action, only two students were present, a mere 2 percent of the student body. As Harry Chase describes most Town Meetings, "a few participate, and the rest are spectators." How can such low participation be accounted for regarding an issue that students clearly feel strongly about?

One reason students may have refrained from participating in debate surrounding the shirt issue is because they remember that the issue was originally labeled non-negotiable by faculty. Following the Town Meeting debate about an alternative to shirts, Susan talked to me about what she thought might happen next.

Susan: I guess some people might try to pick up something about the shirts, try to do something about it, I'm not sure. Some students said the shirts was non-negotiable. They said in the beginning everybody had to wear shirts. They don't think it's worth debating because it's not going to change.

Stacy Smith: So some people might try to do more about it but others think it's not worth it because it's not going to change?

Susan: Yeah.

Stacy Smith: What's your opinion on the subject?

Susan: I think [the pin] would be a good idea for some cases—if you forget your shirt and had to go all the way back to get it, you'll be late. But then you should always remember to wear your shirt anyway. [But we should] try to talk about something different because the shirt issue is not going to change. We're probably just going to spend a lot of time talking about something that's not going to change.

Stacy Smith: Is it fair to say that you kind of like the idea of a pin but don't think it's an issue worth pursuing?

Susan: Yeah.[7]

According to Susan, she and other students do not think that it's worthwhile "to spend a lot of time talking about something that's not going to change." They clearly remember faculty saying that this issue was non-negotiable and have not been informed explicitly of any official change in thinking. Although faculty's intentions may have been to encourage student involvement by including "the student body in the decision making process of what topics are brought to Town Meeting," failure to clarify this intention or explicitly acknowledge a more flexible approach to revisiting items within the school's contract may be confusing for students. Both of the issues that Ms. Taft listed as non-negotiable and part of the contract of being at Winthrop Academy—a shorter day and what to wear— have since been revisited and even taken to the Board of Trustees. Because such non-negotiable issues have been negotiated, and indeed changed in light of Town Meeting resolutions, students may be detecting a message that faculty's control over whether issues are a matter for discussion is arbitrary. They may sense that agenda-setting is not really a process based upon the rule of law, but rather faculty discretion and authority.

We'll Talk Later

In other cases, students are frustrated not by faculty labeling an issue as non-negotiable, but because faculty indicate that now is not the appropriate time for discussion. During one Town Meeting, Ms. Taft, as moderator, responded to an issue that Jabran raised by saying "we can talk about it" and moving on with the formal agenda. Soon after, I asked Jabran how he felt about this exchange.

Stacy Smith: Were you discouraged when [Ms. Taft] said "we'll talk at another time"?

Jabran: It didn't discourage me, I was just making a suggestion, letting it be known what I thought.

Stacy Smith: Are other students this confident?

Jabran: No, they're not. They get discouraged. They don't know how to approach it, they feel discouraged like they might as well not bring it up.

Stacy Smith: How do you know this is how they feel?

Jabran: Guess, feeling, from—it happens to a lot of students. I can tell from what they say after, how they are. They react hostile and it shows. They are mad because they can't say what they want to say. . . . I guess it shows students' impatience. Decisions won't be made right then, they don't realize it's a slow process. . . . I know it's a slow process, especially when it's decisions on a student's future or the school's future. Patience.[8]

In this case, Jabran was not discouraged by the suggestion that "we can talk about it" because he feels confident enough to approach Ms. Taft at a later time and he views decision making "on a student's future or the school's future" as "a slow process." But he explains that for many of his peers, when faculty say they will "talk later" or refuse to immediately make a change that students' desire, students get quite frustrated.

Some students also get frustrated because they perceive that the faculty do not make time to talk even when they are approached.

Natasha: Sometimes, I know sometimes people might be like, like Ms. Taft, you might try to approach her with a situation, but she's always busy, so you feel like "Ms. Taft, God, she never listens." They'll go back to Mr. Asher, I've noticed, they'll go back." Ms. Taft, my goodness, I go to her all the time and she never listens to what I got to say, she's always doing something." So they feel like, they might feel like they're not being heard.

Other students interpret faculty not wanting to talk about an issue as evidence that the issue is not that important. Kerry, who once brought up the shirt issue while Ms. Taft was visiting her Advisory to make a brief announcement, felt this way about Ms. Taft saying "that's a good item for discussion, but I can't talk about it now."

Kerry: I think she was putting it off, because in her opinion it's not that important. But, in my opinion, everything's equally important.[9]

Whereas students perceive that faculty do not listen to them or downplay issues of importance to students, faculty feel that they are doing the best they can to create opportunities for discussion.

Kareem: . . . like with things that affect us, they either say well this item's not up for discussion or *I'll talk about this later on.*

Mark: Talk about it later. They always talk about it after school. But then no one goes to talk about it after school.

Kareem: No one wants to talk about it after school.

Mark and Kareem are referring to faculty's suggestions that students come discuss issues of concern after school hours or during the lunch hour. But students do not want to talk about school things during non-school time. Just as students are frustrated with faculty for wanting to talk later, faculty are frustrated when students are inflexible in their demands for attention. Faculty feel that each and every student concern cannot be addressed during Town Meeting or during limited class time. Shaka Reid expresses this frustration:

> We're all busy. The onus is on you to find time to speak about things that are important to you. Students see the day as from 8 a.m. to 3 p.m. . . . They're not creating effective time for conversation, but trying to smash in time when it's not there. After school I'm still on, but if they're not on, then it's off. I do my home-work at school. I want to hear their concerns and find a time that is good for both of us. So, there's finding a good time versus not being willing to stay at all.

Mr. Reid's perception that many students are not willing to stay at all is reinforced by Mark's comments that "no kids are going to come" talk during non-school time.

Mark: They need to make it so we can give our feedback during a time, not a time where we can come if we want to or not, because if that's the case no kids are going to come. It needs to be mandatory, but not on our time.

Mark admits that he is unwilling to discuss school issues during "his time." He expects faculty to force him to participate by setting mandatory times for discussion. Where faculty exhibit a willingness to work longer hours and make themselves available to students in order for student concerns to be heard, students identify these actions as an unfair expectation to do more school things during what they see as their own time. And each group is frustrated by the expectations of the other.

It's Totally Discouraging

Students become particularly discouraged when faculty state goals for Town Meeting that prove illusory. For some students, discouragement resulted from striving to achieve a shorter school day through what they understood to be formal processes, then failing to achieve this goal as faculty changed the rules along the way. As I mentioned earlier, a Town Meeting resolution was approved by the Board of Trustees to shorten the school day from 3:46 to 3:16 p.m. After the resolution was passed, however, the Winthrop Academy faculty informed students that they could leave at 3:16 only if they earned the privilege by completing all of their homework each week. Some students were very discouraged by this "perfect homework" policy and felt that the resolution to shorten the day was a faculty ruse.

Mark: They didn't shorten the schedule. They just did that to get us to stop from bothering them. A shortened schedule means a shortened schedule; you get out at 3:16 every day.

Kareem: And the whole perfect homework thing is you have to get every question on every lab.

Mark: Before they had, if you missed one question you'd still get credit for the assignment. But now that they do have [the policy], you not only don't get perfect homework, but you get an incomplete on that assignment which you wouldn't have got if you weren't trying to get perfect homework.

Kareem: And towards the end Mr. Simon was talking about the quality of the labs.

Mark: A reading assignment, you can read and not understand it, that doesn't mean you didn't do it, and they still say, it's never

happened to me, but so many other kids, that they'll read something and the next day they really won't understand what's it's
saying and they say "oh, no perfect homework because you
didn't read it." But that's not the case, because I remember me
and Maria, we sat in here one day and the passages for the
Odyssey we were supposed to read and the next day Mrs.
Eichler's like "Maria, can you tell us?" And she was like "I don't
know." I remember that. And you knew she had put in the
time, but she wasn't getting the credit for it.

Qua: Mrs. Eichler, she'll be like "incomplete, this isn't what I want, go
home and do it again." Next thing you know you've got no
perfect homework, then you go home and do it again and she
keeps saying "incomplete" or "it's not enough."

Kareem: And *it's totally discouraging* too because if you miss a question on Friday's homework and you don't get a complete homework, then you're not going to want to do it, you're just not
going to strive for it.

Mark, Kareem, and Qua all appear discouraged by the rules surrounding
"perfect homework" which they perceive to be constantly in flux and
unattainable. This discouragement also seems to have tarnished their faith
in the Town Meeting process. As Mark says, "They didn't shorten the
schedule they just did that to get us to stop from bothering them. A shortened schedule means a shortened schedule; you get out at 3:16 every
day."

At least one faculty member was also disillusioned by the combination
of involving students in a policy decision yet adding faculty-driven stipulations for how the policy would be implemented. Mrs. Eichler disagreed
with shortening the day and, after the resolution was passed, disagreed
with attaching the perfect homework stipulation to leaving school at the
earlier time of 3:16. On both issues, she was outvoted, and abided by the
decision due to her respect for the democratic process. She explains:

> I saw this debate as a setback because it gave students a topic that shouldn't have
> been set forward instead of delineating a constitution and what is basic here,
> what's sacred. Then, when they granted [the shorter day], they granted it with
> bells and whistles. If they win, let them win.

It is interesting to note here that both Mark and Mrs. Eichler refer to the
faculty as "they" who "granted" a shortened schedule. In fact, it was the
overwhelming majority of votes by students that passed the resolution to
shorten the schedule. But Mark's choice of words indicates that he per-

ceives that this decision was ultimately controlled by the faculty who "just did that to get us to stop from bothering them." Mrs. Eichler's words then reinforce his perception that the faculty ultimately controlled how this issue would be framed and how a corresponding school policy would be implemented.

Indeed, most faculty seemed to use Town Meeting in this case as a vehicle to make it appear that students were involved in a decision that in fact had already been made. By doing so, they may have thwarted their civic objective of students gaining a sense of agency. It is important to notice that the three students discussing their discouragement with this process are students who do not frequently participate in Town Meeting. For these three, the "shortening the day" experience appears to have played a role in creating a sense of discouragement whereby they feel that their participation is not worthwhile because it does not make any substantive difference.

The Silent Treatment
Other students report that they refuse to participate in Town Meeting if they are discouraged, frustrated, or angered by other dynamics within the meeting. Some students get frustrated if they are not called upon when they raise their hand and others are upset about the strict procedures that they are expected to follow during Town Meeting.

One student says that if students are not recognized to speak during Town Meeting, they will refuse to raise their hands again in the future.

Natasha: There's like some people, I know sometimes at the end of the year I used to raise my hand a lot, but if you don't get picked on all the time, . . . once [you] raise [your] hand, [you] didn't get picked on that time, [you] ain't gonna raise [your] hand again. . . . And Ms. Taft, she'll call on all the people, then she'll be like "well I don't have time, put your hands down, put your hands down" and then nobody puts their hand up again.

Some other students refuse to participate because they disagree with procedures they have to follow at the beginning of Town Meeting. Students are to enter the Common Room and sit in seats adjacent to members of their Advisory Group. Some perceive this as infantilized treatment and resent being treated like children.

Nichola: Well, the filing in does *not* work.
Stacy Smith: How come?

Nichola: Because people just are not having it, we're not in kinder-
              garten so why should we have to line up and file in?

Daniel: They treat us like 5th graders. Why don't they have us fold
              our hands and take naps? In an ordinary Town Meeting
              they don't have people file in. You must act like an adult.
              But they treat us like children.[10]

In each of these cases, not participating through legitimate avenues
such as being recognized and formally speaking does not necessarily mean
that students are not participating at all. Rather, they are often participating in the covert ways that faculty refer to as "dissolving" by doing things
like coughing, snickering, sucking their teeth or clapping. Students may
also refrain from participating in "legitimate" ways if they disagree with
what is being said by those who are speaking.

Jabran: Students go into a whole new world when they hear something
             they don't want to hear, they release themselves. It's like they're
             giving Town Meeting *the silent treatment*. They think it's bet-
             ter, but it's not. . . . The best Town Meetings are when students
             elaborate on topics, not the ones with grunts and sucking teeth
             because they didn't want to hear what was being said. . . .It takes
             time go get used to. It can't just happen over night. Your confi-
             dence builds as you watch other people speaking. You see that
             talking it out gets more things done than sucking teeth. Some
             subjects people won't like.[11]

Jabran perceives that formal avenues of participation are ultimately more
effective. But many of his peers continue to prefer "the silent treatment"
and "dissolving" over reasoned argumentation.

Blah, Blah, Blah

Unlike students, the majority of faculty are not silent during a typical
Town Meeting. Take, for example, the Town Meeting of Friday, March
21, 1997. Faculty raised the question "What does it mean to be a citizen
at Winthrop Academy?" as part of their deliberations over re-instituting a
Citizenship Grade. Mr. Simon introduced the day's topic.

"Last year, students got a Citizenship Grade. We outlined what a citizen is and
students were ranked by teachers according to how well you did. There is the
potential to do this again this year. But how can we grade you if we don't know

what a citizen is? Since we are all members of this community, we will decide: What does it mean to be a citizen?"

After a short pause, a second-year African American student stands and says "My name is Dameon. Help somebody out when they need help."

A female student behind me lets out a muffled noise; other students around the room cough and whisper.

Then, a first-year African American female, stands, says "My name is Amy. You attend the school." As she sits, a few giggles erupt from other students.

Following a few more suggestions, a second-year white male student stands, introduces himself as "Ryan" and says "I would just like to clarify how we're citizens, do we have rights? I see us being students, not citizens. I don't see how we're different from any other school exactly."

After a brief exchange with the moderator, Ryan says "we're not already citizens because we don't have standards. Shouldn't the question be: How could we be citizens at Winthrop Academy?"

Beth Taft then stands, says "Ms. Taft. Point of clarification, Mr. Moderator. Was that a motion to change the question?"

Ryan stands and says "Yes. What should be the standards to be a citizen at Winthrop Academy?"

After an affirmative vote to change the question, debate continues. Two male faculty members ask questions of clarification regarding the difference between a student and a citizen. Ryan declines to clarify his initial remarks. Shaka Reid remarks that people are not agreeing to a common set of standards. "Thank you, Ryan, this is a much more effective question. Identifying the least thing that we can agree with that helps us to do what we have to do."

Next, Wilman, a first-year African American student stands and introduces himself. He states, "The question doesn't change what we're trying to accomplish. I haven't been treated like a student or a citizen, students should look inside themselves. I have come up against disrespect here. The Citizenship Grade shouldn't be at the end of the year, but on an ongoing basis."

Derrick, a second-year Hispanic student, stands and asks: "What's the usefulness of getting a grade? You're just going to label someone good or bad. Is that going to effect our GPA?"

Mr. Simon responds, in the form of posing a question back to the Town Meeting body, "what's the point of having a grade?"

Mr. Reid stands and begins "I would love to have students contribute to that question." A female student behind me mutters "blah, blah, blah." Mr. Reid continues, "I think [the citizenship grade is] very problematic. I would love student input."

Ms. Taft, stands and says "I would push us to think about standards in classrooms, in addition to being a student, to get at the heart of what it means to participate here at Winthrop Academy. Then, Derrick, part of performance, and if citizenship is to be graded, is something you should have a voice in building."

Mr. Simon says, "we're out of time. As moderator I postpone this question. Think about it during the week, then we'll add to it next week."

Silvia, a second-year African American female student stands, introduces herself, and says "I make a motion to close Town Meeting."

Leilah, a second-year African American female student, introduces herself, and queries Mr. Simon "don't you have to take a vote to postpone the question?"

Mr. Simon, "that is what has to happen. May I have someone second my motion?"

Ms. Taft, "Point of clarification. We'll be working on this in small Advisory Groups. We may not come back to it the next Town Meeting."

Mr. Simon, "may I have a second?"

Leilah, "I second that motion."

Mr. Simon moderates a voice vote that decides in favor of postponing the question.

Lorenzo, a second-year African American male, rises and says "I motion to close Town Meeting." A female behind me laughingly remarks, "he just woke up." She and her friend giggle.

Silvia, "I second that motion."

Mr. Simon moderates a voice vote to close Town Meeting. Students begin to talk to each other and get out of their seats.

Mr. Simon says "sit down." He moderates another voice vote and Town Meeting ends.

This Town Meeting illustrates a tension between "student talk" and "faculty talk" during open debate. Faculty chose this topic for Town Meeting because they wanted to get student input regarding what it means to be a citizen at Winthrop Academy and in creating a new rubric for citizenship grading. And Mr. Simon clearly articulates this desire to students— "We are all members of this community. We will decide." His words suggest that this is a question to be tackled by the entire community.

Student participation is fairly high in this Town Meeting. A number of different students speak. One student challenges and articulates an alternative version of the question at hand. And another student questions the proper procedure for postponing debate at the end of the meeting. But one other dynamic is also in evidence. After Mr. Reid begins speaking toward the end of the meeting, a student behind me mutters "blah, blah, blah." Her tone suggests that she is frustrated by yet another teacher talking. Immediately following Mr. Reid's comments, Ms. Taft gets up to add another point, then Mr. Simon draws the meeting to a close because they have run out of time.

Although faculty intend for Town Meeting to be a forum for student participation, their own participation within this setting may sometimes thwart their intended objective. One student who has served as an Advisory Representative and participated in setting the agenda for upcoming Town Meetings once asked Ms. Taft, "Who will we debate with? The teachers?" Careful attention to the pattern of faculty and student dialogue during Town Meetings suggests why students may perceive that they are debating with teachers, rather than among themselves.

On March 7, 1997, two weeks prior to the citizenship debate, the resolution for Town Meeting read: "The U.S. government should fund research on cloning human beings." Town Meeting members debated this resolution and then voted to endorse or reject it. Mr. Simon introduced the topic by asking "what is the big deal about cloning?" He reviewed some of the recent scientific research findings on cloning sheep and monkeys. Then, he asked for proponents or opponents to speak on the resolution.

Nina, a second-year white student, rose and said she would like to read something she had written on cloning. Mr. Simon invited her to come up to the podium. Once at the podium, she read a speech she had prepared for History class that ended with the question "can souls be Xeroxed?" Next, Jabran, a second-year African American student, went up to the podium to read an essay he had prepared for History class. Immediately following his presentation Kareem, another African-American male, stood to make some comments. He exhorted his fellow students "let your morality and ethics guide you."

Over the next few minutes two female students spoke, then a faculty member, then a female student, then another faculty member. Finally, an African-American student, Leilah, stood and addressed two questions to the moderator: 1) Is the clone at the current age or a baby? 2) Is there an automatic mentality? Following Leilah's questions, Dipan Patel and Max Simon, the school's two science teachers, each offered answers. Then, Brenda Schank, the Director of Programs, posed two additional questions: 1) If you take DNA material from a just viable egg, could you have a clone two months younger than the original mammal? 2) What's the difference between two clones and two identical eggs? Again, Mr. Simon and Mr. Alwan both responded, each speaking for a few minutes. Then, Dr. Chase, a Humanities teacher, posed his version of the distinction between clones and identical twins. This led to a few minutes of exchange between him and Mr. Alwan over the semantics of the difference.

Next, Mr. Navarro, the Spanish teacher, offered his opinion on the resolution—"I say in a free country, with citizens running the government, have the government fund it." Mr. Simon summarized, "us as citizens asking our government to do this versus a trillionaire." Then he said, "in order to move this question we must have a 2/3 majority to stop debate" and he called a vote. Town Meeting members voted against stopping debate. Mr. Simon concluded "we'll continue this debate in the next Town Meeting; continue your conversations in Advisory."

The last ten to fifteen minutes of this Town Meeting were filled with "faculty talk." Students and faculty alike were enthusiastic about the topic of cloning. Two students went to the podium to deliver prepared speeches—not the most common of occurrences during a weekly Town Meeting. And six different students participated in the debate prior to the final period of "faculty talk." Six faculty members also participated in debate. So, in a debate with nearly 100 students and 12 faculty members approximately six percent of the student body spoke, compared with fifty percent of the faculty; and the ratio of "air time" was similar.

Although "faculty talk" can be blamed for precluding student participation within this debate, faculty were placed in a bit of a double bind. Faculty were called upon to explain the scientific and technical intricacies of cloning research. Some faculty members may have also felt compelled to voice ethical considerations in order to raise students' level of ethical awareness surrounding the issue. In each of these respects, faculty's contributions added to the quality of the debate. This double bind suggests that there is a trade-off in practicing civic debate with neophytes between the *quantity* of student talk and the *quality* of views aired. The civic objective that students gain skills in reasoned deliberation contains a tension between faculty modeling quality debate and students practicing persuasive argumentation. In addition, the objective of students gaining a sense of agency may be thwarted when "faculty talk" leads to students disengaging from Town Meeting processes because they do not see them as their own.

Letting *Them* Know

Not surprisingly, in light of the preponderance of "faculty talk" in Town Meeting, when students do participate it seems that their speech is aimed toward influencing faculty, rather than toward persuading their peers. Angel, a Puerto Rican student, explains why he participates in Town Meeting.

> Angel: [I speak in Town Meeting when it's] necessary, to let the faculty know you can help them run the school. Just because we're kids doesn't mean we have the minds of kids, we can have the minds of faculty. We're here five days a week. We know how things are going in the school. We let the faculty know they can be dependent on us, not just on themselves.[12]

Angel's descriptions of equality and interdependence seem at odds with his acknowledgment that faculty run the school. Another student clarifies a similar contradiction when probed:

Daniel: Everybody's on same level . . .
Stacy Smith: Faculty and students?

Daniel: Students. Teachers have a little leeway, we have to give them respect. They do hold power; there are a lot of things they can make us do, and little things we can make them do.

When asked for examples of who makes who do what and how, Daniel explains that students successfully submitted the petition to get more time to change clothes between gym and academic classes. As an example of a not-so-successful issue for students, he raises the issue of wearing Winthrop Academy shirts as school uniforms.

Daniel: [some students were opposed to wearing the shirts, but the faculty said the shirts were mandatory] so we didn't get that one. . . . Some things go your way, some don't. You just deal with it, maybe sometimes you beat the odds.[13]

Daniel's assessment likens participation in Town Meeting to a game of chance with students playing the odds. He claims there are little things students can do to bring the odds toward their favor.

Daniel's fellow student, Jabran, views participation in Town Meeting more as a waiting game than a game of chance.

Jabran: Whenever I say something I really want to be done or attempt to make a change at least it got that far, even if the decision isn't what I wanted, at least it was considered. Everything's not going to go my way, that's not the way life is. Either way you have an effect, whether it comes your way or not. Other teachers might like your idea in time. You might change it just by bringing it up. They might change something five months from now. That's why patience is so important. You might not get your way now, but later on.[14]

For Jabran, patience is a virtue of participation since change is always possible down the road. Patience and optimism allow him to feel that simply being heard is enough to constitute effective participation.

For Angel, Daniel, and Jabran participation in Town Meeting means different things. Demonstrating equality and interdependence, playing the odds, and being patient are among the many ways in which these student's attempt to act like citizens and to have their say in the Town Meeting forum. But, one strand is consistent across all of their stories; each of these students frames his participation in terms of the faculty. Angel wants to "help *them* run the school," Daniel figures he can beat the odds through "the little things we can make *them* do," and Jabran waits for the teacher who "might like [his] idea." When these students have their says it is the teachers they are speaking to.

These students' comments suggest that they view faculty as the real decision makers in Town Meeting. It seems that students' shared perceptions of who their audience is—the faculty—may in turn impact how they speak, and how they listen. Rather than attempting to use speech to persuade their peers to vote with them, students perceive that they are communicating directly with the faculty. Through this lens, "dissolving" may be interpreted as a symbol for students taking control of the agenda. Presuming unequal status between themselves and teachers, students may be transplanting strategies for control that work quite well for them in another unequal setting—the classroom. Misbehavior, rather than being ineffective, is often a quite effective means for students to achieve distinct goals, such as ending Town Meeting, or subverting the faculty's authority. Rather than lacking knowledge of how to participate, students are applying practical knowledge they have gained in classroom settings to meet their own goals. Thus, students employ a variety of strategies to impact those whose votes wield greater impact and ultimately run the school. The problem is that these "dissolving" strategies are examples of coercive power rather than the power of reasoned argumentation.

The Chosen Few

Despite all of these obstacles to participation in reasoned debate among the student members of Town Meeting, some students participate frequently. As Mark, a student who rarely rises to speak, explains, "it's usually the same kids that get up and speak." One impetus for such students to speak is because of their official roles as Advisory Representatives or members of the Student Advisory Council. One such student indicates that she tends to speak because other students expect it of her.

Nichola: Some people have a lot to say, but they'll ask me to say it for them, and I'm not really sure how they want it said. And I wish they were comfortable to say it themselves, but being in the position I'm in, I can't say "well, do it yourself."

Nichola's comments suggest that if she did not occupy the role of Advisory Representative, she probably would not speak so often. If this were the case, other students might feel the need to express their own views.

Students who are not school leaders are also frustrated by the frequency of particular students standing up and speaking again and again during each Town Meeting.

Natasha: There's a certain person, he'll get up and say something; he'll keep on getting up.

Stacy Smith: Saying it a bunch of times?

Nichola: Trying to turn Town Meeting into a debate forum, that's all.

Stacy Smith: What is it then if it's not a debate forum?

Nichola: It's a debate forum, but not a debate between two people.

Natasha: Not between you and somebody else.

Stacy Smith: Not interpersonal?

Natasha: Yeah.

Nichola: That's not the forum for it.

Natasha: For real, cuz he thinks that he gets up and keep on blabbing his mouth like . . . it was him against everybody else. [giggling]

Nichola: My goodness, he just needs help. [giggling]

Despite students' exasperation with their more participatory peers, the less active students allow the frequent talkers to represent their views. The most stark example of one student speaking for the entire student body was provided during the December 6, 1996, debate on the shirt issue.

After the Town Meeting assembly debated the resolution "Winthrop Academy students should have an alternative to shirts, such as pins" for about twenty minutes, one student stood and motioned to bring the resolution to a vote. Just after Mr. Simon called a vote to end debate on the resolution, Ms. Taft stood and asked for clarification.

Max Simon: All those in favor, will say "aye," all those opposed will say "nay." All those in favor of voting, in other words, if we don't agree we'll continue debate. Makes sense. All those who want to vote say Aye. {Ayes voted.} All those who oppose the vote say "Nay." {Nays voted.} The "ayes" have it.

Beth Taft: Point of clarification. The resolution as it reads is a little bit vague, it reads "Winthrop Academy students should have an alternative to shirts, such as pins." If we vote in favor of this are we endorsing the pins or are we endorsing an alternative? {Murmuring among the crowd.}

Max Simon:	{In response to the restless crowd.} You need to understand the clarification.
Beth Taft:	Let me add one further thought to that, Mr. Moderator, which is that if we endorse the resolution, would we then have further debate as to a series of alternatives? Or are we simply resolving that there should be pins instead of shirts?
Max Simon:	As its written now, it says {murmuring; Mr. Simon pauses}. Ladies and Gentlemen. As it reads now, it's not specific, right? It says "such as," that is a suggestion. So, what Ms. Taft is asking is: are we going to vote, say "such as pins," and then have debate on what are the things we're going to use as symbols. In other words you could say, "well, I think my sneakers are my alternative, shows my pride in my school." So, as it's worded now it's not that clear. So, what do we do about that? We can change the wording now?
Beth Taft:	Perhaps a member of SAC can speak to how they put this?
Jabran:	It's supposed to be "such as pins or buttons."
Max Simon:	That's the only alternative?
Jabran:	I think I'm changing my mind because I think we should try to keep it open so we don't just say to the Board that we want pins or buttons so that we keep it open so that they can have a little leeway between the two.
Max Simon:	That's the way it is now.
Jabran:	That's just an example. We want to probably debate a series of alternatives.
Cathy Eichler:	Would the proponents of this resolution, which I heartily oppose, would the proponents of this accept a friendly amendment that would simply put "Winthrop Academy students should have an alternative to the shirts" period? {Some students in the crowd respond "Nope."}
Max Simon:	That's what we're going to debate.
Cathy Eichler:	No, the resolution would then read Winthrop Academy students should have an alternative to the shirts. {Some students say "yeah."} The alternatives then would be . . . {shrugs her shoulders}
Max Simon:	So, we're now going to vote on if you'd like an alternative. Therefore, the next debate is then going to vote on what the alternatives may be.

Cathy Eichler:	No, I believe the proponents may accept a friendly amendment. If they accept the amendment, you can vote it.
Max Simon:	So I ask them?
Cathy Eichler:	{Nods.}
Max Simon:	Student Advisory Council, is it all right if we erase "such as pins" and put a period after shirts? May I have a representative please acknowledge that and say yes or no.
Jabran:	Yes, that's fair enough.
	{Shaka Reid made the changes to the written resolution.}
Max Simon:	All those in favor, we're now going to vote for this resolution. Yes, sir, point of clarification.
Frank Nardelli:	Point of Clarification. I'm not familiar with this procedure so you're going to have to explain to me, am I to assume that one member of the Student Advisory Group is empowered to speak for the entire student body? Or?
Megan:	I'm also a student and a member of the Student Advisory Council and yes Jabran's speaking for the rest of the SAC. It was his idea.
Harry Chase:	Point of Clarification. {Students, moving around and murmuring, appear restless.} I think that this as presently presented is an ill-considered proposal and that if they want it to be taken seriously either by the staff or the Board they must word it very carefully so that when we vote on it we are sure about what we're voting on. They seem to be changing the content of the proposal in midstream here.
Jabran:	I'd like to reply to Dr. Chase' statement. I think what is going to be considered by the staff or the Board is the final thing, the final cut that we make here, so I don't think this has anything to do with the teacher's or the Board's decision. This is our process of Town Meeting. I basically think that this process that we have here is in order to come up with something that would be sufficient enough for the teachers or the Board to come up with a final decision.
Harry Chase:	I would contend, Mr. Moderator, with the answer in saying that alterations that are made on the floor I hardly think can be representative of the whole school body.
Jabran:	I would like to see show of hands who oppose the alterations that we made. {Pause} Any hands? Mr. Moderator I think his question is answered. {Laughter}

Max Simon: I think any alteration, whether or not the resolution was
                as specific as possible or as vague as possible, will then
                influence the decision made about the resolution. There-
                fore, if the resolution is vague and not specific it can be
                rejected by the Board for being vague and not specific
                and be sent back to Town Meeting to be ratified or sent
                back to the SAC to be ratified so it's then specific. So, if
                everyone accepts it the way it is now, that doesn't have
                anything to do with the decision the Board makes. So, if
                it's vague now and the Board says it's vague, that's the
                resolution presented as it is.

Brenda Schank: I want to know, are we allowed now to make a statement
                about the resolution as it's stated to inform students of a
                possibility that could happen as a result of this resolu-
                tion or is that part of debate which we don't have any-
                more?

Cathy Eichler: Debate's been closed. Call the question.

Max Simon: Debate's been closed, I agree. All those in favor of the
                resolution say "Aye." {Ayes voted.} All those opposed
                say "Nay." {Some students begin to murmur "ayes" have
                it}. The "ayes" have it.

                Ladies and gentlemen, the resolution as it stands, we
                will inform you on Monday on the process of the resolu-
                tion. May I have someone make a motion to close Town
                Meeting.

During the course of this Town Meeting discussion, both faculty and
students treated Jabran as the designated speaker for the student body.
This began rather subtly as Mr. Simon asked for a representative of the
Student Advisory Council to respond to a change in the wording of the
resolution and Jabran responded affirmatively. But Jabran's control over
the direction of the resolution became more explicit as he made statements like "*I'm* beginning to change *my* mind." His designated role as
representative of the student body became starkly clear when his jurisdiction was called into question by Mr. Nardelli and Dr. Chase, who both
wondered whether "one member of the Student Advisory Group is empowered to speak for the entire student body?" In response to their queries, another SAC member rose and said that this resolution on the shirts
was Jabran's idea. Next, all of the students at least tacitly supported his

leadership role by not responding when Jabran challenged, "I would like to see a show of hands who oppose the alterations that we made."

In this and other Town Meetings a number of factors appear to coalesce to make Jabran one of the "chosen few" who actively participates. First, Jabran is comfortable speaking in this setting. He raises his hand to be recognized and rises to speak at virtually every Town Meeting, and he usually speaks more than once. Second, Jabran is a member of the Student Advisory Council and therefore occupies an official role that requires that he speak more often than students who are not SAC members. Third, many faculty and students alike defer to Jabran as speaking "for the students," particularly surrounding the shirt issue.

Each of these factors that serves to encourage the active participation of a few students may simultaneously hinder the participation of a large number of other students. Because those students who are quite comfortable raising their hands and rising to speak are frequently recognized first, they tend to take up more air time. Other students who are shy, or need more time to think through their ideas before speaking, are not likely to have even raised their hands by the time a more aggressive student is already speaking and moving the debate in a specific direction. To the extent that the more active speakers and participants are also the student leaders within the school, those students who are members of SAC or Advisory Representatives, they are both more comfortable speaking and feel called upon to fulfill their official roles. Finally, these factors combine to form the expectation, shared by many faculty and students, that these are the students who will participate. Other students are either let off the hook or do not have the time to speak even if they might want to because one of the "chosen few" already has the floor.

A Few Participate and the Rest are Spectators

Winthrop Academy faculty aspire to cultivate in students both *know how*, including skills in reasoned deliberation and ways of being conducive to civil interaction, and *agency* or a sense that what they say matters. Toward these ends, they provide students with a weekly Town Meeting as a forum in which to practice. In many respects Town Meeting is living up to its intended objectives. Students debate a wide array of issues ranging from those directly impacting the school to those of international significance. Students play a direct role in influencing school policy. Students make presentations in front of their peers, vote, suggest agenda items, and write letters to politicians.

Despite these many successes, there are also ways in which Town Meeting is not achieving its intended objectives. Neither the quantity nor the quality of student participation in Town Meeting meets faculty's expectations. As Harry Chase points out, "a few participate and the rest are spectators." Moreover, the spectators are not simply "learning how to listen," but rather are engaging in "dissolving" behaviors as opposed to reasoned discourse.

Students' descriptions of their participation in Town Meeting provide clues to a number of hindrances to their practicing skills and habits of minds necessary for democratic processes. One source of hindrances is attitudinal. Many students are too nervous or scared to participate. Their fears emanate primarily from the anticipation of negative reactions from their peers. These students are afraid that they will be laughed at or jeered while expressing their views. Other students are discouraged; they feel that their participation is not worthwhile either because they will not be able to persuade their peers, because the decision is ultimately in the hands of the faculty, or because they perceive that issues they care about are non-negotiable.

A second source of hindrances is structural—due to constraints on time the participation of some constrains opportunities for participation by others. In Town Meeting active participation by a select few, namely faculty and student leaders who often occupy official roles such as Advisory Representative or Student Advisory Council member, disallows participation by the majority of students who remain silent spectators. A final hindrance to legitimate participation is the "dissolving" behavior that many student spectators choose to engage in. "Dissolving" and "the silent treatment" may each arise in response to student perceptions of the unequal nature of the student/teacher relationship combined with perceptions that faculty are the "real" decision makers within Town Meeting. Thus, rather than engaging in reasoned discourse with their peers, students engage in behaviors that subvert faculty authority by exerting student control over the agenda and pace of Town Meeting.

These multiple hindrances to students practicing democratic participation complicate the realization of faculty's civic educational objectives of *know how* and a sense of *agency*. For Beth Taft, who along with Cathy Eichler is one of Winthrop Academy's strongest proponents of civic education, the gap between ideals and reality suggests that students have not yet adopted Town Meeting as a forum for pursuing their own ends. Ms. Taft explains,

It says to me that students haven't yet learned how to use the tool for their own purposes. *There's a way in which practicing is a form of instruction from just having done it.* I would love to see the day where kids come and want to use Town Meeting for their own purposes. [emphases added]

Much of the success of Town Meeting as a forum for practicing democracy is premised upon Beth Taft's notion that "[t]here's a way in which practicing is a form of instruction from just having done it." Yet, students' experiences of "just having done it" suggest the tenuous nature of practicing civic participation in an educative setting. Because students are not manifestly equal to faculty within the Town Meeting process, and because faculty are concerned with monitoring the behavior of students and elevating the quality of debate, reasoned deliberation among free and equal parties is not really what happens in Town Meeting. As a result, Town Meeting is not yielding faculty's intended outcomes, nor outcomes consistent with the "quality of reasoned deliberations" required by the deliberative model. Thus, in the next chapter I offer some recommendations for bringing Winthrop Academy's *practices for* civic participation within Town Meeting closer to their own intended objectives and to the normative standards of deliberative democratic theory.

Notes

1. Unless otherwise noted, the quotes from faculty in this and the following sections are from interviews conducted in April, 1996.

2. Interview with Max Simon conducted November 2, 1995.

3. Students were asked to report on these items in a written survey administered to the entire student body in May of 1996. The response rate to the survey was over 90% of the 66 students. Specifically, 93% reported that they felt like a member of a community at Winthrop Academy; 64% reported that their voices were heard within the school community; and 60% reported that they participated in decision making within the school. See appendix C, table 6.1 for the entire survey.

4. These students' comments are from interviews conducted in February and March of 1996.

5. Unless otherwise noted, the quotes from students in this and the following sections are from interviews conducted in June 1996.

6. *Winthrop Academy Town Meeting Guidelines*, 6.

7. Interview conducted January 9, 1997.

8. Interview conducted February 9, 1996.

9. Interview conducted March 15, 1996

10. Interview conducted February 13, 1996.

11. Interview conducted February 9, 1996.

12. Interview conducted February 9, 1996.

13. Interview conducted February 13, 1996.

14. Interview conducted February 9, 1996.

Chapter 5

Charter Schools and Democratic Social Reproduction

I. Revisiting the Democratic Potential of Charter School Reform

At the outset of this book I noted that the charter school debate is polemicized between a model of market competition on one hand and charges that charter reform is anti-democratic on the other. I suggested that this polemic overlooks some key potentialities of charter reform in terms of democratic social reproduction. Charters are autonomous organizations within the public educational sphere that provide conditions for voluntaristic, associational school communities. Insofar as charter school reform creates distinct public school communities, some potential goods and some potential dangers may arise.

In terms of goods, charter schooling offers increased and pluralized choices within the public educational sphere. Such choices are especially significant for low-income and historically marginalized families. The organizational structure of charter schooling allows for the institutional representation of these groups' distinct educational interests within public education. In addition, the voluntaristic and associational nature of charters raises the possibility that distinct schools may encourage a sense of belonging in students. A sense of belonging might provide a corrective to the widespread alienation that so often accompanies the contractual, bureaucratic relationships within traditional schools. Finally, the regulatory relief granted to charter schools raises the possibility that they might function as particularly democratic associations where public discourse surrounds common educational concerns and a spirit of civic participationism is cultivated in both parents and students.

Yet a model of charter schools as voluntaristic, associational public school communities also poses some dangers to democratic social reproduction. Charter schools might spur the resegregation of public education as families choose to associate with those who share common interests. Within tightly-knit educational communities students' future choices, especially surrounding their values and sense of identity, may be constrained. Increased participation within such particularistic communities might come at the cost of mutual understanding and tolerance for differences. Inevitably, some students and families will be excluded from the unique missions of specific charter schools. Can this sort of factionalization within public education be reconciled with the political requirements of democratic public life?

In light of tensions between these potential goods and dangers, I raised two overarching questions for charter school reform: Is a pluralized sphere of distinct school communities something we (as democratic citizens of the United States) might want to cultivate? And if so, under what conditions? I proposed to take advantage of the opportunity offered by charter reform to envision an idealized model of public life and to formulate concrete ways to institutionalize this ideal in the structures and practices of public education. Accordingly, I searched for a model of public life that would enable our pluralistic citizenry to maximize the potential goods while minimizing the potential dangers of charter school communities.

In response, I offered deliberative democracy as a normative model for evaluating the legitimacy of institutions and decision-making processes within civil society. I contend that a deliberative model of democratic politics is capable of withstanding the challenges of plurality and complexity faced by our political and educational institutions. Through multiple, associative publics within civil society, and through face-to-face processes of deliberative decision making, deliberative democracy allows for both the representation as well as the reconciliation of difference. Difference is not overcome nor transcended, but it is mediated in such a way that common interests are formed which are equally in the interest of all.

Charter school reform raises unique questions surrounding public interests in educational governance, the distribution of educational opportunities among socio-cultural groups, and civic education. The deliberative model of democratic politics provides charters with normative standards for balancing particular educational interests with public interests in democratic social reproduction. The model clearly demonstrates that charter schools are not necessarily the demise of public education. Charters need not be anti-democratic, as critics fear, but may vitalize a more participatory, more deliberative form of democratic politics within the public educational sphere. Moreover, charter schools embody not only the potential to serve as *arenas of* deliberative democracy, but also to serve as *schools for* deliberative democracy.

In order to inform how each of these potentials might be realized in charter schools, I translated a discourse theory of deliberative democratic politics into a corresponding theory of civic education. I suggested that the deliberative model informs both *practices of* the governance and distribution of public education as well as civic educational *practices for* future democratic participation. I cautioned, however, that it is often in concrete practices that ideal theories exhibit their exclusionary and privileging tendencies. Thus, I undertook a case study of one charter school with an explicit mission of civic education in order to illuminate the complexities of translating deliberative theory into concrete institutional structures and educational practices.

Deliberative democracy requires that its participants are manifestly equal and that all who are affected by a decision are included in the decision-making process. Within a deliberative theory of civic education, participation comes in the form of *practicing for* future involvement in democratic processes. Education for deliberative democracy thereby requires that students are manifestly equal and included within such *practices for* democratic participation. My case study of Winthrop Academy Charter School serves as a critical case for investigating how deliberative democracy's ideals of equality and inclusion are fostered and hindered in deliberate *practices for* future civic participation. In addition, the case provides some glimpses of challenges to the ideals of equality and inclusion within charter schools' *practices of* governance and distribution.

In the following sections of this chapter I demonstrate how the norms of deliberative democracy can be employed to assess the legitimacy of concrete charter school practices and policies. I draw upon the theory's principles as critical yardsticks with which to evaluate whether the policies and practices I observed at Winthrop Academy fulfill public interests in democratic social reproduction. This analysis of Winthrop Academy's experiences elucidates many complexities surrounding the realization of deliberative democratic ideals within *practices of* and *practices for* democratic participation in charter schools.

After applying discourse theory's critical yardsticks to deliberate practices of civic instruction at Winthrop Academy, I recommend some strategies for more fully realizing deliberative ideals within such *practices for* democratic participation. Next, I examine the potential educative influences of *practices of* governance and distribution unique to charter school reform. These discussions illuminate the strengths and weaknesses of deliberative democracy as a normative model for assessing charter school reform as well as ramifications for safeguarding democratic public interests through charter school policy. Finally, I end by making some recommendations for specific aspects of charter school policy and future directions for the reform movement as a whole.

II. Deliberate Instruction: *Practices For*
Democratic Participation

The case study of Winthrop Academy's experiences with civic education presented in the last chapter explored the types of dynamics that foster or hinder equal and inclusive participation in *practices for* democratic citizenship. The case particularly emphasized a complex set of hindrances to students participating in the weekly Town Meeting forum. Whereas some attitudinal hindrances stem from students being nervous and afraid of speaking in front of their peers, a number of other hindrances appear rooted in tensions between the participationist aspects of democratic processes on one hand, and the educative mission of *practices for* democratic participation on the other. These tensions illustrate challenges to a deliberative democratic theory of civic education while also highlighting some sticking points within deliberative theory's ideal procedure.

As I pointed out in chapter 2, a discourse theory of democratic politics offers a participationist model of political community. Seyla Benhabib explains that "on the participationist model, the public sentiment which is encouraged is . . . political agency and efficacy, namely the sense that we define our lives together, and that what one does makes a difference."[1] Deliberative democracy's participationist ethic is sustained within its ideal procedure because all parties are free and manifestly equal and only reason, or "the force of the better argument," prevails.

Schools, however, are not only, nor necessarily, participationist communities. Rather, schools are first and foremost educative communities. In terms of civic education, deliberative democracy requires that schools teach students how to become future participants in democratic decision-making processes. Students need to gain skills in reasoned argumentation, a willingness to abide by background conditions of respect and reciprocity, and a sense that what one does makes a difference. Winthrop Academy brings to life one approach to such a civic education mission and refers to it as education for democracy. Winthrop Academy emphasizes cultivating in students *know how*—including capacities for reasoned discourse and ways of being conducive to civil interaction—as well a sense of *agency*. Teachers view students as "unequals" within the school setting, but simultaneously as "potential equals" within future civic communities. The central question faculty grapple with in achieving this mission is "how do you prepare kids for democracy without being explicitly democratic?" Or, in other words, "how do you teach them to practice?"

Using Critical Yardsticks to Assess
Winthrop Academy's Town Meeting

Winthrop Academy's experiences with Town Meeting as a formal arena of practice starkly illuminate the differences between participatory versus educative communities. Although Winthrop Academy's mission closely reflects the educational imperatives of deliberative democracy, the educative mission itself complicates the realization of these imperatives. This setting, then, provides a rich context for exploring the usefulness of the deliberative model's principles as critical yardsticks for assessing the equality and inclusiveness of civic educational *practices for* democratic participation.

Cognizant that the principles and conditions surrounding deliberative democracy's ideal procedure cannot be translated straightforwardly to the institutional level, Benhabib urges us to consider the principles as "critical yardsticks" for assessing the extent to which institutional practices approach, or deviate from, the normative standard. She adds greater texture to the notion of a critical yardstick in the following passage:

> As a critical theorist, one is interested in identifying those social relations, power structures, and socio-cultural grids of communication and interpretation at the present which limit the identity of the parties to the dialogue, which set the agenda for what are considered appropriate or inappropriate matters of institutional debate, and which sanctify the speech of some over those of others as being the language of the public.[2]

In the following three sections I will address the issues of setting the agenda for debate, limiting parties to dialogue, and sanctifying a language of the public in terms of identifying the complexities of institutionalizing deliberative democracy's requirements for civic education. This discussion highlights the ways in which Winthrop Academy's experiences in Town Meeting both reflect and challenge deliberative theory's claims to mediate social relations of inequality, especially those surrounding race, class, and gender.

Setting the Agenda for Debate

Benhabib's concern as a critical theorist with "identifying those social relations, power structures, and socio-cultural grids of communication and interpretation which . . . set the agenda for what are considered appropriate or inappropriate matters of institutional debate" implicitly reveals her assumption that processes that deem matters inappropriate for debate tend to illegitimately exclude or silence certain groups. This assumption is complicated within educative *practices for* democratic deliberations. Winthrop Academy's experiences suggest that students do not yet know how to select appropriate topics for debate. Nevertheless, their participation in determining the agenda may provide them with an important sense of agency.

Winthrop Academy students identified one of the best Town Meetings as the meeting in which they debated President Clinton's decision to send troops to Bosnia. But students had no part in selecting this topic as an agenda item. Conversely, student Advisory Representatives were intimately involved in selecting the "Gym Day" topic for debate. Many of their peers, however, thought that this topic was "not important," "stupid," and generally not worth talking about. These contrasting instances of agenda setting indicate that including some students in the process of determining an appropriate item for discussion does not mean that all students will find the issue engaging. On the whole, students are most concerned that the topic for debate is important. Students described the best Town Meetings as those in which they "talked about an important topic" and students "took it seriously."

Not surprisingly, students seem more likely to consider a topic important if they know something about it. Regarding the example of the Bosnia debate, Jabran explains that this was one of the better Town Meetings "because students seemed confident in what they were saying. They got to say what they had to say without getting hostile. They talked it out; felt like it was an issue they could really articulate and elaborate on." Jabran stresses that students did not get hostile, but he also emphasizes that they "seemed confident" and "could really articulate and elaborate on" this topic. Perhaps students were confident speaking on this topic because some shared personal experiences with the issue, such as fears that relatives in the Army would be sent into a dangerous situation. Similarly, in other instances, students gained knowledge of a topic from their academic classes. During the debate on human cloning, for instance, two students spoke at the podium. This is not a common occurrence in Town Meeting. Both students presented speeches that they had prepared for their academic classes. And faculty linked the success of this debate to the background preparation that took place within the science and history classes.

Despite the fact that students do not necessarily have to participate in the agenda-setting process in order to feel that the topic is important, access to such processes does seem to provide them with a sense that they have a say within the school community. Many students report that Town Meeting is the place for them to have their voices heard within the school. Students also emphasize the importance of having avenues for issues that they care about to be addressed within Town Meeting. Those students who do not feel as if the agenda includes issues they care about tend to retreat from the process by giving Town Meeting "the silent treatment."

To the extent that students' participation is linked to their sense that the topic for debate is important as well as a sense that they have some opportunity to bring topics they care about to the floor, the pedagogical question becomes: how are "important" topics to be selected? One Advisory Representative, Nichola, feels that a process "of people having ears around to know what to do on the agenda" works well. Nichola is referring to students, mostly Advisory Representatives, simply paying attention to what fellow students are talking a lot about during the week, especially in informal settings such as the lunch room or the hallways. Nichola thinks that this informal process worked more effectively for identifying important topics than a process of Advisory Representatives formally polling students. She explains, "I found that when we'd ask 'what do you want on the agenda?' people'd put little stupid things up there, basketball, and I mean everything else, but . . . when it comes time to say something they won't, and they sit there like everything's hunky dory."

Nichola's perception that "having ears around" proves an effective way of selecting an agenda item that students feel is important reinforces the contention of deliberative democrats that informal processes of opinion-formation are inclusive means of formulating the agenda for formal political debate. Winthrop Academy's experiences, however, illuminate one key sticking point within this process. The Advisory Representatives were those students whose "ears" would absorb the opinions among the student body. Then, the Advisory Representatives would report back to each other and to Ms. Taft on what students were talking about during the Thursday lunch meetings. During this meeting, a topic for the following day's Town Meeting would be determined.

This agenda-setting process placed the onus for filtering and accurately reporting the weight of various opinions to the formal agenda-setting body squarely on the shoulders of the Advisory Representatives. In the case of the "Gym Day" topic, one particular representative, Camara, was especially concerned about this topic. It was her Advisory Group that was at risk of not being allowed to participate in Gym Day because her fellow students were squandering the opportunity by refusing to participate in swim class. Perhaps Camara's own feelings about Gym Day influenced her representation of the topic as "important" more than the actual quantity or quality of opinions she heard from other students. Or perhaps she heard more from her friends or fellow students in her Advisory than from students in other Advisory groups who were not so concerned with Gym Day because they were not at risk of being excluded from participating.

The central point raised for deliberative theory by Winthrop Academy's experiences with agenda setting by "having ears around" is the crucial role played by channels between informal spheres of opinion-formation and formal spheres of will-formation. Habermas insists that as public opinion coalesces around an issue, communicative power will be directed toward the formal spheres of decision making and influence the administrative power of these bodies. But Camara's ability to push through the "Gym Day" topic indicates that the influence of public opinion is susceptible to distortion within the channels that transmit informal communicative power toward formal arenas of decision making. While processes of opinion-formation can be particularly inclusive, processes of agenda-setting with formal political arenas do not necessarily reflect this inclusivity.

Although questions surrounding the processes that translate public opinion into a formal political agenda are noteworthy for deliberative theory, these are not the most pressing questions for civic education. Winthrop Academy's experiences suggest that students learn as much or more about identifying appropriate topics for public debate through the process of debating. In the case of Bosnia, for instance, due to their lack of knowledge surrounding national politics, students would not have identified this topic on their own. But they found the debate worthwhile and important. Within civic education, it is not only agenda-setting processes, but processes that ensue which strongly impact students' sense of agency as well as their willingness to participate according to the background rules of respect and reciprocity.

Limiting the Identity of Parties to Dialogue

Within Winthrop Academy's "education for democracy" students are not parties to public dialogue. Instead, students are participants within educative *practices for* future civic participation. Faculty themselves perceive that student participation in practicing democracy is limited in the Town Meeting forum insofar as "a few participate and the rest are spectators." In the interests of "identifying those social relations, power structures, and socio-cultural grids of communication and interpretation" that may be coalescing to limit student participation, I will outline two key possibilities. First, unequal relationships between faculty and students seem to limit student involvement in formal Town Meeting processes. Second, the procedural style of communication within Town Meeting seems to disproportionately marginalize some cultural groups as well as individual students who are not assimilated into the academic culture of the school. These two limitations of student participation in Town Meeting highlight weaknesses within the deliberative model as well as unique challenges to preparatory *practices for* civic involvement.

An unequal relationship between teachers and students within Town Meeting appears to often preclude rather than enhance students practicing democratic citizenship. Faculty's participation as "teachers" impacts students' participation in a number of ways. To the extent that teachers talk a lot, students have fewer opportunities to participate in debate. When teachers regulate student behavior by setting and enforcing policies for appropriate conduct, students react by giving Town Meeting "the silent treatment" and essentially refusing to participate. When these student spectators do participate, it is most often characterized by "dissolving" behaviors which do not constitute practice in reasoned deliberation nor "ways of being" conducive to civil interaction.

A second source limiting the identities of student participants may be Town Meeting's procedural style for debate. A few students actively participate in Town Meeting debate. Jabran, an African American student, is by far the most frequent participant. His high level of participation is closely followed by that of a few other African American students and a handful of White and Hispanic students; many of these students occupy leadership roles within the school. This pattern demonstrates at least two groups of students whose participation is limited within Town Meeting—students who are not members of the majority cultural group and students who have not bought into the academic culture of the school. In order to discuss how these two groups are excluded from participation, I must first discuss the forms of communication that are sanctified as the "language of the public" at Winthrop Academy.

Sanctifying a Language of the Public

As I discussed in chapter 2, the styles of communication employed by many cultural groups are likely to affect parties' senses of inclusion and manifest equality in the discourse procedure. Political theorist Iris Marion Young describes how the communication styles of dominant cultural groups tend to devalue, and even discourage, participation by members of other cultural groups.

> In many formal situations the better-educated white middle-class people . . . often act as though they have a right to speak and that their words carry authority, whereas those of other groups often feel intimidated by the argument require-ments and the formality and rules of parliamentary procedure, so they do not speak, or speak only [in] a way that those in charge find "disruptive." Norms of assertiveness, combativeness, and speaking by the contest rules are powerful silencers or evaluators of speech in many actual speaking situations where cultur-ally differentiated and socially unequal groups live together. The dominant groups, moreover, often fail entirely to notice this devaluation and silencing, while the less privileged often feel put down or frustrated, either losing confidence in them-selves or becoming angry.[3]

Young also asserts that the "norms of articulateness" within a delibera-tive model of democratic decision-making—norms that favor formal, gen-eral, principled speech "that proceeds from premise to conclusion in an orderly fashion"—privilege the speech culture of white middle-class men over the speech cultures of women and racial minorities.[4] Based upon past empirical research and these sorts of assertions from feminist and cultural theorists, I predicted in chapter 2 that cultured and gendered styles of communication would be potential hotspots for hindering equal and inclusive student participation in civic educational practices.

At Winthrop Academy, communication styles consistent with parlia-mentarian deliberation characterize the speech culture of Town Meeting. Faculty members who are attempting to teach the nuances of this speech culture occupy a privileged position of educative authority in relation to their students. And most of these teachers are "better-educated" and/or "white" and/or "middle-class" people. Young's assertion that "norms of articulateness" privilege some social groups over others suggests that students from racial minority groups as well as girls would likely be deval-ued or silenced with Town Meeting. Silencing of female students, how-ever, is not glaringly apparent at Winthrop Academy. In terms of numbers of students who actively participate in Town Meeting there is no significant gender imbalance. Jabran clearly participates most frequently, but following him the breakdown between males and females is fairly equal.[5] What seems more noteworthy is that the most active students are African Americans; this is a trend which at first glance appears to fly in the face of Young's claim that the speech cultures of racial minorities are likely to be marginalized within formal deliberative processes.

Upon closer inspection, however, Young's fundamental contention that those groups with less "social privilege" remain less privileged with formal deliberative procedures continues to ring true. The fact that African American students tend to dominate active participation within Town Meeting may be attributable in part to their near-majority status at Winthrop Academy. African Americans comprise a full 59% of the student body compared with an average closer to 12% within the American population at large. In this setting, African Americans are not a minority and some degree of social privilege may simply be attached to their status as the largest cultural group of students at the school.

In addition, the particular African American students who participate most frequently within Town Meeting are students who appear to buy into the overall academic culture of the school. Jabran, for instance, is frequently at Winthrop Academy after hours working on homework. He was one of the only students who spoke against shortening the school day because he thought that less time in school would prove a detriment to students' learning. Also recall that Jabran feels comfortable approaching faculty members with his concerns. These characteristics suggests that Jabran is fairly assimilated to the academic school culture at Winthrop Academy. This assimilation to the expected behaviors, or "ways of being," carries over into Town Meeting where he is often first to raise his hand to speak and continues to raise his hand numerous times throughout each debate.

Thus, Jabran is both a member of the majority cultural group at Winthrop Academy and he appears to be assimilated to the mainstream norms of the school's academic culture, including the speech culture of Town Meeting. These two attributes are not shared similarly by many other students at Winthrop Academy. Asian American, Hispanic, and White students do not enjoy majority status within the student population. And a large number of students from all cultural groups are less assimilated to the mainstream academic and communicative expectations of the school's faculty. These other students, the spectators in Town Meeting, may not actively participate either because they are resisting the academic and behavioral norms of the school community or because their own cultural norms simply clash with those expected within Town Meeting.

Many students resist the academic and behavioral norms that Winthrop Academy faculty wish to inculcate in a plethora of other ways. These types of students do not do their homework, they disrupt academic classes, some write graffiti on the bathroom walls and some fight. It appears that most of the students who resist assimilation to the norms of Winthrop Academy's educative community are also those who refuse to actively participate in Town Meeting. Once source of such resistance may be due to these students' backgrounds as members of groups, both race- and class-based groups, whose marginalization within American society has led to the formation of a sort of oppositional culture. Such a culture is characterized by strategies of accommodation, such as passive or covert resistance, to the dominant authority of other groups. According to this reading, some "dissolving" behaviors may be examples of an oppositional culture of resistance to faculty authority that students perceive as arbitrary.

Similarly, other examples of "dissolving" may stem from differences between mainstream and African-American styles of communication. African Americans represent the largest cultural group at Winthrop Academy. Thus, despite Jabran and a few other African American student leaders, a large number of students who resist the school culture are African American. And their participation in Town Meeting tends to be viewed by faculty as "dissolving" behavior. It is interesting to compare faculty's language with Young's assertion that groups who "often feel intimidated by the argument requirement and the formality and rules of parliamentary procedure, . . . do not speak, or speak only [in] a way that those in charge find 'disruptive'" [emphasis added]. Thomas Kochman's research comparing the communication styles of Blacks and Whites indicates that not only educated, white, middle-class people find black patterns of communication disruptive. Blacks who are assimilated to mainstream cultural norms also find such patterns disruptive.

Kochman posits that an African American style of communication is characterized by "the point and counterpoint of argument, [and allows for] spontaneous impulses to speak." This "pattern and pulse" of the black pattern of communication is "quelled by the impersonal manner of the presentation and the number of points made" within parliamentary procedure, for instance.[6] Kochman provides an example of conflicting cultural styles from a meeting that is reminiscent of Winthrop Academy's Town Meeting.

A good example of this occurred at a meeting, described by Joan McCarty, consisting mostly of black community people. The talk centered on male-female relationships. During the question-and-answer period, people were allowed to give their opinions. At one point, a man was giving his opinion when a woman said (after a point had been made, but before the man had finished all he wanted to say) "That's not true, that's not true . . ." At this the black moderator—whom McCarty considered acculturated to middle-class norms—announced, "I just won't listen to any of you. You have to raise your hand. There's no debate, and you cannot ask a question of the person who made the statement." As a result, according to McCarty, "the heat level went down so low that it actually became boring to the people there, despite the fact that the issues were exciting."[7]

This passage suggests a couple of things for Winthrop Academy's experiences with students' participation in Town Meeting. First, the more active participation of African American students, like Jabran, who are buying into the school culture as a whole is consistent with acculturation toward the white, middle-class norms that characterize the parliamentarian speech culture of Town Meeting. Other African American students, on the other hand, who are either resisting acculturation or experiencing this process more slowly may experience two phenomena. Sometimes students may be bored by the speech culture of Town Meeting and, therefore, participate less actively. At other times, students may participate in ways that the faculty view as "disruptive" and consequently refuse to recognize. Like the moderator above who announced "I just won't listen to you," the Town Meeting moderator will not recognize students who do not conform to strict parliamentary procedures.

The lack of participation by Asian American students within Town Meeting's formal procedures provides another possible example of cultural marginalization. Asian American students rarely, almost never, actively participate within Town Meeting debate. This behavior suggests that Asian American communication styles may be at odds with the formal parliamentary procedures of Town Meeting. For example, when discussing the lack of participation by Asian American students, a Japanese friend pointed out to me that within many Asian cultures silence is a virtue. Thus, Asian American students who value silence, or who are uncomfortable with the assertiveness required by debate, may refrain from speaking. There are two caveats to this finding. First, there a very few Asian American students at Winthrop Academy so I am hesitant to make a grand claim about cultural behavior based upon their actions. Second, it is never entirely possible to delineate the influence of culture from individual personality traits; these students may simply be quiet and shy. But the possibility remains that the formal speech culture of Town

Meeting is functioning to exclude Asian American students as active participants.

In sum, the sanctified language of the public within Winthrop Academy's Town Meeting is consistent with norms of deliberation which tend to privilege an educated, white, middle-class speech culture. As a result, those students who participate are more assimilated to those sanctioned norms of articulateness within Town Meeting's parliamentarian procedures. Students who are not assimilated to this speech culture—including Asian Americans, some African Americans, some Hispanics, and some working-class Whites—are excluded from the process. In addition, the participation of all students is limited by their unequal status with faculty members. Thus, both cultural differences *vis-à-vis* the sanctified "language of the public" and inequality between faculty and students limit the participation of students in *practices for* democracy.

Re-Considering Deliberative Requirements for Civic Education

Deliberative democrats are interested in guarding against exclusions from and silencing within deliberative processes because the force of the better argument can only prevail if all relevant perspectives are included. This requirement leads to the two fundamental principles of equality and inclusion—all affected by a decision must be included and manifestly equal within the deliberative process. These conditions do not require, however, that everyone actively participate (i.e., speak) within formal political debate. Rather, the ideal conditions require that all relevant views are aired and that collective agreement is based upon rational discourse.

As I have explained previously, the ends of educative processes are different from those of deliberative processes. Deliberation is aimed at collective agreement; civic education is aimed at providing students with the requisite skills and predispositions that will enable them to participate in future democratic processes. Thus, when students are excluded from *practices for* civic participation, their opportunities for gaining such skills and capacities are limited. Dynamics that exclude Winthrop Academy students from practicing democracy within Town Meeting jeopardize the chances that these students will be prepared to function as equal citizens upon high school graduation in a few short years.

Winthrop Academy's experiences with exclusionary dynamics suggest that *practices for* civic participation will necessarily be specific to the particular types of students who are practicing. In addition, their experiences raise a number of questions for deliberative democracy and for a deliberative theory of civic education. First, to the extent that students from oppositional cultures engage in resistance behaviors, such as "dissolving," the question is raised as to whether student resistance is legitimate or not. More precisely, dissolving may sometimes be a warning sign that Town Meeting's procedures are being used inappropriately. But at other times, it may simply be a case of misbehavior.

For example, if a student is attempting to raise a "point of order" but the faculty moderator refuses to recognize her, and threatens punishment if the student persists in her "mis"behavior, and if students "dissolve" into sucking their teeth in reaction to this incident, dissolving can be usefully viewed as a signal of illegitimate use of authority by the moderator. If, on the other hand, students are incessantly laughing and clapping just to take up time within Town Meeting because they see this forum as part of school, they see school as a teacher-controlled place, and they "will do anything against the teachers," as one student said to me, then "dissolving" is an example of student coercion. In the latter case, the pedagogical question becomes: How do you teach students who distrust all forms of authority to value and participate in forums of shared democratic authority?

Second, another set of questions is raised for deliberative theory around cultural differences in communication styles. Within deliberative politics, an Asian American citizen who views silence as a virtue and who determines that his perspective on a policy issue has already been aired by another speaker may decide not to speak during deliberation. Asian American students, on the other hand, need to learn skills in persuasive argumentation that will prepare them to be manifestly equal as citizens in future deliberative arenas. In other words, they need to gain skills and capacities that will allow them to participate effectively should they choose to. Thus, the question raised for civic education is: Should some students be coerced into practicing in order to become free and equal participants as citizens? A deeper question raised for deliberative theory by this example of cultural differences is whether the theory's conception of "free and reasoned discourse" is culturally biased. In other words, does manifest equality simply translate into all students learning the skills required of the procedures? Or should the procedures themselves be revised?

Winthrop Academy's experiences with civic education suggest that inequality inherent to teacher/student relationships, as well as inequalities that accompany cultural differences and majority versus minority status within a school community, complicate the realization of deliberative ideals within *practices for* democratic participation. Ideals, however, are just that. The use of "critical yardsticks" to identify ways in which educational practices fall short of normative ideals also illuminates how these undesirable consequences might be minimized. In the next section I offer some recommendations for bringing Winthrop Academy's *practices for* civic participation within Town Meeting closer to their own intended objectives and to the normative standards of deliberative democratic theory. Then, I draw upon Winthrop Academy's experiences to raise questions surrounding *practices of* distribution and governance within charter school reform and to make some recommendations regarding charter school policy.

How Do You Teach Them To Practice?—A Pedagogy for Fulfilling Public Interests in Civic Education

Winthrop Academy's experiences with civic education suggest that teaching democratic participation is no easy task. The nature of democratic participation centers around the equality and free consent of the participants. Educative processes of teaching future citizens how to participate, on the other hand, are not necessarily premised upon these principles. At Winthrop Academy, the civic mission is one of "education for democracy" whereby students and faculty are inherently unequal because faculty are adults and they have something to teach students in the way of becoming capable of equal democratic participation. For Beth Taft, this "education for democracy" mission raises the question "can you get students to buy into practicing democracy if they don't have full power in the school?" Students' participation in Winthrop Academy's Town Meeting sheds some light on her question. First, students inequality *vis-à-vis* faculty impedes their ability to actually practice democratic participation. Second, the inequality between students who are differently situated in relation to Town Meeting's "language of the public" marginalizes some groups of students.

Many of the attitudinal and structural hindrances that complicate faculty's civic objectives point to tensions between "education for democracy" and democratic participation. The educative mission of "education for democracy" essentially disallows authentic democratic participation because it necessitates: 1) an unequal relationship between students and faculty, and 2) faculty regulation of the quality of participation. In light of these educative constraints, Taft's contention that "[t]here's a way in which practicing is a form of instruction from just having done it" is problematized because students do not really do "it." Students do not participate in democratic processes whereby their status is equal to that of all other members and their consent is freely given.

Winthrop Academy's experiences with practicing for democratic participation demonstrate how difficult an educational objective "having done it" is to achieve. In this setting, "having done it" consists of three elements: skills in reasoned deliberation, ways of being appropriate for civil interaction, and a sense that what you say matters. Without instruction, students do not learn skills in reasoned debate. Without regulation, students do not learn ways of being appropriate for civil interaction. And without experience based upon practice, students do not gain a sense that their voice matters.

Yet, the educational requirements of these three elements sometimes seem to pull in different directions. For example, as faculty regulate ways of being within Town Meeting, they reinforce the hierarchical nature of their relationship with students thereby disallowing the equality between participants necessary for decision-making processes based upon reason alone. Similarly, as faculty participate in Town Meeting in order to improve the quality of debate, they usurp valuable opportunities for students to practice deliberating. Thus, the final goal of cultivating in students a sense that what they say matters is stymied insofar as students do not actually experience democratic processes in which their say ultimately prevails.

Tensions within Winthrop Academy's vision of "education for democracy" complicate the relationship between faculty teaching and students practicing civic capacities. Faculty's roles as instructors and regulators essentially disallow the conditions under which students might authentically practice democratic participation and gain a sense that what they say makes a difference. Perhaps alleviating some of the tensions between "educating for democracy" and "participating in democracy" might create conditions more conducive for students to practice *know how* and gain a sense of *agency*. The following recommendations are intended to mediate the tension in civic education between practicing and participating.

Mediating Unequal Status between Teachers and Students
1. Clarifying Teachers' Authority: As Winthrop Academy faculty straightforwardly explain, and students clearly perceive, the role of a faculty member in Town Meeting is not that of just another member. Rather, faculty act as regulators of behavior and as instructors of the quality and content of debate within this forum. And many of their actions within these roles tend to hinder opportunities for students to participate. Perhaps both clarifying and limiting these faculty roles within Town Meeting would foster more opportunities for student participation.

One way to clarify their status as instructors and regulators within Town Meeting would be for faculty to explicitly claim their status as what Mr. Reid labels "first among equals." In this manner, faculty's hierarchical status in relation to students would be made explicit and distinctly separate them from students who share equal status only with their peers. Once the unequal status of the faculty/student relationship within Town Meeting is clarified, its implications for equal participation among students could be minimized in a number of ways. Faculty might choose to act simply as regulators and instructors of processes that students participate in rather than participating themselves. Such decisions might depend upon whether the topic for debate is a "grand issue"—an issue of national or global significance—where faculty and students share more equal status versus an issue of school policy where faculty's authority may have a chilling effect on student participation. Also, the regulatory versus the deliberatory aspects of Town Meeting might be more clearly delineated. According to Mrs. Tolkoff's sentiments, Town Meeting is not the ideal place for regulation since it should be "for confirmation, not separation." Perhaps regulatory events such as announcements of absences and reminders regarding school policy could be confined to the Monday morning all-school meetings and avoided during the Friday sessions.

2. Clarifying Jurisdiction: Students' comments about Town Meeting indicate that they are unlikely to participate if they do not find the issue important or do not feel that their input will make a substantive difference. This suggests that *know how* may not necessarily precede *agency*. Rather, students may need a sense of agency in order to engage in practice. As democratic theorist Benjamin Barber insists:

> . . . knowledge and the quest for knowledge tend to follow rather than to precede political engagement: give people some significant power and they will quickly appreciate the need for knowledge, but foist knowledge on them without giving them responsibility and they will display only indifference.[8]

Faculty may select topics, such as the Bosnia debate, that students will feel are important. But in order for students to experience a sense of ownership over Town Meeting as their own forum, it seems crucial that the jurisdiction surrounding what sorts of issues are negotiable within Town Meeting is clear to students. A school constitution or contract could set the parameters for the types of decisions subject to Town Meeting authority. Such a process was begun within the *Town Meeting Guidelines* that went into effect during the 1996-97 academic year. Such moves toward clarification protect faculty's educational prerogatives from the majority rule of students as well as protecting students from arbitrary faculty authority. Clear jurisdiction also informs students as to the sorts of issues they claim control over so that they can practice defining and addressing issues that they care about, as well as learn valuable lessons from having to live with the consequences of democratic processes.

Winthrop Academy's experiences with "education for democracy" and Town Meeting as a forum for practicing democracy demonstrate that various aspects of their mission are sometimes at odds with one another. Town Meeting as an educative forum sometimes gets in the way of Town Meeting as a participatory forum where students can actually engage in democratic processes. Perhaps greater ownership over this forum might encourage students' sense of agency and foster their engagement in practicing skills of reasoned deliberation and democratic ways of being. Faculty might facilitate the educative processes within Town Meeting by limiting their roles to explicit instruction, minimizing regulation, and clarifying students' jurisdiction such that "practicing [becomes] a form of instruction from just having done it."

Making the Language of the Public Accessible to All Students

Another response to Beth Taft's question "can you get students to buy into practicing democracy if they don't have full power in the school?" has more to do with inequality between students themselves than inequality between students and faculty. In this regard, students who appear to be "buying into" practicing democracy are students who are "buying into" the school as a whole. These students are taking on official leadership roles such as Advisory Representative, or member of the Student Advisory Council, among others. In addition, students who are buying into democratic processes are members of student groups whose numbers outweigh those of other groups within the school. Namely, many of "the chosen few" who participate are African American students who represent 59% of the student population. Each of these dynamics suggests that students who feel more closely affiliated with the accepted ways of being, or the accepted culture of power, within the school are included in civic educational practices whereas many other students are marginalized from these practices.

Deliberative democratic theory accounts for social inequality by bracketing it from formal procedures so that participants will be manifestly equal. In addition, the theory relies on the power of reasoned deliberation to transform cultural differences into shared understandings. Winthrop Academy's experiences reinforce the claims of feminist theorists and others who insist that "bracketing" is not sufficient to keep inequality from impacting formal procedures and that plurality is inextricably tied to the very concept of reason. Reason does not transcend difference; rather, reasonable outcomes are constituted through difference.

Unequal relationships, such as those based upon majority versus minority status in a given social setting or those based upon access to norms of social privilege, inevitably permeate formal arenas of decision making and disrupt the ideal of manifest equality. The deliberative model of democratic politics would be strengthened by attending to these infiltrations and buttressing the formal procedures so that inequality is addressed rather than ignored. The procedures might be buttressed in any number of ways.

1. Creating an Inclusive Language of the Public: Young suggests that parliamentarian deliberation, because of its privileging tendencies, be expanded toward a more "communicative democracy." Communicative democracy would include not only argumentation but a number of other communicative forms such as greeting, rhetoric, and storytelling. According to Young, this ideal of communicative democracy is more inclusive than deliberative democracy because it "requires a plurality of perspectives, speaking styles, and ways of expressing the particularity of social situations as well as the general applicability of principles."[9] At Winthrop Academy, such an expanded conception of "communicative democracy" might serve to recognize some of students' "dissolving" behaviors as legitimate political behaviors. Such recognition may include more spectators in practicing participation by decreasing their boredom and disenchantment with formal processes that devalue or silence their voices.

Other options for buttressing formal procedures include my suggestion from chapter 2 that participants acknowledge inequalities and account for them by enacting measures, down to the most minute aspects of the deliberative process. Strategies here might include a fixed rotation of speakers so that air time is more evenly split among participants, or structuring participation by representatives of cultural groups so that no groups are consistently excluded. At Winthrop Academy, for example, requiring all students to speak at Town Meeting a specific number of times within an academic year would increase the participation of Asian American students as well as provide them with opportunities to practice the parliamentarian style of communication. Another option might be to increase forums for student participation through additional councils or committees. Not only would such forums provide a greater number of students with opportunities for direct participation in reasoned discourse, but the smaller settings might be more comfortable for students who are reticent to speak in front of large crowds.

Suggestions for increasing the inclusiveness and equality of formal decision-making procedures, however, do not address all of the tensions within educative *practices for* democratic participation. In educational settings, inequalities that are structured into the teacher/student relationship are not necessarily illegitimate. Thus, the task for making educative processes more inclusive and egalitarian is not to abolish inequality between teachers and students, but rather to identify and minimize the ways in which this inequality obstructs students from gaining civic capacities that will allow them to participate as equals in future civic communities.

For example, Young's corrective of "communicative democracy" is intended to expand "legitimate" forms of reasoned discourse from the privileged norms of deliberative argumentation to include other communicative forms more often employed by women and racial minorities. Young contends that:

> These norms of "articulateness" [unique to argumentative deliberation] . . . must be learned; they are culturally specific, and in actual speaking situations in our society exhibiting such speaking styles is a sign of social privilege. Deliberation thus does not open itself equally to all ways of making claims and giving reasons.[10]

Because deliberation is not equally accessible to all participants, Young proposes to broaden the forms of communication and styles of speaking that citizens may draw upon as they seek to make decisions together. In one respect Young's argument urges educators to sanctify a "language of the public" that is more pluralistic and more inclusive than parliamentarian deliberation. And this could be achieved by employing the strategies I discussed above. But this corrective does not go far enough in terms of an educative mission of preparing students for equal future participation in economic, political, and social institutions.

2. Providing Students with Cultural Capital: Young points out that mainstream "norms of articulateness" are signs of social privilege that must be learned. Therefore, the responsibility falls to educators to convey to students the types of attributes that comprise the "cultural capital," or prevalent "language of the public," that students will be expected to demonstrate within a variety of institutions. As Sam Asher of Winthrop Academy succinctly explains:

> There are certain moves you make in society that get you power. Some kids grow up with it. Our kids, kids here in the city, we're raising generations of kids who don't have access to that power. I want them to have structure so that at least they'll have the choice to buy into that or not. Our job is to teach them that.

Although the mainstream "language of the public" excludes some students from participation, students also need opportunities to become familiar with and practice this language.

Winthrop Academy's experiences demonstrate that ideals of equality and inclusion are not easily realized within *practices for* civic participation. The educative mission of a preparatory civic community sets up an unequal relationship between faculty and students. As a result, students do not practice authentic democratic participation. Inequality gets in the way of deliberation based upon the force of reason alone and interferes with students gaining a sense that what they say matters enough to actually effect change. Moreover, some groups of students appear to be marginalized by the speech culture of parliamentarian deliberation. This speech culture may silence students from cultural groups whose styles of communication markedly differ. In addition, students who are resisting assimilation toward the norms of the school's culture may exclude themselves from civic participation because they view it as just another "school thing."

Thus, practitioners of civic education within charter schools are faced with two key challenges in making *practices for* democratic participation inclusive and equal among students. First, teachers are faced with the task of alleviating tensions between actual relationships of inequality within the school, including their unequal status with students, and the manifest equality necessary for practicing democratic participation. Second, teachers are faced with the task of striking a balance between broadening the language of the public to include more communicative forms while simultaneously providing all students with opportunities to master privileged communicative forms that will provide them with valuable access to economic, social, and political institutions.

III. Educative Influences: *Practices Of* Democratic Participation

In chapter 2 I explained that the distribution of educational opportunities as well as the governance of charter schools impact democratic social reproduction insofar as these processes exert "educative influences" on current and future citizens. In this section, I draw upon Winthrop Academy's experiences to examine some educative influences of *practices of* governance and distribution unique to charter school reform. Specifically, I consider *practices of* charter school governance and distribution in terms of deliberative democracy's principles of inclusion and equality. I highlight areas for concern surrounding the exclusion of certain stakeholder groups by specific charter schools. In the final section, I will recommend how charter school policy might mediate such exclusions.

Distribution of Charter Schools

The voluntaristic and associative characteristics of charter schools heighten the likelihood that charters may cultivate a sense of community among their members. A sense of community might provide students with a sense of belonging that would be preferable to a widespread sense of alienation among today's youth, especially those from marginalized social groups. A possible downside to voluntaristic, associative communities, however, would be the factionalization of the body politic around particularistic group identities. Group factionalization might threaten a sense of civic identity as well as tolerance and mutual understanding among groups.

The organizational structure of charter schools closely reflects Joshua Cohen's model of "associative democracy." Within Cohen's associative strategy, groups of citizens come together to pursue common interests. Because the issue of concern is too complex or disperse for centralized governmental action to prove effective, such associations take up a regulatory role. These sorts of localized associative democracies are both arenas of and schools for deliberative democracy. Charter schools, as autonomous public institutions with regulatory control over disperse and complex educational issues, have the potential to function as deliberative arenas that comprise associative democracy.

Because deliberative associations arise in order to address common concerns, they need not be factionalizing. I argued in chapter 2 that as deliberative arenas which arise within contexts of shared concerns, Cohen's associations are at once particularistic, pluralistic, and participatory. They are particularistic in that common concerns bind members together. Yet, they are pluralistic in that people with very different identities come together to address these concerns. And, they are participatory because members deliberate together in order to solve their common problems.

Winthrop Academy's experiences shed valuable light on my claims that charter schools provide the organizational structure for associative democracies. Through my case study research at Winthrop Academy I found that parents and students who choose to attend a charter school do seem to share some common interests. Parents and students alike emphasize attending a safer, smaller school that offers more hope for meeting their needs than the schools they previously attended. For many families, a charter is viewed as the last, best hope for a child's education.

These interests are not necessarily the same as those of the founders and or the staff of a charter school. At Winthrop Academy, the founders are committed to their vision of democratic civic education. Many other faculty members joined the school primarily because they were interested in working in a school outside of the traditional system where they could educate kids in a way they see fit. Faculty at Winthrop Academy are also drawn to the fact that it is a "teacher-driven" school where teachers and classroom needs drive decision making.

This finding—that stakeholders are drawn to a charter school for many different reasons, including reasons that do not closely coincide with the school's unique mission—draws into question my initial speculations that the particularistic missions of a charter school may: 1) encourage a sense of school as communy, or 2) serve as common basis for deliberative decision making. In terms of the community-constituting aspects of charter schools, Winthrop Academy students overwhelming report that they feel like a member of a community within the school. If this sense of community is not to be attributed to common interests surrounding the school mission, perhaps it is due to the small size of the school or students' perception that faculty really care about them. Each of these factors—size and caring—was emphasized by students when I asked them what the Winthrop Academy community is like.

If size and caring are the community-constituting forces at Winthrop Academy, these are factors that are not unique to charter schools and that are subject to change as the school grows and as faculty change. But perhaps common interests play more of a role in creating a sense of community than is readily apparent from the seeming disconnect between the school's mission and participants' reasons for association. A lack of identification with the school's mission does not necessarily mean that stakeholders do not have common interests.

Cohen contends that within his model of associative democracy issues of common concern provide the bases for cohesion among diverse groups of people. He explains:

> The solidarities characteristic of such efforts will be the bonds of people with common concerns . . . who treat one another as equal partners in addressing those shared concerns. In short, these efforts—which could have very wide scope— have the potential to create new "deliberative arenas" outside formal politics that might work as "schools in deliberative democracy" in a special way. Deliberative arenas established for such coordination bring together people with shared concrete concerns, very different identities, and considerable uncertainty about how to address their common aims.[11]

At Winthrop Academy, faculty, students, parents, and Board Members address shared concerns by deliberating together in Town Meetings, Faculty Meetings, and Board Meetings. These stakeholders do not seem to be associating primarily around the common mission of civic education.

Perhaps their "considerable uncertainty about how to address their common aims"—creating a public school better than those they have previously experienced—downplays the importance of the mission. Yet, neither have stakeholders rejected the school because of this mission. They have chosen to become part of the school knowing full well that its mission is civic education. Then, once stakeholder are members of the school, they participate in building a common mission together. You see evidence of this in faculty's discussions regarding the civics curriculum. Moreover, the success of the school itself becomes a common mission.

The common interests that draw parents, students, and faculty to charter schools may be more multiple and complex than those stated in the school's mission statement. But these interests overlap and intersect, allowing for political cohesion and community solidarity to be built through deliberation. In addition, such multiplicity and plurality within Winthrop Academy's associative community demonstrates that charter schools do not necessarily factionalize the public school population according to identity groups. Rather, people with very different identities are struggling to build and pursue a common mission at Winthrop Academy. Their experiences do suggest, however, that charter schools exhibit some segregatory tendencies in relation to students who are discipline problems and students who have special education needs.

Students Who Violate Community Norms

As I noted in chapter 1, in their research on the relationship between the communal aspects of Catholic schools and academic achievement, Bryk et al. concluded that Catholic school communities equalize achievement across social groups. The researchers noted that membership within Catholic school communities is marked by the voluntary nature of the association and the idea that participation is "not an inalienable right. . . . Students who seriously or chronically violate the community's norms must leave."[12] The notion that participation in a school is not an inalienable right is much more problematic for public schools than it is for private Catholic schools. Nonetheless, public schools cannot evade the question of how to deal with students who chronically violate the community's norms, and Winthrop Academy encountered such dilemmas a number of times in the two-year span of my research.

Voluntaristic membership and core norms are features central to the concept of a "school as community." Chronic violation of norms is both a signal that a student does not really want to be a member of a specific community as well as a threat to the community's integrity, and sometimes to the very safety of its other members. At Winthrop Academy faculty have been faced with the question of whether a particular student should remain a member of the community. At least two types of cases arose during the school's first two years of operation: cases where a student chronically violated behavioral norms and cases where a student violated norms so egregiously that faculty were concerned for the safety and well-being of other students. Examples of chronic violations included verbal harassment of students and faculty, physical assaults on students, stealing from students or the school, defacing school property, disrupting academic classes, and failing to meet academic and disciplinary obligations. Instances of egregious violations of community norms included illegal drug use and the involvement of Winthrop Academy students in criminal bank fraud.

Under Massachusetts charter legislation "a student may be expelled from a charter school based on criteria determined by the board of trustees, and approved by the secretary of education, with the advice of the principal and teachers."[13] According to these regulations, Winthrop Academy could potentially expel students who are either chronic or egregious violators of the school's norms. At the end of their first two years, however, they had not done so. Only one student, a student allegedly involving other Winthrop Academy students in criminal activity, had been asked not to return to Winthrop Academy. Other chronic violators left the school, but not because they were expelled. Rather, these students chose not to remain at the school under the disciplinary stipulations that Winthrop Academy articulated to them.

The questions raised by Winthrop Academy's experiences with violators of school norms are questions of discipline and expulsion within public charter schools. In schools where membership is voluntary, what do educators do with those students who refuse to play by the rules? Charter schools will be hard pressed to pursue distinct missions or create a sense of school community if violators remain in the school. And a key underlying premise of charter reform is that individual students will be best served within particularistic schools. This leaves open the possibility that students will sometimes face a poor match with a school they choose and will benefit from transferring to another school. But the risk remains that students who are discipline problems will simply be "dumped" back into the traditional school system. This is precisely the nature of the concern raised by critics who fear that charters will "cream" the most desirable students and leave the dregs behind.

Winthrop Academy struggles to determine whether a particular student should remain in its community by attempting to balance the rights and needs of an individual student against the good of the entire student body. In some instances, faculty feel that the good of the whole school demands that one member leave. But this raises questions surrounding the public good: Are public interests served by sending the most troubled students back to traditional public schools? Should charters consider the "good of the whole" within the confines of their own school walls? Or should considerations of the "good of the whole" include the entire system of public education? Similar questions are raised surrounding the capacity of charter schools to accommodate special needs students.

Special Needs Students
Charter schools face similar tensions between creating distinct school communities versus the interests of individual students and the overall public education system with the case of "special needs" students. In Massachusetts "special needs" students are students who have learning disabilities and require special services or provisions in order to meet school achievement standards. Charter schools in the state are subject to the same Special Education laws as other public school districts, but they do not have financial resources similar to those of most districts with which to address special needs.

Beth Taft, Winthrop Academy co-founder, contends that Special Education laws are forcing charters to become the sort of one-size-fits-all schools they seek to avoid. She explains:

> There are Special Education regulations that apply just as forcefully to charter schools as regular public schools. These regulations stipulate that a student be provided with the services he needs to learn in the least restrictive environment. Hence, whereas I might conclude, as an educator and as a manager of a small school with a limited budget, that a 16-years-old learning-disabled freshman reading on the third-grade level cannot be expected to master what Winthrop Academy requires within the constraints of our schedule and the time usually allotted to high school, I would not be allowed to suggest (let alone require) that this child attend another school. Rather, I would be expected to find a way for him to read Shakespeare alongside his more advanced peers, and would be held accountable for finding the resources to ensure this success. In our school, this would mean ignoring the fact that at least 74 percent of those reading below grade level are not learning disabled—they're just poorly prepared. Rather than investing properly in those who are behind where they should be but are still capable of succeeding in our school, we are pushed to re-create the very one-size-fits-all program that we had sought to reform.[14]

Taft's example illuminates multiple tensions between Winthrop Academy's academic expectations, the overall preparedness of their student body, the needs of Special Education students, and their limited fiscal budget. These tensions are faced by many charter schools and raise a number of questions: How are the needs and rights of special needs students to be balanced against the needs and rights of other students? How can charters, with their limited resources, address the needs of these students? What does "inclusion" within public education entail for special needs students? Should policies surrounding Special Education be reformed in light of charter schools' unique situations? If so, how should such decisions be made?

Taft's comments imply that special needs students might be better served by attending a school other than Winthrop Academy, most likely a school where the academic standards are not so high. In addition, the majority of non-special needs students would be better served by this option because more of Winthrop Academy's resources could be directed toward improving their poor basic skills. In Taft's view, Winthrop Academy's commitment to academic excellence is jeopardized by Special Education regulations which require that inordinate time and money be funneled toward special needs students.

Taft's concerns are valid ones. Winthrop Academy has undertaken no simple task in their endeavor to bring a student body that is overwhelmingly underprepared to a level of parity with students from more privileged, more reputable school systems within four high school years. Special Education regulations take valuable resources that could be devoted toward this endeavor with 74 percent of the school's student body and demand that, instead, these resources are used for a small percentage of students.

But what are the alternatives to charter schools abiding by Special Education regulations? If Winthrop Academy were to reject all students at risk of not meeting their high academic standards, they would be participating in a form of institutionalized tracking whereby more skilled, better prepared students would attend schools with high academic expectations and less skilled, ill prepared, and special needs students would attend schools with lower expectations. This alternative seems at odds with Winthrop Academy's commitment to inclusion within their own school; they refuse to track students in classes by academic ability.

In addition to tracking students at an institutional level, not serving special needs students within charter schools could create the same sort of dumping ground effect possible for students with discipline problems.

A Deputy Superintendent of Eaton's public school system expressed this type of concern during a discussion panel on charter reform. She said:

> [In our public schools we have] severe populations in special needs. I'm interested to see how charters do with this. . . . that when kids have problems, we don't get them out in those informal ways we all know how . . . Who gets dropped? We know who the disenfranchised are.[15]

Charters would not be living up to their public school mandate to serve all students by institutionalizing a school-level system of tracking special needs students or by informally dumping special needs students back into traditional public schools. But charters are faced with a rather untenable dilemma in the face of current Special Education regulations. Like school districts, charters are expected to earmark the resources necessary to meet the educational requirements of special needs students. Yet charter schools are much smaller and have many fewer resources with which to meet special needs. Charters are in a disadvantaged position in relation to most school districts when it comes to meeting Special Education requirements because they do not enjoy similar economies of scale. In light of this dilemma, Special Education regulations need to be revisited with the aim of softening the tension between public charter schools responsibilities toward special needs students and their financial capacity to meet students' needs. The deliberative principle of inclusion would require that representatives of charter schools be involved in formal processes by which Special Education policies may be revised.

The interests of students who violate norms and special needs students within charter schools raise a difficult set of questions surrounding the boundaries of public school communities within the public educational sphere. As charter schools weigh the interests of individual students against the greater good of their educative communities, the interests of "the many" may legitimately win out. The majority of students within a given charter school may be better off without special needs students or students who violate school norms within their ranks. But will the entire system of public education be better off by creating alternative enclaves for these students or dumping them back into traditional schools? As members of charter school communities associate together and undertake democratic decision-making processes to regulate their interactions they would do well to keep in mind that "the public" does not stop at their school walls. The exclusion of groups of students who are difficult to include in charter schools not only segregates the sphere of public education according to categories of "undesirable" students, but it also adversely affects the quality of existing schools that those students return to and minimizes chances that those students will be adequately prepared for equal future participation within other institutions.

Governance of Charter Schools

Winthrop Academy's experiences also illuminate potential hotspots surrounding inclusion and equality within *practices of* charter school governance. The regulatory relief and building-level governance of charters raise possibilities that decision making in these arenas may be more inclusive than in traditional public schools.[16] But inclusiveness and egalitarianism in decision-making processes appear to be more at the mercy of individual commitments than a matter of charter school policy.

Deliberative democracy's ideal procedure for decision making requires that all affected by a decision are included in the process. Much standard practice in the realm of public education does not meet this ideal of inclusion. School administrators and union representatives negotiate school contracts; neither parents nor students are included in this process. Administrators and school district boards often set curriculum and set other school policies; these processes often marginalize or exclude the perspectives of teachers, parents, and students.

The building-level governance that characterizes charter schools has the potential to expand such decision making processes. Within charter schools, faculty, parents, and students might join the ranks of politicians, union representatives, and administrators as participants in processes of public education governance. Winthrop Academy has brought to life this potential for expanded inclusion in many ways. Students participate in Town Meeting and the Student Advisory Council. Parents are members of the Board of Trustees and have their own advisory board. And faculty members make most decisions surrounding curriculum and day-to-day school policy.

This potential for inclusion, however, appears to be at the discretion of the school's founders. Winthrop Academy's founders are committed to the ideal of a teacher-driven charter school, they believe in the importance of including parents' perspectives in school policy decisions, and they stress the importance of students participating in the school community in order to prepare them for civic participation in future communities. But founders of other charter schools may not exhibit a similar commitment to including the perspectives of faculty, parents, and students in decision making. Ultimately, in the Commonwealth of Massachusetts, only the school's Board of Trustees is accountable for educational governance. Inclusion in governance within the state's charter schools need not be expansive; it could be narrowed to the Board of Trustees and its delegates, such as a school principal.

Not only is school governance placed squarely in the hands of a charter school's Board of Trustees, but these boards tend to be hand-picked by the school's founders. The charter legislation in Massachusetts says nothing about who should be included on these boards or what types of interests should be represented. As far as the legislation dictates, founders of a charter school could select their best friends as members of the board with no thought to representing the interests of the school's faculty, parents, students, or members of the surrounding community.

Compounding this issue of inclusion is the issue of equality among board members. At Winthrop Academy, for example, the Board of Trustees includes the two founders, an additional faculty member, two parents, and a number of community members. All of these roles *vis-à-vis* the school and its educative mission complicate achieving manifest equality within the Board's decision-making processes. Founder Cathleen Eichler straightforwardly acknowledges such difficulties, particularly tensions that arise between the status of founders as compared to the status of other faculty members:

> [Winthrop Academy] is a hierarchical community, I'm part of it. There is shared power, but there are those of us who are more powerful than others. Democracy doesn't mean that each member has the exact same power. We appoint and delegate for the good of the whole. Along with responsibility comes power. Some things are hierarchical but not necessarily antithetical to the democratic process, like appointees and delegates. For example, you can be concerned about input and autonomy without necessarily being democratic. We do not have a democratically arrived-upon curriculum. Because I am able to shut my door [and teach what I want], it is not democratic.
>
> I am also more secure than my peers. As a founder I am bound by the school's five-year charter. The rest of the faculty is subject to one-year contracts. I am more secure than my peers. I have much more ready recourse, safety nets, in the case that my position is challenged. It would be hard for Winthrop Academy to continue without me, for political reasons as well as our original contract with the Commonwealth, which would minimally require litigation. I try to minimize this by standing back at Town Meeting, standing back in staff discussion, [etc.]. But it's not egalitarian. How are you going to legislate that?

Similar issues arise surrounding the participation of parents and community members who do not share status with faculty members as educational "experts" and students whose perspectives are not even represented on the Board of Trustees.

Before addressing how attentiveness to inclusion and equality on charter school boards might be legislated, one final issue must be raised. To whom is a charter school's Board of Trustees accountable? What if a board decides by means of a "democratic" majority vote something that abridges the rights of certain individuals or groups? In Massachusetts, the Department of Education has the authority to revoke a school's charter. But, unlike the state legislature, this department is comprised of appointed bureaucrats whose decisions are not subject to formal conditions of deliberation. Bureaucrats are expected to simply carry out the will of the legislature. Nevertheless, in cases where charter school legislation is vague or the performance of a particular school is in question, there are few protections to ensure that decisions within state-level bureaucratic departments are not made in an entirely arbitrary fashion.

States may grant charter schools the regulatory relief to govern themselves. But what, then, is the appropriate structure for relationships between charter schools and other public bodies such as state and federal governments? And in what manner are parents and local community members to be included in processes of holding charter schools accountable? The deliberative democratic theory's models of informal spheres of opinion-formation versus formal spheres of will-formation and "associative democracy" do not say much about such questions of public oversight. Thus, this is an area where both deliberative democratic theory and charter school policies require further development. In the following section I point out some additional issues that require attention and suggest specific ways these issues might be addressed in future stages of charter school reform.

IV. Future Directions for Charter School Reform

The concrete experiences of Winthrop Academy Charter School during its first two years of operation shed light on the actual goods and dangers that accompany charter school reform. The school's experiences with civic education, distribution, and governance say a great deal about institutionalizing the ideals of deliberative democracy within the concrete practices of charter school reform. Winthrop Academy brings to life the possibility of charter reform as a movement toward a model of "associative democracy" whereby charters schools are both arenas of deliberative decision making and schools for deliberative democracy. Within such arenas, students may gain a sense of belonging, school governance may be more inclusive, and an ethic of civic participationism may be cultivated among both youth and adults.

Yet these possibilities are simply that—democratic *potentials* that may well not be realized within the charter school movement. More time and empirical research are necessary in order to assess whether public goods outweigh drawbacks within the reform movement as a whole. But in the interest of maximizing opportunities for the democratic potentials of charter schools to flourish, I now conclude by offering a few suggestions in the areas of public debate surrounding school choice, public policy regarding charter schools, and future research.

Public Debate About School Choice

The level of political attention across the country focused upon school choice suggests that the time is ripe for some type of choice options to be implemented and tested. An important question that remains: Which options should be offered within the realm of public education? Common rhetoric in school choice debates sets up both "choice" and the "existing system" that choice opposes as monolithic entities. As historian of education David Tyack points out:

> . . . in national policy talk about education, choice has become a word to conjure with. An extraordinary range of reformers rally around the magical concept, united by opposition to the public school "monolith" but agreeing on little else.[17]

Just as *every* aspect of traditional public schooling is not problematic, every form of choice is not equally desirable. Tyack contends, "there are many choices to be made about 'choice' and no one correct answer."[18]

Although no one choice option rises above all others as the "best" form, there are principled ways to distinguish between and evaluate various options. Careful attention to public interests in school choice—interests such as democratic participation, equity concerns, and civic education—allow us to identify some forms of choice as more appropriately "public" than others. Based upon such principled interests, Tyack concludes that vouchers or tax credits—two approaches to choice that allow parents to spend public dollars on private schools of their own selection—are extraordinarily risky and therefore inappropriate as reform strategies within the public educational realm. Tyack's overriding concern with these options is that within a market free-for-all where parents and schools compete for selection to elite institutions, choice will function as a sorting machine to the disadvantage of poor and racially marginalized parents. In other words, market-based choice will not provide equitable educational opportunities to families with unequal access to resources such as information and influence.

In light of such concerns, Tyack concludes that choice plans should be limited to public schools; public dollars should not be devoted to choice options in the private sphere.[19] If school choice were constrained to the public sphere, a number of choice options would remain available including charter schools, magnet schools, open enrollment, and pilot schools, among others. With careful consideration of public interests, one option is preferable to the others as a reform strategy for future consideration.

According to many models of school choice that fall under the umbrella of traditional school districts—magnet schools, pilot schools, and open enrollment, for example—families are granted some level of consumer choice, but their voices are highly circumscribed by the ultimate authority of schools' administrative structures. In the case of charter schools, on the other hand, reform expands not only democratic choice among citizens, but also the potential for democratic participation in school governance.

As educators, policy makers, and legislators debate various school choice options, it is imperative that we keep public interests in public education at the forefront of our considerations. Democratic participation in school governance, equity concerns, and the preparation of future citizens are all issues in which we have a common stake as citizens of a democratic society. Careful attention to these shared interests suggests that choice options within the public sphere that maximize the participation of parents and students in local school communities are most consonant with the public goods of democratic civic life. Charter schools provide one such institutional strategy for public education reform.

Some types of school choice are more desirable in terms of fulfilling public interests in education. Expanding the lens with which we view school choice options to include the democratic—rather than market-oriented—goods of specific types of choice might allow us to clarify preferable options and minimize legitimate resistance to those choice plans that threaten public education. As we consider alternative organizational models that expand the "public" that is included in educational decision making, such as charter schools, we may also build coalitions of public constituencies committed to playing out the struggles of shared civic life where it matters the most—in the education of future citizens.

Charter School Policy

The next question then becomes: How can charter school reform be implemented in ways most likely to fulfill legitimate public interests? The primary form that charter school policy takes is the state-by-state legislation that authorizes the creation of charter schools. Thus, in light of lessons learned from Winthrop Academy's experiences with charter schooling and democratic social reproduction, I recommend a few items be incorporated into such legislation. These items include additional wording within charter legislation concerning civic education, student expulsion, Special Education, and the selection of charter school boards. Charter reform advocate Ted Kolderie offers a "Model Charter School Law" that is intended for use by "a bill drafter in any state . . . to produce proposed legislation" (see appendix B for a complete draft of the model law).[20] I recommend some revisions to this model law that would apply not only to proposed legislation, but to existing legislation within many states.

Section 8 of Kolderie's model law lists seven "requirements for public education" including the non-sectarian status of charter schools; open enrollment; accountability to a public authority for performance; free tuition; subjectivity to state and local health, safety, and civil rights requirements; anti-discrimination language; and subjectivity to financial audits. I would add to these requirements some language surrounding the responsibilities of all public schools to provide students with civic education in preparation for their future roles as citizens. As public schools responsible for determining their own curriculum, charter schools would then decide for themselves precisely what would constitute such a civic education.

Section 6 of Kolderie's model charter law outlines "eligible pupils." This section stipulates that charter schools must be open to all students within a state who fulfill the application requirements. Charter schools may specialize in certain students such as a particular age group or students considered at-risk. But charters may not segregate according to race or ethnicity, nor limit admission based upon "intellectual ability, measure of achievement, or aptitude or athletic ability." Kolderie explains that the basic thrust of this section "is to let the school target certain populations (often those not doing well in the conventional system) and, in general, to require it to meet the test of a common public school. It may not 'cream' able kids or 'nice' kids or create a white neighborhood school."[21] I would add specific language to this section indicating that not only the students a charter admits, but those they lose or expel, as compared to those they retain, will be investigated as evidence of whether the charter is adequately serving all eligible pupils. Schools will face revocation of their charter for disproportionately "dumping" not-so-nice or not-so-able kids from their rosters.

Section 9 of Kolderie's model law outlines provisions to be included in a school's original charter document. Point 2 of this section stipulates that a sponsor of charter schools should require, as part of the charter document, a plan outlining "[t]he governance structure of the school. . . ." among other things.[22] Although according to Kolderie the school and the sponsor need not reach agreement at the time of the original charter document as to all of the details surrounding the school's governance, I would argue that the sponsoring agency should express some concern for how various public interests are to be represented within the governance structure. For instance, such language might mandate that the interests of faculty, parents, students, and community members affected by the charter school must all be represented in some fashion within the school's governance structure.

Further Research into Charter Schooling

In addition to informing how charter legislation and policies might regulate *practices of* democratic participation, Winthrop Academy's experiences suggest directions for future research. First, the regulatory relief from district and state statutes afforded to charter schools allows decisions to be made at the school level. This regulatory relief fosters the sort of inclusion in decision making referred to above, in part by enabling Winthrop Academy faculty to give students jurisdiction over some issues of school policy. In addition, problems can be identified and addressed with an immediacy that is often impossible within bureaucratic structures. At Winthrop Academy such opportunities for school-level decision making are used as opportunities for students to practice civic participation within the school community. Experiences within the school's preparatory civic community are intended to cultivate in students an ethic of participationism that they will take with them to other civic communities. Comparative research would illuminate whether Winthrop Academy students participate more actively in future civic communities than their peers from schools that do not offer similar opportunities for practice in civic participation.

Second, opportunities for Winthrop Academy students to address issues that they really care about, or perceive as important, combined with a forum in which they can have a say, instill in many students a sense that their voices are heard within the school. And this sense that their voices are heard may be connected to a widespread perception among students that they are members of a community at the school. Future empirical research might investigate whether students at other charter schools share this sense of belonging and compare whether students in charter schools are more likely to feel like a member of the school community than are students within traditional public schools. In addition, research might explore whether a sense of belonging improves student achievement or mitigates drop out rates, particularly for students from historically marginalized groups.

Third, Winthrop Academy's struggles to reconcile their mission of civic education and academic excellence with students who violate the school's norms and with Special Education requirements also illuminate some potential dangers of charter school reform. Because public charter schools are open to all comers, it is highly likely that Winthrop Academy is among many charters faced with such struggles. Early research indicates that charter schools are not necessarily producing the creaming effects that critics feared. Emerging evidence indicates that the charter movement as a whole is serving students of color as well as students who are labeled at risk.

But creaming may not be the trend to watch for. Rather, dumping students with behavioral problems and special learning needs back into traditional public schools may be a cause for concern. Charters are hard pressed to live up to their mandate of developing distinct school cultures with limited resources while simultaneously retaining students who chronically violate school norms or who require an inordinate amount of their finite staff and fiscal resources. Future research into the creaming effect, which thus far has focused upon the types of students that charters admit, needs to pay similar attention to the types of students that leave charters and where they end up.

Fourth, and finally, school governance at Winthrop Academy is teacher-driven, but is careful to include the perspectives of parents and students, and is held accountable to community members who serve on its Board of Trustees. In these respects, Winthrop Academy's governance structure is inclusive of stakeholders groups that tend to be marginalized by the decision-making processes of traditionally hierarchical and bureaucratic school districts. Yet this inclusiveness appears to be at the discretion of the school's founders. Further research is required to evaluate the types of stakeholder groups who are included in or excluded from the governance structures of charter schools. And charter school legislation needs to address more clearly issues of representation within these public bodies.

Conclusion

The verdict is still out on whether charter schools will serve our students well, and on whether they will serve primarily as a privatizing or as a democratizing force in public education reform. Yet, as more schools are created and more conclusive results become available, it is important to keep in mind the democratizing *potential* of charter school reform. Each of the suggestions offered in this chapter is in the interests of maximizing the potential of charter schools to serve as *arenas of* and *schools for* deliberative democracy. Deliberative ideals provide charter schools with normative standards for assessing the extent to which their *practices of* and *for* civic participation are consistent with public interests in democratic social reproduction.

Deliberative democracy's vision of a vibrant, decentered public sphere is reflected in virtually every aspect of the charter school movement. Charters bring conversations about the proper role, scope, and purposes of public education out of the offices of policy wonks and into our kitchens as parents discuss what type of school their children should attend. Charters bring policy making out of state legislatures and into neighborhood centers where community members debate the appropriateness of a particular charter school for their city or town. And charters bring professional discussions about how to best teach children out of the administrative buildings of school districts and into our school hallways as teachers think about where their talents and energies would be best devoted, and sometimes choose to bring their dreams to life in a school of their own. The potential here that is most often overlooked is the possibility of vibrant political debate and action surrounding the proper role and function of the public schools that we all share. To the extent that charters spark and sustain such debate, they will have achieved one measure of success.

Notes

1. Seyla Benhabib, *Situating the Self: Gender, Community and Postmodernism in Contemporary Ethics* (New York: Routledge, 1992), 78–81.

2. Ibid., 48.

3. Iris Marion Young, "Communication and the Other: Beyond Deliberative Democracy," in *Democracy and Difference: Contesting the Boundaries of the Political*, ed. Seyla Benhabib (Princeton: Princeton University Press, 1996), 124.

4. Ibid., 124.

5. This claim, however, is based only on the sheer numbers of males or females who speak in Town Meeting. A more detailed analysis of speaker frequency and/or air time according to gender might yield a result indicating higher male participation.

6. Thomas Kochman, *Black and White: Styles in Conflict* (Chicago: University of Chicago Press, 1981), 27.

7. Ibid.

8. Benjamin Barber, *Strong Democracy*, (Berkeley & Los Angeles: University of California Press, 1984), 234.

9. Young, 132.

10. Ibid., 124.

11. Joshua Cohen, "Procedure and Substance in Deliberative Democracy," in *Democracy and Difference: Contesting the Boundaries of the Political*, ed. Seyla Benhabib (Princeton: Princeton University Press, 1996), 112–13.

12. Anthony Bryk, Valerie E. Lee, and Peter B. Holland, *Catholic Schools and the Common Good* (Cambridge, MA: Harvard University Press, 1993), 313.

13. Commonwealth of Massachusetts 1993 Education Reform Act, Chapter 71, Section 89. For the complete text of Section 89 see Appendix A.

14. This passage is from a journal article written and published by Beth Taft (pseudonym) in 1996. In the interests of confidentiality I am not providing the citation information for the article.

15. This panel discussion on charter schools took place in Eaton (pseudonym) in October 1996. In the interests of confidentiality I am not providing further information about the location or participants.

16. Specifically, because Winthrop Academy is autonomous from the authority of the local School Committee and local union regulations it makes its own decisions surrounding its budget, the hiring and firing of teachers, and the specific content

of its curriculum. Within these areas, then, decision making *may* include more stakeholders than it does within the local public school system where appointed members of the School Committee or school administrators have discretion over these decisions. The Massachusetts charter school legislation provided in appendix A stipulates, however, that charter schools are subject to "the provisions of law regulating other public schools." Thus, Winthrop Academy's regulatory relief from local district control is constrained by state-level mandates such as special education requirements as well as procurement, health, and safety regulations.

17.   David Tyack, "Can We Build a System of Choice That Is Not Just a 'Sorting Machine' or a Market-Based 'Free-for-All'?" *Equity and Choice* 9, no. 1 (1992): 13.

18.   Ibid., 15.

19.   Ibid.

20.   This law is presented in full in appendix B and in Joe Nathan, *Charter Schools: Creating Hope and Opportunity for American Education* (San Francisco: Jossey-Bass, 1996), 203–18.

21.   Nathan, 206.

22.   Ibid., 210.

Appendix A

Massachusetts Charter School Legislation[1]

Massachusetts Education Reform Act of 1993— Chapter 71. Section 89. Charter schools.

Section 89. A charter school shall be a public school, operated under a charter granted by the secretary of education, which operates independently of any school committee and is managed by a board of trustees. The board of trustees of a charter school, upon receiving a charter from the secretary of education, shall be deemed to be public agents authorized by the commonwealth to supervise and control the charter school.

The purpose for establishing charter schools are: (1) to stimulate the development of innovative programs within public education; (2) to provide opportunities for innovative learning and assessments; (3) to provide parents and students with greater options in choosing schools within and outside their school districts; (4) to provide teachers with a vehicle for establishing schools with alternative, innovative methods of educational instruction and school structure and management; (5) to encourage performance-based educational programs and; (6) to hold teachers and school administrators accountable for students' educational outcomes.

Persons or entities eligible to submit an application to establish a charter school shall include, but not be limited to, a business or corporate entity, two or more certified teachers or ten or more parents. Said application may be filed in conjunction with a college, university, museum or other similar entity. Private and parochial schools are not eligible for charter school status.

The secretary of education shall establish the information needed in an application for the approval of a charter school; provided, however, that said application shall include the method for admission to a charter school. There shall be no application fee for admission to a charter school.

Applications to establish a charter school shall be submitted each year by February fifteenth. The secretary of education shall review the applications no later than March fifteenth.

The secretary of education shall make the final determination on granting charter school status and may condition charters on the charter school's taking certain actions or maintaining certain conditions. No more than twenty-five charter schools shall be allowed to operate in the commonwealth at any time. Of these, no more than five shall be located in the city of Boston; no more than five shall be located in the city of Springfield; and no more than two shall be located in any other city or town. Under no circumstances shall the total number of students attending charter schools in the commonwealth be allowed to be greater than three quarters of one percent of the total number of students attending public schools in the commonwealth.

A charter school established under a charter granted by the secretary shall be a body politic and corporate with all powers necessary or desirable for carrying out its charter program, including, but not limited to, the following:

  (a) to adopt a name and corporate seal; provided, however, that any name selected must include the words "charter school";
  (b) to sue and be sued, but only to the same extent and upon the same conditions that a town can be sued;
  (c) to acquire real property, from public or private sources, by lease, lease with an option to purchase, or by gift, for use as a school facility;
  (d) to receive and disburse funds for school purposes;
  (e) to make contracts and leases for the procurement of services, equipment and supplies; provided, however, that if the board intends to procure substantially all educational services under contract with another person, the terms of such a contract must be approved by the secretary, either as part of the original charter or by way of an amendment thereto; and provided, further, that the secretary shall not approve any such contract terms, the purpose or effect of which is to avoid the prohibition of this section against charter schools status for private and parochial schools.
  (f) to incur temporary debt in anticipation of receipt of funds;
  (g) to solicit and accepts any grants or gifts for school purposes;

(h) to have such other powers available to a business corporation formed under chapter one hundred and fifty-six B that are not inconsistent with this chapter.

Charter schools shall be open to all students, on a space available basis, and shall not discriminate on the basis of race, color, national origin, creed, sex, ethnicity, sexual orientation, mental or physical disability, age, ancestry, athletic performance, special need, or proficiency in the English language, and academic achievement. Charter schools may limit enrollment to specific grade levels or areas of focus of the school, such as mathematics, science, or the arts.

A charter school may establish reasonable academic standards as a condition for eligibility for applicants. Preference for enrollment in a charter school shall be given to students who reside in the city or town in which the charter school is located. If the total number of students who are eligible to attend and apply to a charter school and who reside in the city or town in which the charter school is located, or are siblings of students already attending said charter school is greater than the number of spaces available, then an admissions lottery shall be held to fill all of the spaces in that school from among said students. If there are more spaces available than eligible applicants from the city or town in which said charter school is located and who are siblings of current students, and more other eligible applicants than spaces left available, then a lottery shall be hold to determine which of said applicants shall be admitted. There shall be no tuition charge for students attending charter schools.

A student may withdraw from a charter school at any time and enroll in a public school where said student resides. A student may be expelled from a charter school based on criteria determined by the board of trustees, and approved by the secretary of education, with the advice of the principal and teachers.

A charter school may be located in part of an existing public school building, in space provided on a private work site, in a public building, or any other suitable location. A charter school may own, lease, or rent its space.

A charter school shall operate in accordance with its charter and the provisions of law regulating other public schools; provided; however, that the provisions of sections forty-one and forty-two shall not apply to employees of charter schools. Charter schools shall comply with the provisions of chapters seventy-one A and seventy-one B; provided, however, that the fiscal responsibility of any special needs student currently enrolled in or determined to require a private day or residential school shall remain with the school district where the student resides.

Students in charter schools are required to meet the same performance standards, testing and portfolio requirements set by the board of education for students in other public schools.

The board of trustees, in consultation with the teachers, shall determine the school's curriculum and develop the school's annual budget.

Employees of charter schools shall be considered public employees for purposes of tort liability under chapter two hundred and fifty-eight and for collective bargaining purposes under chapter one hundred and fifty E. The board of trustees shall be considered the public employer for purposes of tort liability under said chapter two hundred and fifty-eight and for collective bargaining purposes under chapter one hundred and fifty E. Teachers employed by a charter school shall be subject to the state teacher retirement system under chapter thirty-two and service in a charter school shall be "creditable service" within the meaning thereof.

Each local school district shall be required to grant a leave of absence to any teacher in the public schools system requesting such leave in order to teach in charter schools. A teacher may request a leave of absence for up to two years.

At the end of the two year period, the teacher may make a request to the superintendent that such leave be extended for an additional two years, and approval for said request shall not be unreasonably withheld or he may return to his former teaching position. At the end of the fourth year, the teacher may either return to his former teaching position, or, if he chooses to continue teaching at the charter school, resign from his school district position.

Notwithstanding section fifty-nine C of this chapter, the internal form of governance of a charter school shall be determined by the school's charter.

A charter school shall comply with all applicable state and federal health and safety laws and regulations.

The children who reside in the school district in which the charter school is located shall be provided transportation to the charter school by the resident district's school committee on the same terms and conditions as transportation is provided to children attending local district schools. Students who do not reside in the district in which the charter school is located shall be eligible for transportation in accordance with section twelve B of chapter seventy-six.

Each charter school shall submit to the secretary, to each parent or guardian of its enrolled students, and to each parent or guardian contemplating enrollment in that charter school an annual report. The annual report shall be issued no later than August first of each year for the preceding school year. The annual report shall be in such form as may be prescribed by the secretary of education and shall include at least the following components:

(a) discussion of progress made toward the achievement of the goals set forth in the charter;

(b) a financial statement setting forth by appropriate categories, the revenue and expenditures for the year just ended;

Individuals or groups may complain to a charter school's board of trustees concerning any claimed violation of the provisions of this section by the school. If, after presenting their complaint to the trustees, the individuals or groups believe their complaint has not been adequately addressed, they may submit their complaint to the secretary of education who shall investigate such complaint and make a formal response.

A charter granted by the secretary of education shall be for five years. The secretary of education may revoke a school's charter if the school has not fulfilled any conditions imposed by the secretary of education in connection with the grant of the charter or the school has violated any provision of its charter. The secretary may place the charter school on a probationary status to allow the implementation of a remedial plan after which, if said plan is unsuccessful, the charter may be summarily revoked.

The secretary shall develop procedures and guidelines for revocation and renewal of a school's charter.

Notwithstanding the foregoing, no school building assistance funds, so called, shall be awarded to a charter school for the purpose of constructing, reconstructing or improving said school.

Charter schools shall be funded as follows: If a student attending a charter school resides in a community with a positive foundation gap, the district of the city or town in which said student resides shall pay to the charter school an amount equal to the average cost per student in said district. If a student attending a charter school resides in a community that does not have a positive foundation gap pursuant to chapter seventy, the district of the city or town in which said student resides shall pay to the charter school an amount equal to the lesser of (1) the average cost per student in said district; (2) the average cost per student in the district in which the charter school is located.

Note

1. The Massachusetts charter school legislation has been amended since 1993. I have included here, however, only the 1993 legislation because that was the existing policy when Winthrop Academy's charter was approved and when the school began operation in 1995-96.

Kolderie's "Model Charter School Law"[1]

Model Bill Provisions	Comments
Section 1: Background. This section allows the creation of charter schools. Charter schools are declared to be part of the state's program of public education.	*Essentially, in charter school legislation, the state says it is all right for more than one organization to be offering public education in the community—or put another way, that it is all right for somebody other than the local board of education to start and run a public school.*
Section 2: Purpose. The purpose of this law is to: 1. Improve student learning. 2. Encourage the use of different and innovative learning and teaching methods. 3. Increase choice of learning opportunities for pupils. 4. Establish a new form of accountability for public schools. 5. Require the measurement of learning and create more effective, innovative measurement/ assessment tools.	*The movement for charter schools is not really about the charter schools themselves. It is about systemic change—about the state creating the dynamics that will make the system a self-improving system*

6. Make the school the unit for improvement.
7. Create new professional opportunities for teachers, including the opportunity to own the learning program at the school site.

Section 3: New schools, existing schools.

1. Charter schools may be formed either
   a. By creating a new school. A proposal for a new charter school may be made by an individual, a group of individuals, or an organization. Individuals are most commonly teachers or parents. Organizations could be, for example, community groups, universities, community colleges, hospitals, zoos, or museums.
   b. By converting an existing school. In the case of an existing public school, the proposers will be the principal, teachers, and/or parents at the school.
2. A board of education, on its own motion, may convert all or some of its schools to charter status.

Section 4. Sponsor. The organizers may apply to, and the school may be sponsored by, any of the following:

One process can probably handle both new schools and conversions, even though in a conversion, two additional questions will have to be answered. The sponsor will have to decide whether enough support exists among teachers and parents for it to grant a charter. (The law should leave this as a matter of judgment on the sponsor's part.) And where a public school is converting to a charters chool, the district will need to provide for students and teachers who choose not to remain after the change.

A question is whether a charter school may be created out of an existing nonpublic school. Answers vary. Some states prohibit this. Some, such as Minnesota, feel it is all right for a school, as it is for a student, to transfer from the private to the public.

The opportunity for an applicant to go either to a local board or to some other responsible public body for its charter is the single most important provision

1. The board of a school district.
2. The state board of education (or if not the board, the state superintendent).
3. The board of a public post-secondary institution.
4. The board of a unit of general local government, such as a city or a county.
5. A new state body created to sponsor or oversee charter schools.
6. Such other responsible public body as the legislature may designate.

Section 5. Number of Schools. The number of charter schools shall not be limited.

Section 6. Eligible pupils.
1. Charter schools shall be open to any student residing in the state.
2. A charter school shall enroll an eligible pupil who submits a timely application, unless the number of applications exceeds the capacity of a program, class,

if charter school legislation is to have the dynamics the legislature wants. The idea is not to bypass local boards but to encourage them to respond more positively within the district framework to teachers and parents who want changes and improvements and to say to those interested in a new school (as local boards do in states with such laws), "Charter with us!"

The state wants everybody to improve. So the law should expose every district to the possibility that a charter school may appear in its area. Small "pilot" programs that authorize only a handful of charter schools fail this test. Some states do "cap" the allowable number of charter schools at any given time and then raise the cap over time. But again, a state that wants the maximum stimulus to change and improvement will not limit the opportunity for charter schools to appear.

Charter schools will be different schools. So students get to choose whether to come.

Letting students cross a district line to get to a charter school provides a larger enrollment grade level, or building. In that case, all applicants shall have an equal chance of being admitted (that is, pupils shall be accepted by lot).

3. A charter school may elect to specialize in:
    a. Pupils in an age group or grade level.
    b. Pupils considered "at risk."
    c. Residents of a specific geographical area where the population percentage of people of color is greater than the percentage of people of color in the congressional district in which the geographical area is located, as long as the school reflects the racial and ethnic diversity of the area.
4. The school may not limit admission to pupils on the basis of intellectual ability, measure of achievement, or aptitude or athletic ability.
5. Private schools converting to public status under the charter school law may not give preference in admissions to prior students.

Section 7. The school as a legal entity. The charter school, new or existing, shall organize under one of the forms of organization available under the laws of the state: for example, nonprofit, cooperative, partnership, public benefit corporation, and the like. Or a new form may be established for charter schools.

base for innovations and diffuses the financial impact.

The idea is to let the school target certain populations (often those not doing well in the conventional system) and, in general, to require it to meet the test of a common public school. It may not "cream" able kids or "nice" kids or create a white "neighborhood school."

The law may require the charter school to become a legal entity or may simply permit that step. The law should not require the school to remain a part of the local district. This is critical to provide the autonomy the school requires for its success.

Section 8. Requirements for public education.

1. The school must not be affiliated with a nonpublic sectarian school or religious institution. The school must be nonsectarian in its programs, admission policies, employment practices, and all other operations.
2. The school must admit students as provided in section 6.
3. The school is accountable to public authority for performance as provided in section 9.
4. The school may not charge tuition.
5. The school must meet all applicable state and local health, safety, and civil rights requirements.
6. The school may not discriminate.
7. The school is subject to financial audits in the same manner as a school district.

This section and section 6 contain the provisions that distinguish charter schools from voucher programs and public education from private. In private education, a school can pick and choose its students, can teach religion, can charge tuition, and is not accountable to public authority for student performance.

The idea, though, is basically to shift away from an auditor's mentality—away from a control system based on process to a control system based on performance.

Section 9. The charter document.

The state will simply require that the major issues in the operation of the school be thought through in advance and written into the charter document, which must be signed by the school and the sponsor.

1. The school and the sponsor must come to a written agreement on the following:
    a. The educational program: the school's mission, the students to be served, the ages and grades to be included, and the focus of the curriculum.

It is a good idea (it is California's approach, for example) simply to list the questions that school and sponsor must answer and to be open to whatever answer they want to give. Some states do narrow charter schools' discretion, to require certified teachers or to specify the term of the agreement, for example.

b. The outcomes to be achieved and the method of measurement that will be used, including how the school will meet state-required outcomes.

c. The admissions procedures and dismissal procedures under state law.

d. The ways by which the school will achieve a racial and ethnic balance reflective of the community it serves.

e. The manner in which the program and fiscal audit will be conducted.

f. How the school will be insured.

g. The term of the agreement.

h. The facilities to be used and their location.

i. The qualifications to be required of the teachers.

j. The arrangements for covering teachers and other staff for health, retirement, and other benefits.

Setting a term is essential, to establish that this is a school that will be continued only on an affirmative showing of student and fiscal performance. The setting of a term establishes the public character of the charter school and its accountability to public authority.

2. The sponsor must require that the school include, as an addendum to the charter document, a plan covering the following items, although the school and the sponsor need not reach agreement at this time on the terms for these items:

a. The governance structure of the school.

b. The management and administration of the school.

c. In the case of an existing school being converted to

charter status, alternative
arrangements for current
students who choose not to
attend the school and for current teachers who choose
not to teach in the school
after conversion.
d. The learning methods to be used.
e. Any distinctive learning techniques to be employed.
f. Internal financial controls.

Section 10. Causes for non-renewal or termination.

1. At the end of the term, the
sponsor may choose not to
renew the agreement on any
of the following grounds:
   a. Failure to meet the requirements for student perfor-
mance stated in the agreement.
   b. Failure to meet generally
accepted standards of fiscal
management.
   c. Violation of law.
   d. Other good cause shown.
2. During the term of the agreement,
the sponsor may act to terminate
the agreement on any of the
grounds listed above. At least 60
days before not renewing or
terminating a contract, the
sponsor shall notify the board
of directors of the school of the
proposed action in writing.
The notice shall state the
grounds for the proposed
action in reasonable detail and
that the school's board of
directors may request, in writing,

an informal school hearing before
the sponsor within 14 days of
receiving the notice A termina-
tion shall be effective only at the
conclusion of a school year.

3. The school may appeal the
   sponsor's decision to terminate
   or not renew the agreement to
   the state board of education.

4. When an agreement is not
   renewed or is terminated, the
   school shall be dissolved under
   the provisions of the statute under
   which the school was organized.

5. If an agreement is not renewed
   or is terminated, a student who
   attended the school may apply
   to and shall be enrolled in another
   public school. Normal application
   deadlines will be disregarded under
   these circumstances.

**Section 11. Exemption from
statutes and rules.** Except as
provided in this section, a charter
school is exempt from all statutes
and rules applicable to a school
board or school district, although
it may elect to comply with one or
more provisions of statutes or rules.

*In return for accepting the
accountability represented by
the requirements placed on the
charter school to get its charter
affirmatively renewed at regular
intervals and to attract and
hold its student and parent
community, the charter school
has the other "rules" for public
schools waived up front. This
"superwaiver" is better (and
fairer) than requiring each charter school to petition for the
waivers it needs, one at a time.*

Section 12. Teachers.

1. The charter school will select
   its teachers, and the teachers
   will select the school.

*A charter school that aims to
have a distinctive character
must be able to maintain the*

2. If the teachers choose to be employees of the school, they shall have the rights of teachers in public education to organize and bargain collectively. Bargaining units at the school will be separate from other units, such as the district unit.

3. Alternatively, the teachers may choose to be part of a professional group that operates the instructional program under an agreement with the school, forming a partnership or producer cooperative that they collectively own.

4. Teachers leaving a current position in a public school district to teach in a charter school may take leave to teach. While on leave, they retain their seniority and continue to be covered by the benefit programs of the district in which they had been working.

5. Teachers not previously teaching in a public school district may be made eligible for the state teacher retirement program. Alternatively, the state may add to the financing of the school an amount equal to the employer contribution for teacher retirement so that the school may set up its own program.

Section 13. Revenue. The state will provide the charter school with the full amount of revenue for each student that would be available if the student were enrolled in a regular school.

integrity of its teacher group. So the idea is both for the teachers to choose the school and for the school to choose its teachers.

Model charter school legislation breaks with the long-held assumption that if you want to be a teacher, you have to be an employee. It opens up a new option for teachers: to form a separate group that will provide the learning program under an agreement with the school. This will give teachers full control of the professional issues they have been unable to win through bargaining as employees.

States vary considerably in their provisions for financing K-12 education. Generally, the idea is for the charter school to receive the same amount that would have been available for

each student under traditional
arrangements and to receive that
revenue directly from the state.

1. The state will pay directly to
the school the average amount
per pupil spent statewide for
operating purposes, plus
weightings and categoricals.

*Think about it this way. The state
now requires each community to
pay each year a certain propor-
tion of its wealth toward the
cost of educating its children.
With whatever dollars this levy
raises, the community pays for
the education of as many kids
as those dollars will cover. The
state pays in full for all the
remaining kids.*

*This lets us think of district
enrollment as a box full of kids:
the bottom layer (say 60 percent)
all green, fully paid by the community; topped off by a 40
percent layer all gold, fully paid
by the state. Thus, the notion
that there is a "local" portion and
a "state" portion of educational
funding never applies to the
funding of an individual student.*

*A student moving to a charter
school is assumed to be a kid off
the top of the box—fully state
paid. The state pays the full
amount—say $4,000—to the
charter school, where the student
now is in attendance, rather than
to the district, where the student
is no longer in attendance.*

*This view will fit a state with a
foundation formula, where the
state is contributing some part*

of the revenue, at least, for every district. Most states have some kind of foundation formula.

School districts always object when a charter law is proposed that a charter school will "take away our money." But the system of financing schools is pupil driven. When enrollment goes up, the district has more money; when enrollment goes down, it has less money. Kids moving to a charter school are another kind of enrollment change. The state payment changes accordingly. The district adjusts, just as it would if the students moved to another district or another state.

2. A charter school may receive other state and federal aid, grants, and revenue as though it were a district.

   Section 11 applies here, too.

3. The school may receive gifts and grants from private sources in whatever manner is available to districts.

4. Special education will be, as now, an obligation of the district of residence. The charter school must comply with the requirements of law with respect to pupils with disabilities, as though it were a district.

Section 14. Immunity.

1. The charter school may sue and be sued.

   Accidents happen: people sue. Someone has to buy insurance. It should be the school.

2. The sponsor of a charter school, members of the board of the sponsor organization in their official capacity, and employees of a sponsor are immune from civil or criminal liability with respect to all activities related to a charter school they approve or sponsor.

Section 15. Length of school year.
The charter school shall provide instruction for at least the number of days required by state law. It may provide instruction for more days if not prohibited by state law.

Section 16. Leased space.
A school district may lease space or sell services to a charter school. A charter school may lease space or secure services from another public body, nonprofit organization, or private organization or individual.

Perhaps the district could lease space at a price reflecting its operating costs for that space.

Section 17. Transportation.
Transportation for pupils enrolled at a charter school shall be provided by the district in which the school is located for students residing in the district in which the school is located, and to and from the border of the district for nonresident students. Districts may provide transportation for nonresident students.

Most laws simply establish the principle that transportation to the public charter school will be provided through the district in which the school is located. Students coming from another district are usually responsible for getting themselves to the border of the district in which their school is located. School bus professionals are quite creative and practical about working out arrangements from that point on.

Section 18. Initial costs. A sponsor may authorize a school before the applicant has secured space, equipment, personnel, and so forth, if the applicant indicates authorization is necessary for the school to raise working capital.

Section 19. Information. The state department of education must disseminate information to the public, directly and through sponsors, both on how to form and operate a charter school and on how to enroll in charter schools once they are created.

Section 20. General authority. A charter school may not levy taxes or issue bonds secured by tax revenues.

Note

1. This model law was developed by Ted Kolderie and is taken from Joe Nathan, *Charter Schools: Creating Hope and Opportunity for American Education* (San Francisco: Jossey-Bass Publishers, 1996), 203–18. According to Nathan, 203 "[t]he following can serve as a model charter school bill that a bill drafter in any state can use to produce proposed legislation. This model bill relies on findings from considerable experience around the country."

Appendix C

Methodological Appendix

I. Orientation to the Research:
Melding a Critical Interpretive Methodology

In this appendix I situate myself within, as well as distinguish myself from, a critical research orientation by: 1) defining what is commonly meant by critical education research, 2) outlining and responding to some common criticisms of critical research, and 3) describing a specific approach to critical research that draws upon Habermas's theory of communicative action, as well as insights from postmodernism and interpretivism, to meld a viable brand of critical inquiry. After establishing this orientation, I describe how I applied my "critical interpretivist" approach to the research design and methodology.

Although critical research undoubtedly falls under the umbrella of qualitative or interpretive research paradigms in education, it defies clear-cut placement within various typologies common to the field.[1] This is due in large part to the broad amalgamation of theoretical and research traditions that critical orientations draw from. Recent surveys of critical education research describe its indebtedness to symbolic interactionism, ethnography, ethnomethodology, neo-Marxism, feminism, postmodernism, and poststructuralism, to name a few. The core affinity critical researchers identify between these diverse traditions centers around a concern for enhancing the structuralist, or functionalist, critique provided by Marxism with parallel emphases on local understandings and human agency. In sum, "[critical researchers] search for representations of social reality capable of providing social explanations sensitive to the complex relationship between human agency and social structure."[2] Because most critical research in education is ethnographic in nature, including my case study, I will emphasize critical ethnography in my methodological considerations.[3]

Yet my emphasis on ethnography will be situated within a discussion of broader research traditions.

Throughout the 1990s, the critical orientation appeared to congeal around a few key premises. The following characterization of critical research was offered by Joe Kincheloe and Peter McLaren in 1994 and endorsed by Phil Carspecken in his 1996 book *Critical Ethnography in Educational Research.*

> We are defining a criticalist as a researcher or theorist who attempts to use her or his work as a form of social or cultural criticism and who accepts certain basic assumptions: that all thought is fundamentally mediated by power relations which are socially and historically constituted; that facts can never be isolated from the domain of values or removed from some form of ideological inscription; that the relationship between concept and object and signifier and signified is never stable or fixed and is often mediated by the social relations of capitalist production and consumption; that language is central to the formation of subjectivity (conscious and unconscious awareness); that certain groups in any society are privileged over others and, although the reasons for this privileging may vary widely, the oppression which characterizes contemporary societies is most forcefully reproduced when subordinates accept their social status as natural, necessary or inevitable; that oppression has many faces and that focusing on only one at the expense of others (e.g., class oppression versus racism) often elides the interconnections among them; and finally, that mainstream research practices are generally, although most often unwittingly, implicated in the reproduction of systems of class, race and gender oppression.[4]

This passage provides a useful launching point for familiarizing oneself with critical research because it alludes to some of its major distinguishing features. To begin, deep connections to the Marxist tradition appear in the frequent invocation of constructs such as ideology, false consciousness (described as "subordinates [accepting] their status as natural"), and social reproduction. In addition, we get a glimpse of the orientation's epistemological assumptions, or claims about the nature of truth and knowledge, in references to "facts and values," "concepts and objects," and "signifier and signified." Finally, we are told from the outset that the role of the researcher is that of social and cultural critic.

In what follows I explore each of these features in depth through a discussion of the most common criticisms they inspire. This serves a dual function of distinguishing the criticalist stance from other approaches to qualitative research while simultaneously addressing arguments frequently made against it. The three main criticisms I take up all derive from a common source: critical research's supposed utopianism. Detractors from different camps charge that utopian tendencies result in biased research which mistakenly presupposes a unitary reality and lacks utilitarian value.

Values and Research: The Question of Bias

Critical researchers face many challenges as they attempt to undertake research that mediates between the "is" and the "ought." One common problem is the charge that critical research is biased by a particular value orientation. This charge is not unique to critical education research, but plagues other strands of interpretive research as well. Criticalists do not believe in the possibility of completely objective or neutral research. Instead, they share with many interpretivists assumptions about the unavoidability of values influencing all stages of a research project, from what questions are asked to how the findings are derived and presented. For criticalists and interpretivists alike, in the words of Richard Quantz, "the question becomes not should we impose our values, but how should we, as researchers, deal with our values?"[5] A common response to this challenge is to advocate that researchers be up front about their values and rigorous in revealing and challenging their own assumptions as evidence is collected, analyzed, and reported.

Despite the commitment of most criticalists and interpretivists to rigor and quality, traditionalists (here I am broadly referring to positivists and post-positivists) often charge that an explicit value orientation distorts evidence and flaws conclusions.[6] Criticalists and interpretivists respond to this charge in a few different ways, some reflecting their similarities and others highlighting their differences. First, both camps would likely object that blatant distortion of evidence "is as rare [among their practitioners] as in other methods of ethnography."[7] Second, as already stated, both camps take issue with traditionalists' notion that research, or the pursuit of knowledge, can take place either outside of or from a neutral position *vis-à-vis* values or theoretical frameworks. Accordingly, they might together explain to traditionalists that data are not simply collected. Rather, data are produced as a result of complex interactions between a researcher's values, existing theoretical frameworks, and the case at hand.[8] At this point, similarities give way to key differences between criticalists and interpretivists. The differences emerge from the varying ways in which they describe how and why a researcher produces knowledge.

Epistemological and Ontological Claims: Unitary or Plural Realities?

In much of the literature on qualitative research, critical theory and interpretivism are presented as dichotomous or incongruent paradigms. As the previous section demonstrates, such characterizations are off base in that they overlook some key similarities. Both approaches stress the contextual nature of knowledge within interpenetrating realms of facts and values. They do diverge, however, in their willingness to engage in normative evaluation of value positions and, as a result, in their end products. In order to present some of the starkest contrasts between critical research and other strands of interpretivism, I will focus upon one strand of interpretive research known as constructivism.

Constructivism, as defined and championed by Egon Guba and Yvonna Lincoln, is an approach to knowledge and qualitative research that focuses on meaning and enriched understanding. For constructivists, epistemological questions are best accounted for with a relativist account of reality. Social realities are the "multiple, apprehendable, and sometimes conflicting . . . products of human intellects . . . that may change as their constructors become more informed and sophisticated." Thus, no one account of reality or, in other words, no one knowledge claim, is more "true" than another. Rather, claims are only more "informed and sophisticated."[9]

Criticalists have a particularly hard time stomaching the relativist proclamations of constructivism. They disagree with relativism at two levels: normative and epistemological. At the normative level, criticalists find "informed and sophisticated reconstructions" useful in that they help us to understand how individuals make sense of their world. But, they find that the constructivist's passion for understanding lacks a guiding normative vision. What especially bothers criticalists about constructivism is an absence of substantive concern with the ways in which local meanings reflect social relations of domination and oppression. Satisfied with sense making and epistemological relativism, constructivist accounts run the risk of moral nihilism. Gary Anderson explains that critical ethnographers avoid this pitfall by drawing attention to the ways in which:

> . . . informant reconstructions are often permeated with meanings that sustain powerlessness and [the ways in which] people's conscious models exist to perpetuate, as much as to explain social phenomena. Critical ethnographers, therefore, attempt to ensure that participants in research "are not naively enthroned, but systematically and critically unveiled."[10]

Criticalists insist that any research that fails to engage in critical analysis, whether traditional or interpretivist, unwittingly adopts a value position that reinforces the existing social order. In Habermasian terms, "the mere acceptance of . . .'meaning,'" which is indicative of constructivism, ". . . [remains] trapped in a hermeneutic circle that fails to transform . . . [R]esearch that takes this 'hermeneutic' position' serves the 'practical interest' which seeks harmony and integration at the expense of freedom." Committed to the belief that research always serves some interests, criticalists choose what Habermas labels the "emancipatory interest." They aspire to conduct research that will lead toward "emancipation and democracy."[11]

Criticalists and constructivists are each skeptical of the consequences of the other camp's approach to intersections between values and epistemology. Criticalists charge constructivists with reinforcing status quo power relationships by refusing to adopt a critical value orientation. In response, constructivists accuse criticalists of falling into the same trap that bedevils traditional research: belief in a single reality. Traditionalists reinforce existing power relationships as a result of their ill-fated attempts at "neutrality." Criticalists, by combining theories of oppression with a commitment to emancipation, use research to bring about a desired transformation. Either way, reality is reduced to a unitary phenomenon that can be sufficiently explained as to be directed toward particular ends.[12] Criticalists's insistence on a normative commitment weds them to a faulty epistemology.

The constructivist critique of critical research highlights two different issues. The first issue is ontological differences between criticalism and constructivism. The second issue is a critique of critical research as it is commonly practiced. For constructivists, reality itself is constructed and, therefore, only exists through the perceptions of local actors. Criticalists, on the other hand, posit that reality exists apart from our perceptions of it. In this case, it is not reality that is multiplistic, but actors' perceptions of and meanings attributed to specific "objects" of reality. Carspecken, a criticalist, casts doubt on constructivism's ontology of multiple realities apprehended through local understandings. He insists that "[c]onstructivism begs important questions about human communication and human understanding." For instance, if multiple realities are "constructed" by individuals and/or groups, and if one can never attain an insider's view of another's reality,

> then how is it that we could even know that other realities exist? Would not this very idea be the product of just one reality? If the idea is that we can gain partial understandings of other cultural realities, then some sort of transcultural standards must exist by which these partial understandings can be judged as such.[13]

Carspecken draws into question constructivism's ontological assumptions. If reality itself is so multiplistic and partial, how could we as humans ever hope to communicate or reach agreements, let alone identify standards with which to recognize one another's perspectives as partial?

Critical epistemology, again, is rooted in an ontological assumption that reality is unitary. But individual's perceptions of reality are bound by context: historical, social, and cultural. Accordingly, truth claims are multiplistic and indeterminate. The tradition of critical epistemology flowing from the American pragmatists through Habermas argues that truth claims are only valid to the extent that they are agreed upon by all members of a given community. Truth claims are based upon the consent of a community of inquirers. Thus, truth itself is not unitary but fallible and provisional because another community in a different time may agree upon an alternative explanation. Critical epistemology, then, accounts for multiplicity and plurality of perspectives without requiring epistemological or normative relativism.[14]

Even if one finds the ontological and epistemological claims of criticalists more convincing than those of constructivists, Carpsecken does not go far enough in making the case for critical research. Carspecken attempts to debunk constructivism without addressing a compelling problem—the tendency of critical research to posit unitary social concepts that fail to account for plurality and multiplicity. In other words, critical research has difficulty mediating between the "ought" and the "is" in its own practice. Skeptics' assertions that critical research tends toward totalizing explanations of culture and society are often on the mark. Consider, for example, the following claim by Quantz, a supporter of critical research: "Critical ethnography's contribution . . . lies principally in its ability to make concrete the particular manifestations of *marginalized cultures* located in a broader sociopolitical framework" [my emphasis].[15] Quantz's reference to marginalized cultures reveals two implicit assumptions in much critical research. First, that such things as marginalized cultures exist, and, second, that critical research will function to emancipate these cultures.

The first assumption—that there is such a thing as a marginalized culture—brushes over the ways in which *all* cultures have both accommodating and marginalizing tendencies. The second assumption—that critical research will emancipate this marginalized culture—locates the researcher as the emancipator. In both instances, the researcher and the research are placed in privileged positions of identifying and revealing what is marginal and what is emancipatory. Moreover, members of the culture are cast as victims of false consciousness rather than as reasoning human agents. As a result, whereas critical ethnography prides itself on making particular cultural manifestations concrete, its tendency to invoke totalizing constructs such as what Reba Page calls its "familiar whipping boy—

'the system,'" sometimes has the opposite effect of causing social actors and their unique understandings to "retreat from view."[16]

Such problems with unitary explanations of social reality indicate that criticalists could benefit from constructivist insights surrounding multiple understandings within local contexts. Although the constructivist epistemology may not be entirely convincing, its emphasis on the multiplicity of experience may serve as a corrective for the totalizing and deterministic tendencies of critical research's systemic approach. Before discussing how criticalists might make better use of constructivism's insights, I will describe a final criticism of critical research: lack of utility.

Utopianism versus Utilitarianism

In a survey article entitled "Ethnography and Participant Observation," Paul Atkinson and Martyn Hammersley admonish qualitative researchers to keep in mind the following:

> . . . Above all, it is of considerable importance that we do not lose sight of what has hitherto been the goal of ethnographic research, namely, the production of knowledge. We should not replace this with the pursuit of practical goals that, although sometimes valuable in themselves, are no *more* worthy in general terms of our time and effort than the pursuit of knowledge. This is especially so when these goals are of a kind that we may be much less able to achieve. It is true that conventional research never changes the world at a stroke, and that often it may not have much effect even over the long term. But that does not mean that it is of no value. It is also worth remembering that changing the world can be for the worse as well as for the better. Utopian attempts to do politics by means of research are of no service to anyone [emphasis in text].[17]

Criticalists deny that the pursuit of knowledge can take place in isolation, or that, if it could, this would be just as worthy as pursuing knowledge for the sake of just social change. But Atkinson's and Hammersley's position adds another wrinkle to arguments against critical research. For these authors, the main problem with critical theory's utopian agenda is not that its "radical" orientation will bias research, nor that its "conservative" epistemology misreads reality. Rather, they insist that utopianism is of no use to anyone. Research that self-consciously politicizes itself loses the utility it might otherwise offer to the very people it intends to serve.

This emphasis on utility mirrors another more compelling criticism from sympathizers of critical research who hold that it is not fulfilling its emancipatory potential. Here, the argument is that critical research tends "towards social critique without developing a theory of action that educational practitioners can draw upon to develop a 'counter-hegemonic' practice in which dominant structures of classroom and organizational meaning are challenged."[18] In other words, criticalists are quite good at fulfilling their roles as social and cultural critics, but they fall short when it comes to articulating a positive agenda for institutionalizing educational practices that would challenge the existing social order.

In sum, criticalists and constructivists share the conviction that social research takes place in an interpenetrating realm of facts and values. The two orientations share doubts about the objective nature of knowledge, or the possibility that it can be shared in any universal form or fashion, and assumptions that values infiltrate all acts of knowing. But the two camps diverge in their approaches to the confluence of facts and values. Constructivism settles for epistemological and normative relativism in response to plural realities. Criticalism, on the other hand, refuses to throw up its hands to epistemological relativism or the impossibility of shared standards for judging moral worth. Criticalists draw upon a normative framework of democratic values which also drives their epistemology. Truth is only arrived at via consent. Nevertheless, constructivism poses important challenges to critical theory, including lingering questions about totalizing theoretical constructs such as "the system" or "social reproduction." Can critical theory both utilize such constructs and accommodate the multiplicity of meaning that comprises human agency? Do these constructs place the researcher in a privileged position of "knower" or "emancipator" while relegating participants to roles as "victims of false consciousness"?

Critical research struggles with mediating between the "ought" and the "is." Research products often fail to live up to research ideals. In addition, the emphasis on social critique is not matched with corresponding theories of social action. Much recent work in response to these dilemmas calls for a strategy of "resistance postmodernism" to strengthen the tradition's transformative potential. After outlining a few conceptual problems with this approach, I will recommend a strategy of "critical interpretive" research as an alternative democratic remedy.

"Blurred Genres"[19]

Present-day critical researchers are attempting to address the enduring criticisms discussed above—structuralist accounts undermining human agency, the all-knowing researcher, and critique versus action. One strategy for doing so is to balance the critical tradition's deep connections to Marxist theory with postmodernism's anti-foundationalist insights.

A relationship is forged between the historical and materialist social critique of critical theory and the profound skepticism of some postmodern theories. According to McLaren and Kincheloe:

> The synergism of the conversation between resistance postmodern and critical theory involves an interplay between the praxis of the critical and the radical uncertainty of the postmodern. As it invokes its strategies for the emancipation of meaning, critical theory provides the postmodern critique with a normative foundation (i.e., a basis for distinguishing between oppressive and liberatory social relations). Without such a foundation the postmodern critique is ever vulnerable to nihilism and inaction. Indeed, the normatively ungrounded postmodern critique is incapable of providing an ethically challenging and politically transformative program of action.[20]

This strategy avoids constructivism's epistemological relativism, which often slides into moral nihilism, by aligning with "resistance postmodernism" and its penchant for politicizing difference in the name of transformative critique.[21] To put it another way, "resistance postmodernism" merges the contributions of constructivism on multiple perspectives, and of skeptical or "ludic" postmodernists on the relationships between plurality/difference and power relationships, with critical theory's commitment to making use of social and historical critique to intervene in material relations.[22]

Resistance postmodernism's conciliatory strategy between postmodernism and critical theory is at once a necessary and a worrisome move. One of the great philosophical questions as we enter the 21st century is how to combine the "radical uncertainty" of postmodern anti-foundationalism with any sort of normative framework; without foundations, from whence do normative standards derive? Kincheloe and McLaren clearly prefer normative foundations to nihilism, but they provide us with no clear indication of the normative basis from which critical research proceeds. I posit that this ambiguity stems, at least in part, from critical research's vast theoretical legacy. As I pointed out early in this chapter, critical research calls upon, and often collapses categories between, neo-Marxist critical theory, postmodernism, poststructuralism, feminism, and "Freirian empowering research."[23] Such "blurred genres," while in some respects illuminating theoretical gaps and enriching the possibilities of critical research, simultaneously run the risks of logical schizophrenia and sloppy scholarship. For instance, Marxist theory combines a holistic sociological explanation for oppression with a normative commitment to particular ways in which social, economic, and political relations should be ordered. Postmodernism, on the other hand, generally rejects normative frameworks as "grand meta-narratives" that reflect and perpetuate power relationships. In addition, postmodern social critique tends to focus on the fragmented and intersecting nature of power relations, also rejecting holistic sociological models.

In the early years of critical research, Anderson claims, this ". . . uneasy alliance . . . raised serious questions about the compatibility of theory-driven social agendas on one hand and phenomenological research methods on the other. To many, their marriage seemed, at once, both an epistemological contradiction and an inevitability."[24] Inevitability, however, is a poor excuse for lack of clarity. The important question becomes, given the epistemological contradictions, how, if at all, might they be overcome? Rather than simply accepting logical inconsistency as inevitable, or making a righteous claim about justice trumping persuasive argumentation, I believe it is more useful for critical researchers to distinguish the particularities of specific theoretical strands and to make explicit where one locates oneself. Recalling that Habermas's critical social theory attempts to resolve the postmodern dilemma noted above—how to derive shared normative standards without shared foundations—I will orient myself within the critical research tradition by: 1) explicating two distinct strains of neo-Marxist critical theory and affiliating myself with the Habermasian strand, and 2) utilizing some of his conceptual distinctions to make a case for a critical interpretive strategy that softens boundaries between critical theory and constructivism.

Critical Interpretive Inquiry

When criticalists prominently tout "neo-Marxist" theory as one among many influences, they are not only invoking entire traditions that are epistemologically at odds, they are over-generalizing the coherence of the Marxist legacy. At least two strands of this legacy share common roots in the Frankfurt School and the birth of critical theory with Max Horkheimer's "Traditional and Critical Theory" in the 1930s.[25] First-generation critical theorists, namely Adorno, Horkheimer, and Marcuse, produced a scathing critique of Enlightenment rationality which culminated in such works as *Dialectic of Enlightenment* (1947) and *One-Dimensional Man* (1964).[26] Habermas, trained as a critical theorist within this tradition, rejected the nihilistic implications of the earlier scholars' rejection of rationality. He cast doubt upon their dire conclusions by drawing into question their reliance on the functionalism of Marx's account and their narrow interpretation of rationality as purely instrumental. Habermas developed his theory of communicative action in response to such theoretical problems.[27]

To a large extent, the problems with critical education research discussed earlier—difficulty balancing structuralism and human agency, privileging the theoretician/researcher, and stressing critique over action—trace back to gaps within Marx's theory that continue to plague critical theorists to the present day. Habermas distances himself from first-generation critical theorists due to their inability to resolve these issues satisfactorily. Although detractors and supporters alike question whether he has done any better, much of his project of critical *social* theory is an explicit attempt to reconcile these enduring tensions. I will explain how his complex sociological model makes room for such reconciliation by explicating Benhabib's distinction between the "explanatory-diagnostic" and "anticipatory-utopian" strands of critical theory, and a parallel distinction between "critique" and "discourse." Both of these distinctions help to mediate between the theory's normative framework for what society *ought* to be like and its sociological assumptions of what social life *is* like.

According to Benhabib, Habermas begins to narrow the gap between structuralism and human agency by:

> introduc[ing] a more differentiated sociological model which in the first instance distinguishes between "social" and "system" integration and which denies that there is a "functional fit" between the economy on the one hand and culture and personality on the other. Briefly explicated, the distinction between "system" integration and "social" integration is the following: by the former is meant a mode coordinating social action through the functional interconnection of action consequences, whereas "social integration" refers to the coordination of action through the harmonizing of action orientations.[28]

This sociological model has implications for the relationship between philosophy and social science which are reflected in Benhabib's distinctions between the explanatory-diagnostic and anticipatory-utopian strands of critical theory. Both categories are concerned with the partnered notions of crisis and transformation, but they split tasks and responsibilities. The explanatory-diagnostic aspect emphasizes the use of empirical analysis to reveal contradictions and dysfunctionalities within the present system. The anticipatory-utopian dimension complements the concept of systemic crises with that of lived experience. It is concerned with present-day social action and concrete experiences of "suffering, humiliation, aggression, and injustice" in order to anticipate how the crises of today can

be transformed through "resistance, protest, and organized struggle" toward a more desirable future.[29]

Critical social theory's distinctions between system and social integration and between explanatory versus anticipatory dimensions of critique
provide bases for a more interpretivist approach to critical research than
that allowed by functionalist theories. The attention given to lived experience within critical social theory makes more room for accounts of human agency within empirical analyses of domination and crisis. In addition, the requirements of social integration reconfigure the role of the
theoretician/researcher from that of outside expert to internal participant. Benhabib explains:

> Social integration means that individuals orient their actions to one another be-
> cause they cognitively understand the social rules of action in question . . . at
> least two individuals know the pertinent action context and orient themselves to
> it. Whereas system integration can occur even when there is a discrepancy be-
> tween intention and consequence, social integration cannot take place unless
> action consequences are compatible with the intentions of social actors. It follows
> that whereas action systems can be analyzed, and in fact can only be grasped
> from the external perspective of the third, of the observer, social integration must
> be analyzed from the internal perspective of those involved. . . . In the one case
> the consequences of social action proceed "behind the back of individuals"; in
> the latter case the occurrence of social action needs to be explained via a recon-
> struction of its meaning as grasped by social actors.[30]

Social action "explained via a reconstruction of its meaning as grasped
by social actors" sounds remarkably similar to constructivism. The key
difference is this: whereas constructivism settles for "informed and sophisticated reconstructions" as its end product, critical social theory seeks
to wed such reconstructions with both systemic analysis and critique, all
in the name of utopian social transformation. Critical social theory's belief
that integration between actors is possible rejects the epistemological relativism of constructivism, and its normative critique rejects the parallel
slide toward moral relativism that characterizes ludic postmodernism. Yet,
critical social theory is able to embrace constructivism's insights regarding emic meaning because its sociological model pairs systemic and social
action, thereby elevating the lived experiences of human agency to equal
footing with structuralist explanations of reality. Both accounts are necessary for relevant empirical analyses of the potential of crisis and transformation which can mediate between the *is* and the *ought*.

Critical social theory also offers a preferable role for researchers than
that of privileged observer. Whereas functionalist "systems" are observed

and analyzed from an external vantage point, empirical analysis of lived experience must be pursued from the internal perspectives of the actors themselves. This approach to empirical analysis represents a marked departure from Horkheimer's insistence that the intellectual's "own thinking . . . should in fact be a critical promotive factor in the development of the masses."[31] First-generation critical theorists insisted that the theoretician/researcher operate from outside and impart knowledge that would transform social conditions. Their position drew objections from others wondering how the "privileged epistemic situation of the critical theorist" could be reconciled "with its emancipatory intentions."[32] According to Benhabib, Habermas responds to this objection by distinguishing between *critique* "in which an asymmetrical position of knowledge between the theorist and members of a society obtains" and *discourse* "where all are equal to decide upon a common course of action in free and unconstrained debate."[33] Although this conceptual distinction will not do away with asymmetries of power and knowledge, Habermas's model of discourse ethics provides a critical yardstick for evaluating whether researchers' efforts fall more toward the privileged position of the critic or the equalized position of participant in democratized deliberations surrounding knowledge and truth claims.

To conclude, Habermas's critical social theory offers a normative framework, a sociological model, and the broad strokes of an empirical methodology which allow critical researchers to coherently combine interpretive insights with social critique and utopian leanings. Interpretivism lends critical theory a methodological paradigm for reflecting the lived experiences of social actors, from within their emic perspectives, with all of their plurality. Interpretivism's methodological imperatives encourage critical researchers to incorporate perspectives without labeling them *a priori* as powerless or marginalized, thus making room for complexity as well as guarding against exclusion of any voices. Critical theory, on the other hand, offers interpretivism an epistemology based upon the premise of winning consent of those involved and enhancing the particularity of local understandings with social and historical analysis. In doing so, it provides interpretivism with a normative framework for systematically questioning the implications of meaning and social action, thereby avoiding moral relativism. Thus, a merged interpretivist approach to critical research not only encourages but actively calls forth mediation between the system and social action, between structure and human agency, and between the "ought" and the "is."[34] And it does so according to democratic norms that legitimate truth claims as well as the role of the researcher as one consenting member of the inquiry community. As Carspecken reminds us:

> The act of conducting research will always be value driven, but the validity claims
> of the researcher must meet certain standards to avoid bias. Those standards are
> rooted in democratic principles that are required by a careful examination of the
> concept of truth. Thus, validity claims and values connect intimately through the
> relationship of democratic principles and truth. Truth claims presuppose the limit
> case of winning the consent of other people when power relations are equalized.[35]

Critical interpretive research commits itself to applying democratic principles to the research process itself as it explores the ways in which local meanings and social systems interact to produce domination alongside consensual social relations. In the next section I describe how I applied this research orientation which I call "critical interpretive ethnography."

II. Applying a Critical Interpretive Approach to Design and Methodology

The focus of my case study at Winthrop Academy evolved as my relationship developed with the school, and as my critical interpretivist orientation was flushed out. The story of this evolution is largely a chronological one. The following discussion represents a reflective journey that both describes and considers the methodological steps that I took throughout the case study research. I look back on the early stages of building a relationship and determining a research agenda with Winthrop Academy faculty. Next, I explain my methods of data collection and analysis. I also consider challenges to these strategies and to pursuing research democratically. Then, I assess the research project in terms of three quality criteria and end by evaluating the types of evidence that indicate the extent to which the research has been successful.

Attempting Democratic Deliberation in Building a Research Agenda

During the summer of 1995 Beth Taft and Cathy Eichler were busy preparing for the school's September opening. After learning about Winthrop Academy from a phone call to Massachusetts' Department of Education, I reached Cathy by phone and arranged a meeting. From the outset of our relationship, I stressed my willingness to volunteer and to be involved with Winthrop Academy's community. In this initial meeting with Cathy,

I consciously put my own research agenda on the back burner for two reasons. First, I was concerned to demonstrate that I wanted to give something to the school, not simply take research data. Second, I wanted to create a research agenda that would be mutually beneficial to myself and to the school. So I wanted to take some time getting to know the school, its mission, and its priorities before arriving at a concrete set of research questions.

Over the next six weeks I met with Cathy, began meeting other faculty members, and communicated with all of them through memos to begin a dialogue surrounding the research agenda. In a memo of August 12, 1995, for example, I suggested the focusing question: "How can we create and sustain public institutions that promote common political ideals while respecting value differences?" By August 28th, the question had evolved to: "As public institutions, how can charter schools promote common political ideals and civic participationism while respecting particular cultural identities and value differences?" The memos from those weeks provide a record of my uncertainty surrounding the focus of the research as well as my efforts to involve Winthrop Academy in the process of creating a clearer focus. In the interests of clarifying a set of focusing questions in a timely manner I hoped to meet with the faculty to discuss some possibilities.

Wednesday, September 6, 1995, was the first official day of school at Winthrop Academy. I stayed after, waiting to speak with Beth about an opportunity to meet with the faculty to discuss focusing questions. This was the first time that Beth and I had had an opportunity to talk; we had only met briefly previously. I explained to her my interest in studying democratic community building and my desire to define a research agenda in conjunction with the staff. Beth asked how soon this would need to happen. I said as soon as possible in case we wanted to collect information early on from faculty, parents, and staff about perceptions or expectations for comparison at a later point.

Beth stated that she would not want me to meet with families or students because she did not want them to feel that they were being experimented with. She said that regardless of what was in my head, students would perceive me as a researcher and it was important that they did not feel as if the school was an experiment, but rather their school. She said that I could ask individual teachers if they wanted to be interviewed, but that the priority was on the school doing well, not my research agenda. I asked if it would be okay for me to take notes during Town Meetings and she said yes. She asked if I had read the vision statement in the handbook;

I said yes. She said that their mission is to be open, but that the priority was on building the school, not studying it. She said that she would talk to the rest of the faculty and get back to me, but she was unsure when. I learned that faculty meetings were on Friday mornings and said that I would put down on paper what my research interests were so that she could discuss the research with the faculty. Then, possibly, I could come to the next meeting to talk over specific questions. She said, frankly, this was not a priority and she was not sure whether they would get to it over the next two meetings. I said that regardless I would get something on paper so that they could discuss it at their convenience.

I was a bit disheartened after this conversation. Cathy had been fairly encouraging regarding Winthrop Academy's interest in my research. Beth was forthright that her priorities were beginning a school, not a research project. This early conversation marks the beginning of two persistent challenges in pursuing democratic research: conflicting priorities and time. As much as I wanted to create a research agenda in conjunction with the faculty, this agenda was far from the top of their list of priorities during the first weeks of a brand new school. Accordingly, the research was not likely to be a topic during a time-constrained faculty meeting that week. On the other hand, as a researcher, the need to identify a focus for the research was close to the top of my list of priorities. In order to facilitate what movement I could, I drafted a memo to all faculty and distributed it prior to their faculty meeting on Friday, September 8th. In the memo I articulated my interest in "undertaking a study that will assist the faculty of Winthrop Academy in assessing the extent to which your own goals are met over the course of this first school year."[36] I indicated my willingness to derive research questions that would address both my own research agenda and the needs of the school.

That Friday afternoon, following Town Meeting, I learned that the faculty had discussed the memo during their morning meeting. Beth indicated that she and I could discuss the memo the following week and Cathy said things were "a go." I met with another faculty member who said that he was interested in the study primarily for documentation purposes or "keeping track of what [they were] trying to do." He invited me to come to his class at any time. I left the school that day feeling for the first time that the research would indeed move forward. But, I still needed feedback from the faculty as to how we should focus our energies.

Due to busy and conflicting schedules it was not until October 18, 1995, that Beth and I met to discuss a research focus. Beth was very clear that faculty would find it helpful to investigate the question: "What would a successful Town Meeting look like?" By this time, the school community had participated in approximately six Town Meetings. These events had not "looked" quite how the faculty had originally envisioned them. But they were having a difficult time putting a finger on exactly why or what might be done differently.

To begin exploring these questions, I interviewed each of the five core faculty members (Sam Asher, Cathy Eickler, Shaka Reid, Max Simon, and Beth Taft) during the first week of November. I followed this interview protocol:

1) What would a successful Town Meeting look like?
   a. What are the criteria for a successful Town Meeting?
   b. How can these criteria be measured?
2) What is the purpose of Town Meeting at Winthrop Academy?
   a. What are its educational objectives?
   b. Explicitly, how is Town Meeting an aspect of civic education?
   c. Is Town Meeting related to the community-building process?
3) Is there anything you would like to add re: Town Meeting?

I based the first set of questions in direct response to the faculty's request. I derived the second set of questions from my own interests in the school's civic mission and the concept of "school as community." In addition, I felt that attention to the purposes of Town Meeting would elucidate the question of what a successful Town Meeting would look like. Following these interviews, I developed an observation guide for Town Meeting. I solicited faculty feedback on the guide during a faculty meeting on December 1, 1995.

Once the focus of the case study research became focused upon Town Meeting, I constrained my overarching question—how are deliberative democratic ideals institutionalized in one charter school's approach to *practices for* citizenship?—to this setting. As I explored this question within Town Meeting's practices, I paid special attention to the impact of plurality, or differences, and social relations of inequality on the institutionalization of the ideals of equality, inclusion, and participation.

The foregoing discussion demonstrates the steps I took over my first weeks at Winthrop Academy to build a reciprocal, democratic research process. From the outset, I indicated my commitment to participate in, rather than simply study, the school community. In addition, I attempted to initiate a democratic research process that would be equally in the interests of all. These dual commitments to reciprocity and democratic ideals both facilitated and complicated my ensuing research endeavors. Without such commitments, I do not believe access to Winthrop Academy would have even been possible. I learned over time that the school had many other researchers approach them who were turned away. Especially during the early weeks and months, the school was constantly approached by researchers, educators, and journalists seeking information about new charter schools. Winthrop Academy could not address all of these requests and simultaneously run a school; and the latter was clearly the priority. As Beth clearly stated, the mission of the school is to educate, not to experiment with students or families.

But I want to make clear that I did not approach Winthrop Academy in an opportunistic or instrumental manner in order to gain access. I firmly believe that reciprocity and democratic ideals are appropriate standards for social research, particularly in the field of education. I also believe that one learns more about a school community from within. Reciprocity, equality, and participation, however, also complicate the research process. In the following sections, I will touch upon key places where such complications arose as I describe my methods of data collection and analysis.

Methods of Data Collection

My data collection methods at Winthrop Academy included observation, interviewing, a written-response survey, and document review. Even before the faculty and I tailored the research to focus on Town Meeting, I began observing school events. From the first week of school I observed Town Meetings as an unofficial member. I use the term "unofficial" because I was not a voting member of Town Meeting; I did not speak or participate in any manner. But I was distinguished from other public guests of Town Meeting.

Almost every week visitors to Winthrop Academy would attend to observe Town Meeting. Occasionally one of these guests would make an announcement about a special event, but none had voting privileges. Such guests were acknowledged by signing in and wearing a name tag. They were also officially welcomed by the moderator at the beginning of Town Meeting. Sometimes these visitors were asked to leave the Common Room, the official space of Town Meeting, for moments that the faculty identified as "private" within the Winthrop Academy community. Public apologies by students, for example, were not witnessed by visitors. But I was not asked to leave the room at these times. The first time such an instance took place, I looked imploringly at Beth wondering whether I should stay or go. Her look indicated to me that I was not required to leave. From then on, I remained in the room when other visitors were asked to leave. Once, when I happened to step out to use the restroom and returned along with visitors following a public apology a student behind me murmured "she didn't have to leave." As her comment suggests, students and faculty alike seemed to view me as a permanent fixture of Town Meeting, although not as a participating member.

In addition to observing Town Meetings, I also sat in on a Math class beginning the first week of school and continuing throughout the 1995-96 academic year. My primary role in this Math class was to tutor a student with special needs. As Cathy had indicated in our initial meeting, the school aspired to hold all students to a common curriculum. Essentially this means that Winthrop Academy began with a commitment not to track students. This commitment was challenged by students with special learning needs, especially those students who had previously been taught in special education classrooms. Cathy was particular concerned about one student, Susan, who exhibited very poor math skills. Cathy and I agreed early on that I would tutor Susan each week in Math as well as attend math class with her one day per week.

I considered my primary role in the Math 4 class as a tutor. But, I also made use of the time to observe the class. I combined content-related math notes, which I relied on heavily during the tutoring sessions, with process-related classroom notes. I especially noted instances when students directly referred to the civic mission of the school and when the teacher emphasized reasoned deliberation among class members. These classroom observations allowed me to examine how the civics mission related to the academic curriculum outside of Town Meeting and how relationships between teachers and students differed between the classroom and Town Meeting settings.

I also observed special events at Winthrop Academy. I attended holiday parties, observed the day the Governor of Massachusetts came to the school to present new charters, and accompanied the school on a hike up a mountain in New Hampshire as well as on a field trip to New York City. In each of these instances my role combined elements of observer and participant. At special celebratory functions I would help out by answering the phone, directing traffic, or setting up. On the field trips I spent much of my time with Susan. The nature of her disabilities seems to have resulted in a difficulty making friends among her peers. In addition, she has some trouble keeping up with the crowd. So I would be a pal to her as well as make sure she did not get lost in the hectic shuffle of all-school outings.

Within these roles, I witnessed and was a part of moments that created the culture of the school. The trip up the New Hampshire mountain, for example, has become a metaphor within the school for achievement, interdependence, and ecological awareness. The park motto "take out what you bring in" is often invoked to try to get students to clean up after themselves in school! The field trip to New York was intended to tie into the civic mission by familiarizing students with other important U.S. cities as well as key places such as Ellis Island and the Statue of Liberty. Faculty stressed these themes with class assignments based upon students' visit to these sites. Participation in such events provided me with a lens to view how the civic mission was integrated throughout the school's curriculum.

Another source of observational data was faculty meetings. The first faculty meeting I attended was on December 1, 1995. My purpose for attending was not to observe, but to discuss the Town Meeting observation tool with the faculty. But toward the end of that meeting, the faculty started discussing that day's Town Meeting. Beth wanted to show a clip from a speech President Clinton had recently made regarding sending U.S. troops to Bosnia. Some of the other faculty were wary that students were not ready to engage such a topic. I remember Beth saying something along the lines of "well, let's give it a try." She showed a clip in Town Meeting and moderated a debate in which students were quite engaged. At the end of the session, she announced to students "this is by far the best Town Meeting we've had."

The intersections that arose that day between faculty's differing expectations and the actual performance of students in Town Meeting caused me to begin thinking that it would be helpful for me to have clearer insight into faculty's intentions surrounding Town Meeting. Then, soon after Christmas break another event occurred that strengthened my conviction that I needed more data on faculty's explicit intentions for Town Meeting. At the end of January, faculty instituted a new procedure whereby students entered the Common Room prior to each Town Meeting by filing in and sitting with their Advisory Group. In addition, Town Meeting was to end and students were to return to their Advisory rooms if any students acted inappropriately. I was not aware of this change until it actually occurred. And that day, a student disrupted Town Meeting and the entire student body was sent back to their Advisory rooms until dismissal time. Because I did not know what had precipitated this policy or what faculty were trying to achieve, I felt at a loss to adequately interpret or analyze what appeared to be a seminal event.

Thus, the next week I began approaching the faculty to ask them to consider my observation of Faculty Meetings. Everyone agreed and I began attending Faculty Meetings in February, 1996. I intended to use these observations to look for two things: 1) what types of decisions were made at what levels (e.g., Town Meetings vs. Faculty Meetings vs. Board Meetings), and 2) how faculty decisions regarding the civics curriculum played out as they were implemented. In other words, I planned to use observations from Faculty Meetings in order to compare the faculty's articulated goals with actual outcomes as evidenced by observational notes from Town Meetings and interviews.

As I was discussing my intentions for observing Faculty Meetings with Beth, she mentioned another issue. She said that Winthrop Academy was in the midst of struggling with the question "how do you build a democratic process among faculty?" In creating a brand new decision-making process within the school, faculty were trying to decide if all members needed to be involved in all decisions or, if not, what decisions should be made by whom. Because this question reflected my interest in institutionalizing the procedural aspects of deliberative democracy, and because I thought it would be useful to compare a democratic process among faculty with a parallel process among students and faculty, I identified this question as a third area of focus in my observations of Faculty Meetings.

Two final sources of observational data were Board Meetings and agenda-setting meetings for Town Meeting. Just as I attended Faculty Meetings in order to compare what types of decisions were made at various organization levels within the school, I also attended Board Meetings for this purpose. In addition, a couple of issues generated by students in Town Meeting were eventually brought to the Board for review. In these instances, I observed the Board Meetings with an eye toward tracing the evolution of the decision and the roles of distinct bodies. An additional layer within this process was added in the spring of 1996 as Beth Taft attempted to involve students in the process of setting an agenda for Town Meeting. Beth began hosting meetings during the lunch hour on Thursdays that any students were welcome to attend to discuss and choose an agenda item for the following day's Town Meeting. I attended four or five such meetings from March to May 1996.

I buttressed the observational record that was created from all of these sources with semi-structured interviews and an open-ended written survey. All of my interviews at Winthrop Academy were semi-structured; I loosely followed an interview guide combining predetermined questions with follow-up probes and questions unique to specific individuals. Because the total number of faculty was quite small during the first year I did not need to worry about selection criteria; I simply interviewed all of them.[37] As I discussed above, I interviewed each of the five core faculty members in November 1995 regarding what a successful Town Meeting would look like. In February and March of 1996 I interviewed six students to gain their perspectives on community, citizenship, and participation at Winthrop Academy. In terms of selection criteria, I attempted to interview a pool of students that represented the gender and ethnic breakdown of the school population. But I quickly became aware that other factors, such as a student's willingness to be interviewed, might constitute relevant criteria for selection.

As I conducted interviews with students I became aware of two issues that suggested that face-to-face interviews may not be the ideal way to collect data on students' perceptions of Town Meeting. First, I realized that the types of questions I was asking students were fairly straightforward, such as "do you feel like a member of a community at Winthrop Academy." These sorts of questions did not require much probing or follow up. Second, I experienced difficulty getting access to students. I could not interview students during school hours, so interview times were constrained to study periods or after school. Not all students were willing to lend their time to being interviewed. I feared that my sample (which so far was demographically balanced including 3 boys and 3 girls; 2 African American, 1 Hispanic and 3 White students) was being skewed by students who were predisposed toward a willingness to be interviewed. I sensed that students who were not "buying in" to the school were also those who were not volunteering to be interviewed.

My concern about what types of students declined to be interviewed was magnified by a new role I had taken on within Winthrop Academy. In March 1996, I began supervising the computer room for one period on Monday afternoons. I took on this duty because the faculty asked me to. My responsibilities in the computer room were to make sure that students were engaged in academic work and not wasting time or disrupting other students. The following is an excerpt from my notes after the first day of supervision:

> Diablo and Luke were talking and not doing any work. I got into it with Luke. He muttered "all day man" meaning that I had been "on him" all day. When Diablo returned to his work, Luke told him that he had sold out. By having to discipline the students—ask them to keep quiet, stay on task, or leave the room—I feel like I am becoming an arm or symbol of teacher authority. I am very concerned that this compromises my role as a researcher, especially in light of the "us vs. them"

sentiment that I sense among the students. I voiced these concerns to [3 members of the faculty] . . . none of them seemed to realize or care that this stance both compromises the quality of the environment in the computer room and my role as a researcher. My preference would be not to take on this position. If I continue I think I'll try a one warning policy. This stance would at least minimize my negative interaction with students while allowing me to maintain control of the environment.

Despite my discomfort taking on this responsibility, the faculty had no other alternatives for supervision, so I agreed to continue the duty. I supervised the computer room a total of eight or ten times from March through June 1996.

My desire to expand the student interview sample, combined with a desire to downplay any skewing effect that my role as computer-room supervisor might have on students' willingness to be interviewed, provided the rationale for creating an open-ended survey for distribution to the entire student body. The survey was intended to inform students' perceptions of community, citizenship, and democratic participation at Winthrop Academy, particularly surrounding Town Meeting. I began drafting the survey during April, 1996. During this same period of time, I was engaging in a first attempt at analysis of civic participation in Town Meeting. This effort was spurred by a conference paper that I presented at the annual meeting of the New England Educational Research Organization (NEERO).

After I drafted an initial version of this paper I shared it with all of the Winthrop Academy faculty and asked for their feedback. One or two faculty members responded with written feedback. Because of the critical interpretivist orientation of the study and my commitments to an open, democratic research process I did not feel comfortable presenting these initial findings at NEERO without more extensive feedback. So I arranged individual interviews with each of the five core faculty members. These interviews served as a member check on my interpretations. The interviews were extremely useful; they yielded a couple of key conceptual distinctions including "education for democracy," as opposed to democratic education, and students as "potential" rather than actual equals with the school community.

The preliminary analysis and conceptual distinctions that resulted from the NEERO paper were taken into consideration as I developed the written survey for students. I drafted a survey, then reviewed this draft with faculty during a Faculty Meeting. We made several additions and changes and chose a date in early May for the survey to be administered (see table 6.1).

Table 6.1 Civic Education at Winthrop Academy: Student Survey

At Winthrop Academy our mission is civic education. This survey is a way for us to measure how we're doing in our efforts to achieve this mission. The survey is anonymous—you should <u>not</u> include your name. Please answer the following questions based on your experiences at Winthrop Academy.

Gender: _____ Female   Race/Ethnicity: _____ Asian/Pacific Islander
        _____ Male   _____ Black
                                            _____ Hispanic
                                            _____ White
                                            _____ Other (_____)

1) Please rank your level of agreement with the following statements (circle one):

1	2	3	4
Strongly Disagree	**Disagree**	**Agree**	**Strongly Agree**

a. I am a member of a community at Winthrop Academy:
                     1   2   3   4

b. My voice is heard at Winthrop Academy:
                     1   2   3   4

c. I participate in decision making at Winthrop Academy:
                     1   2   3   4

d. Winthrop Academy is preparing me to become a democratic citizen:
                     1   2   3   4

e. Public service is a valuable component of my education at Winthrop Academy:
                     1   2   3   4

2) What is the Winthrop Academy community like?
    (Please describe the community using a few sentences and as much detail as possible.)

3) How is Winthrop Academy different from other school communities?

4) In what ways do you "have a say" at Winthrop Academy?

5) What does it mean to be a citizen at Winthrop Academy?

6) In what ways have you participated in Town Meeting?
    (Please **check** <u>all</u> that apply, then **circle** the <u>most important</u> form of participation.)
    _____ I have asked for an item to be included on the agenda.
    _____ I have made a motion.

_____ I have made a speech.
_____ I have stood to be recognized and voiced an opinion.
_____ I have voted.
_____ I have participated in other ways. (Please describe)

7) So far, which Town Meeting do you think was the best? Why?

    So far, which Town Meeting do you think was the worst? Why?

8) How is Winthrop Academy preparing you to become a democratic citizen?

9) In what ways are your academic classes preparing you for citizenship? Specifically, what have you read, studied, or learned about in class that will help you to become a citizen?

10) What is the most important reason for public service at Winthrop Academy? (Please rank the following reasons #1–#5 with 1 as most and 5 as least important.)
    _____ Applying classroom learning in real life situations
    _____ Becoming a socially responsible citizen
    _____ Developing career skills
    _____ Helping local communities
    _____ Helping overworked people

11) What rules do you believe are valuable at Winthrop Academy? Why?

    What rules are not valuable at Winthrop Academy? Why?

12) What is the role of the pledge at Winthrop Academy?

13) Have you taken or do you intend to take the Winthrop Academy pledge?
    _____Yes _____No Why/Why Not?

Faculty administered the survey to students on May 6, 1996, in their classrooms. For the 9th grade students, the survey followed a bout of standardized tests that students took within their Advisory Groups. As they completed the survey, most students appeared anxious to get done. I would surmise that they were out of patience because they had just completed a few hours of testing and were anticipating lunch. The 10th graders completed the survey both during and following public service field trips that same week. I got the impression from their teacher that they were rather hurried and not able to fully concentrate on the survey.

As a result of these conditions, the quality of the survey data was mixed. The response rate was quite high: approximately 90% of the student body with a total of 58 students completing the survey. But at least one quarter of the questions were left blank or answered with a "don't know." Other answers were quite short. Nevertheless, the data collected provided strong indications of students' perceptions of membership within the Winthrop Academy community and participation in Town Meeting. And I was able to expand upon this data with follow-up interviews in June 1996.

At the end of June students participated in juried assessments of their academic work. The jury schedule was such that a handful of students were in the school building each day for a few hours of assessment, then they were free to leave. I was able to take advantage of this scheduling to conduct six focus group interviews with students. I interviewed a total of fifteen students: 8 girls and 7 boys; 7 African American, 3 Asian American, 1 Hispanic, and 3 White. As with my earlier student interviews, this sample was selected primarily upon availability and student willingness to be interviewed; some students who I asked declined and my sense is that those were students who were more alienated from the school. Both samples reflect the gender distribution of the school and closely approximate the ethnic distribution, although the Asian American population is slightly overrepresented (15% in the sample versus 3% in the student body). Numerically, this overrepresentation was difficult to avoid because there were so few Asian Americans in the school (4). I also think that the overrepresentation was justified because a smaller sample would have problematized any generalizations about Asian American students as a group.

My final method of data collection was document review. I collected a wide variety of school documents including the charter, handbooks, curriculum materials, and assessment tools. In addition, I reviewed newspaper articles from the local and national press. In some cases these documents were simply informational. From newspaper accounts I learned about the backgrounds of the faculty and their visions for the school without having to conduct additional interviews. I approached the school documents with an eye toward the civic mission—I looked for how this mission was portrayed in promotional materials as well as how the mission was communicated to students through the "explicit" curriculum of formal school documents and assessments.

All in all, my two years at Winthrop Academy yielded observational notes from approximately 50 Town Meetings, 35 Faculty Meetings, 5 agenda-setting meetings, 5 Board Meetings, and numerous special events; survey data from 58 of 65 students during the first year; fifteen interviews with the core faculty members (3 interviews each with five faculty members); 6 individual and 6 focus group interviews with a total of 20 students; and a plethora of documents.

Challenges to Data Collection

Despite the overwhelming amount of data, there remained areas where the record could have been more complete. Two primary challenges complicated data collection: time, or timing, and my ambiguous role with students. First, concerning timing, events inevitably occurred while I was not at the school. In such instances, my lack of a first-hand account made it more difficult to attach meanings to the event in order to guide follow-up activities or analytical comparison. In addition, time constraints often made it difficult to gather individual perceptions of what had happened or, more specifically, what faculty's intentions were. Beth, in particular, was very busy and unable to sit down and talk as often as I might have liked. It was fairly common for her to refer me to someone else when I asked for an account of a particular situation. Consequently, I gathered other perspectives on the situation, but not hers. Most of the other faculty were able to take a few minutes to answer questions when I sought their perspectives.

Second, my role with students as an adult and as an authority figure sometimes complicated data collection. For example, in December 1996 the issue of school uniforms (shirts) was raised in Town Meeting. This issues had been raised in many different forms by students since the very first Town Meeting. Because I had identified shirts as an important evolving topic for discussion, I wanted to gather students' reactions to the Town Meeting.

A few days after the Town Meeting in question, I ran into a couple of students in the hallway one of whom, Deidre, was a Student Advisory Council (SAC) member. Since the SAC has placed the shirt topic on the Town Meeting agenda, I thought it would be especially useful to explore her perspective on the meeting. I said hello and asked how Friday's Town Meeting had gone. Deidre responded by saying "Oh, what did I miss?" Her friend, Mona, pointed to a resolution posted on a nearby bulletin board that said "Winthrop Academy students should have an alternative to shirts, i.e. pins." Deidre thrashed her arms around appearing frustrated and disappointed that she had missed this Town Meeting and said "I'll have to watch the tape." Town Meeting was videotaped each week by a student—a duty that I oversaw in my capacity as resident researcher. I said to Deidre that I had the video and would bring it back on Friday unless she needed to see it earlier. She said, "I don't know if they'll let me take it home over the weekend." I checked with a teacher who said that this decision was up to me as the "archivist" and joked that we would need a "major credit card as a deposit" if we ever hoped to get the tape back from Deidre. Uncertain whether Deidre would return the tape, I returned to the hallway and said "we need to keep the tapes here in school, so you can watch it on a TV here after school. Would you like me to bring it back early so that you can watch it one afternoon this week?" She then stepped up to the teacher's door and asked "we can't take the tapes home?" I heard him respond "what's the problem, we have all this equipment here, watch it here after school." After a couple more minutes of exchange, Deidre said, as she began walking away "never mind, you all are making such a big deal, like Blockbuster, I'll see it whenever." I said, "OK, it will be here on Friday." Mona said "thank you," then Deidre said "thank you" and they walked off.

The important point that I want to stress from this exchange is the tension that arose between my role as researcher and as an adult within the school community. In this case, as I made a decision with a faculty member about making data available to a student, I was labeled by the student as one of "you all." This statement implies that she saw me as one of the faculty, or at least as an adult authority figure similar to those at Blockbuster Video stores. Thus, an exchange that began with my hope of gaining her perspective on the shirt topic ended with her acting frustrated with me because I executed a decision that she was not happy with. Not only did I miss an opportunity to hear her views, I also was unable to ask her friend any questions because they walked away as comrades, in solidarity against the "you all" that I represented. In such cases—my supervision of the computer room led to other comparable instances—my role as an adult within the school was in tension with building a rapport with students that would encourage them to see me as a confidante, or at least not as a member of a warring camp.

Although I am unsure whether a perception of me as one of "them" was widespread among the student body, some students who appeared alienated from the school community were often difficult to approach. For instance, students who did not participate much in Town Meeting were also reticent to answer my questions about why. Some of these students appeared shy; others appeared bothered by an adult trying to talk to them. Whatever the reason, I had trouble convincing students who appeared marginalized to share their perceptions of the school and Town Meeting with me.

Time and my role *vis-à-vis* students represented challenges to data collection insofar as they limited my access to the perspectives of particular members of the Winthrop Academy community. Each of these constraints, however, was counteracted to a certain extent because I was in the field for a good length of time (two years) and my samples of student and faculty interviewees were fairly large and representative of the population. Moreover, my role as a participant within the school community provided me with access to many situations and sources of information that another researcher would not have obtained.

Data Analysis

I structured data analysis according to an interpretivist emphasis on three levels of analysis: 1) attention to participant's internal perspectives, 2) face-to-face processes of meaning making, and 3) broader social contexts. In terms of the first two levels of analysis—attention to internal perspectives and face-to-face processes—my initial analytical foray accompanied my preparation for the NEERO paper discussed above. I began by reading through the early interviews with faculty regarding what a successful Town Meeting would look like, the Town Meeting observational record, and student interviews. I compared the accounts offered by each of these sources and searched for similarities and tensions between them.

This initial analytic endeavor yielded a comparison of faculty accounts of civic participation as "civilized debate" with the unintended outcome of students' "dissolving" behaviors. I shared this account with each of the five core faculty members as a member check on validity and to encourage further insight into Town Meeting dynamics. These discussions, in April 1996, led to an emphasis on the nature of students' equality as a "potential" equality and raised questions surrounding what it means for students to "practice" civic participation. Thus, the notion of participation as practice among potential equals became a sensitizing concept for ensuing analysis.

After Winthrop Academy's first school year ended, I began to review the composite data record. I approached various data sources for layers of meaning surrounding the civic education mission and began an initial category system. This category system contained categories such as "Dynamics Fostering Student Participation," "Dynamics Hindering Student Participation," and "Venues for Public Discourse," among others. Although the category system held together fairly well and captured most of the data, it did not seem particularly emergent. Rather, I realized that these categories were theory-driven; they reflected the questions I had set out at the theoretical level. I was conflicted as to how to reconcile such top-down categories with an interpretivist approach to case study research.

Sensing that my theoretical framework was getting in the way of emergent categories I attempted to read through the data again looking for more "ground-up" interpretations. I was able to identify plenty of patterns that I could label with participants' own words, yet they still fit within the original category system. I realized that the questions that I had asked in many of the interviews constructed the data in ways that closely paralleled my theoretical concerns. Thus, I eventually reconciled the theory-driven and interpretivist aspects of the project by clarifying for myself that what was emergent was not the analytical framework itself, but what these categories meant and how they were interpreted within this particular context. Comfortable with this approach, I returned to the original category system, careful to look for meanings, perspective, and processes internal to the Winthrop Academy community.

As I began to tighten the category system, I sought to gauge its validity through triangulation between data sources and through member checks. I compared categories across the interview and observational record searching for gaps and contradictions. When I found them, I searched through the record yet again for alternative explanations. After I felt that the data were adequately represented within the categories, I wrote up an initial draft of the case study and made it available to the entire Winthrop Academy faculty via their e-mail system. This approach encouraged dialogue among members of the faculty, as well as with myself, and facilitated a process of refining the interpretations toward fuller and more complete understandings.

In terms of the third level of interpretive analysis—broader social contexts—I returned to the challenges surrounding social plurality and inequality that I highlighted in chapter 2. Specifically, I revisited the Town Meeting observational record with a specific eye toward identifying the ways in which differences and unequal relationships impacted the formal *practices for* civic education within this forum. I drew upon the categories of inequality stressed by critical theorists such as Iris Marion Young and Nancy Fraser, namely gender and race, as sensitizing concepts for assessing the equality and inclusiveness of Winthrop Academy's educative civic practices.

Quality Criteria

Quality criteria are the standards upon which the findings of a research project are judged to be valid. In keeping with my critical interpretivist orientation I chose three quality criteria to focus upon: credibility, catalytic validity, and generalizability. In this section I will outline the ways in which I tried to meet these criteria and the kinds of things that would serve as evidence of success.

Credibility, also referred to as trustworthiness, is intended to ensure that the researcher's interpretations are plausible to the study's participants.[38] As I have discussed above, I attempted to determine whether my interpretations were plausible by making my work available to the school's faculty and seeking their feedback. Such detailed member checks—checks that tested not only the quality of the data but of my interpretations and analysis—were quite successful to the extent that I received feedback from participants. After the NEERO paper, for instance, I actively set a time with each core faculty member for discussion. These discussion yielded a number of fruitful analytical distinctions surrounding faculty's approach to their civic education mission and its implementation within Town Meeting. The final case write-up, however, has not undergone such a rigorous member check as a test of credibility. Because of time constraints at the end of a busy school year, few faculty had time to read the case study. And those that did read the initial draft never provided me with any substantive feedback.

Catalytic validity is concerned with the capacity of the research to further participants' understandings and to undertake transformation.[39] The difficulty with this criterion, so defined, is its implicit suggestions that: 1) the researcher understands more and hence facilitates participants' understandings; and 2) transformation is an objective state that can be identified through the research process and consequently achieved. As I discussed in my critique of some aspects of critical theory, I want to avoid each of these implications. I prefer to think of enhancing participants' understandings through a process of providing a sort of "critical mirror" for them to reflect back on their own experiences. As a result of such reflexive processes, participants would then make their own subjective and contextualized decisions surrounding what transformation might look like and how it might be undertaken.

There is some evidence that these sorts of processes accompanied my research at Winthrop Academy. Following the NEERO paper, for example, the faculty began discussing the types of issues in which students engage during Town Meeting. Cathy and Beth, in particular, were drawn to a distinction between "grand issues" of national import versus issues of school policy. In her interview with me, Cathy had posited that students would be more equal to faculty vis-à-vis such "grand issues." Therefore, Cathy and Beth came up with a Town Meeting topic that combined an examination of the first amendment with a hypothetical scenario involving hate speech within a school. Following two Town Meeting debates, students rated this Town Meeting one of the best on the May, 1996 student survey. This example demonstrates for me how the research process enhanced faculty's understandings of Town Meeting in such a way that they sought to undertake, and actually implemented, some transformational strategies. To the extent that increased student engagement and participation are evidence of democratic transformation, the faculty's strategies were successful.

According to Lawrence Stenhouse, the generalizability criterion emphasizes the extent to which descriptive case studies provide useful evidence for comparison, critique, and theory testing.[40] In a similar vein, Reba Page and Linda Valli explain that in the case of interpretive case studies, generalizability comes in the form of vicarious experience rather than in the form of making grand claims based on findings within one setting.[41] Robert Donmoyer refers to the audience for such vicarious experience as research consumers.[42] I hope to reach two audiences, beyond the Winthrop Academy community, as research consumers: 1) those concerned with charter school reform at the level of policy making; and 2) teachers within charter schools, or other public schools, interested in the complexities of democratic civic education. To the extent that this case is accessible to these audiences, and that my analysis lends depth to their understanding of the theoretical and practical issues, it will meet the generalizability criterion.

The generalizability criterion is difficult to measure because it involves audiences that I will not necessarily come into contact with. I have sought to make the case more accessible to research consumers by making the language accessible to a wide audience, rather than jargon-filled. I have also dispersed the work through a variety of conference presentations, journal publications, and through this book. In terms of the success of the case as "vicarious experience," I think that to the extent that the write up is plausible to members of the Winthrop Academy community it reflects actual experience as closely as possible. In this manner, the case presents an outside audience with access to one school's particular experiences that non-members would not otherwise have had.

Notes

1. I am referring to "interpretive" here in a very broad sense akin to Fred Erickson's description of interpretive research as encompassing a wide variety of approaches including "ethnographic, qualitative, participant observation, case study, symbolic interactionist, phenomenological, constructivist, or interpretive." Erickson insists that the crucial distinguishing criterion of interpretive research is "using as a basic validity criterion the immediate and local meanings of actions, as defined from the actors' point of view. . . ." See Frederick Erickson, "Qualitative Methods," in *Research in Teaching and Learning, Volume 2*, Frederick Erickson and Robert L. Linn (New York: Macmillan Publishing, 1990), 77–78. Later in this section I will delineate this general approach to interpretivism from the "constructivist" approach advocated by Guba and Lincoln, among others, which stresses relativism among local meanings. See, for example, Egon G. Guba and Yvonna S. Lincoln, "Competing Paradigms in Qualitative Research," in *Handbook of Qualitative Research*, eds. Norman K. Denzin and Yvonna S. Lincoln (Thousand Oaks, CA: Sage Publications, 1994), 109–111. I concur with Phil Carspecken that the neat typologies in the methodological literature that strictly separate categories (e.g., case study/ethnography; qualitative/interpretive/constructivist/critical) are cause for much "angst," *Critical Ethnography in Educational Research.* (New York: Routledge, 1996), 2. Often attempts to illuminate differences between the categories downplay strong similarities and result in confusion rather than elucidation, if not outright misrepresentation.

2. Gary Anderson, "Critical Ethnography in Education: Origins, Current Status, and New Directions," *Review of Educational Research* 59, no. 3 (Fall 1989): 251. See also Richard A. Quantz, "On Critical Ethnography (with Some Postmodern Considerations)" in *The Handbook of Qualitative Research in Education*, eds. Margaret D. LeCompte, Wendy L. Millroy, and Judith Preissle (San Diego: Academic Press, Inc., 1992), 447–505; Joe L. Kincheloe and Peter L. McLaren, "Rethinking Critical Theory and Qualitative Research," in *Handbook of Qualitative Research*, eds. Norman K. Denzin and Yvonna S. Lincoln (Thousand Oaks, CA: Sage Publications, 1994), 138–57; and Carspecken, *Critical Ethnography in Educational Research.* The strand of critical research that I am focusing on is not inclusive of the "action" orientation represented in other strands such as participatory action research and teacher action research, among others.

3. For a few examples of critical ethnography see Peter McLaren, *Schooling as Ritual Performance: Towards a Political Economy of Symbols and Gestures* (New York: Routledge, 1993); Kathleen Weiler, *Women Teaching for Change: Gender, Class, and Power* (South Hadley, MA: Bergin and Garvey Publishers, 1988); and Jay Macleod, *Ain't No Makin' It: Leveled Aspirations in a Low-Income Neighborhood* (Boulder, CO: Westview Press, 1987).

4. Kincheloe and McLaren, 139–40; Carspecken, 4.

5.   Quantz, 472.

6.   Quantz, 473–74 and Carspecken, 16 both refer to such charges.

7.   Quantz, 473–74.

8.   Ibid., 459.

9.   Guba and Lincoln, 109–11. Constructivism's insistence that truth claims can be more or less informed or sophisticated suggests that the orientation is not completely relativistic. What is left unclear is what sorts of criteria count in determining what types of claims are more informed or sophisticated.

10. Anderson, 253 with citations from J. B. Thompson, *Critical Hermeneutics* (Cambridge: Cambridge University Press, 1981), 143.

11. Quantz, 461; 473. Quantz is drawing here from Jurgen Habermas, *Knowledge and Human Interests* (Boston: Beacon Press, 1971). For additional arguments that non-critical research reinforces the status quo, see Paul Atkinson and Martyn Hammersley, "Ethnography and Participant Observation," in *Handbook of Qualitative Research*, eds. Norman K. Denzin and Yvonna S. Lincoln (Thousand Oaks, CA: Sage Publications, 1994), 252.

12. Carspecken, 16.

13. Ibid., 17.

14. For a more complete discussion of critical epistemology, see Carspecken, Chapter 4, and Jurgen Habermas, *Between Facts and Norms* (Cambridge: MIT Press, 1996), Chapter 1.

15. Quantz, 462.

16. Reba Page offers this critique in "Do-Good Ethnography," *Curriculum Inquiry* 24 no. 4 (1994): 480. This article is a review of Michelle Fine's critical ethnography *Framing Dropouts: Notes on the Politics of an Urban Public High School* (Albany: SUNY Press, 1991).

17. Atkinson and Hammersley, 254.

18. Anderson, 257.

19. This is Clifford Geertz's phrase from *Local Knowledge* (New York: Basic Books, 1983). Anderson, 249 also draws upon Geertz's concept.

20. Kincheloe and McLaren, 144.

21. Kincheloe and McLaren, 143–44 attribute both terms "ludic" and "resistance" postmodernism to Teresa Ebert, "Political Semiosis in/or American Cultural Studies," *American Journal of Semiotics 8*, (1991): 113–135. They characterize ludic postmodernism as "an approach to social theory [which generally occupies itself with a reality constituted by the continual playfulness of the signified and the heterogeneity of differences and] that is decidedly limited in its ability to transform oppressive social and political regimes of power." They contrast this with "resis-

tance postmodernism" which appropriates and extends ludic critique by adding to it a "form of materialist intervention" through social and historical analysis.

22. Ibid.

23. These traditions include the work of first-generation critical theorists of the Frankfurt School (namely Adorno, Horkheimer, and Marcuse), Foucault, Lyotard, Derrida, Freire, the over-generalized injunctive "feminists," and others. See Kincheloe and McLaren, "Rethinking Critical Theory and Qualitative Research"; Anderson, "Critical Ethnography in Education"; Quantz, "On Critical Ethnography (with Some Postmodern Considerations)"; and Carspecken, *Critical Ethnography in Educational Research.*

24. Anderson, 252.

25. Max Horkheimer, "Traditional and Critical Theory," in *Critical Theory* (New York: Herder and Herder, 1972), 188–243.

26. Theodor Adorno and Max Horkheimer, *Dialectic of Enlightenment* (New York: Herder and Herder, 1947) and Herbert Marcuse, *One-Dimensional Man* (Boston: Beacon Press, 1964).

27. Seyla Benhabib, *Critique, Norm, and Utopia: A Study of the Foundations of Critical Theory* (New York: Columbia University Press, 1986), 128; 260.

28. Ibid., 230.

29. Ibid., 227.

30. Ibid., 231.

31. From Horkheimer's "Traditional and Critical Theory" cited in Quantz, 464.

32. Benhabib, 274 notes that theorists including Gadamer and Giegel raised these questions.

33. Ibid., 274–75.

34. I am not suggesting that Habermas is the only social theorist who asserts the importance of or offers a model for bridging the agency/structure dichotomy. Indeed, sociologists such as Anthony Giddens are well known for work in this area. Moreover, much ethnography in the tradition of Clifford Geertz stresses the interrelationships between local interpretations and broader social significance. See, for example, Clifford Geertz, *The Interpretation of Cultures* (London: Hutchinson, 1975) and Geertz, *Local Knowledge.* Rather, what I am arguing for is the advantage of drawing upon Habermas's critical social theory for critical education research due to the confluence between the theory's epistemological presuppositions and democratic principles at normative and empirical levels of analysis. For those who do not share the normative convictions of critical democratic theory, Carspecken argues that the methods of critical research remain useful because of the persuasiveness of its epistemological commitments. See Carspecken, 6.

35. Carspecken, 8.

36. Memo to Winthrop Academy faculty, September 7, 1995.

37. Although the fact that my interviews were conducted during the school's first year resulted in a dearth of new faculty's perspectives on the civic mission and Town Meeting practices over the second year.

38. See Yvonna Lincoln and Egon Guba, *Naturalistic Inquiry* (Beverly Hills, CA: Sage, 1985); and Kincheloe and McLaren, 151.

39. See Patti Lather, *Getting Smart: Feminist Research and Pedagogy with/in the Postmodern* (New York: Routledge, 1991) and Kincheloe and McLaren, 152.

40. Lawrence Stenhouse, "A Note on Case Study and Educational Practice," in *Field Methods in the Study of Education,*" ed. Robert G. Burgess (Philadelphia: The Falmer Press, 1985), 263–71.

41. Page and Valli, 7–8.

42. Robert Donmoyer, "Generalizability and the Single-Case Study," in *Qualitative Inquiry in Education: The Continuing Debate*, eds. Elliot W. Eisner and Alan Peshkin (New York: Teachers College Press, 1990), 192–97. Donmoyer's conception of generalizability from a single-case study stresses 1)accessibility to the case allowing "research consumers" valuable new information to accommodate into their existing cognitive structures; 2) the researcher's perspective lending theoretical and conceptual depth to constructs; and 3) decreased defensiveness from vicarious experience increasing the chances of accommodation versus resistance of new constructs.

Bibliography

Adorno, Theodor, and Max Horkheimer. *Dialectic of Enlightenment.* New York: Herder and Herder, 1947.

Anderson, Gary. "Critical Ethnography in Education: Origins, Current Status, and New Directions." *Review of Educational Research* 59, no. 3 (1989): 249–70.

Appiah, K. Anthony. "Culture, Subculture, Multiculturalism: Educational Options." In *Public Education in a Multicultural Society: Policy, Theory, and Critique,* ed. Robert K. Fullinwider, 65–89. New York: Cambridge University Press, 1996.

Arendt, Hannah. *Human Condition.* Chicago: University of Chicago Press, 1958.

Asante, Molefi K. "The Afrocentric Idea in Education." *Journal of Negro Education* 60 (1991): 170–80.

Astrup, R. E. "Charter Schools: A Dissenting View." *Education Week,* 23 September 1992, 29.

Atkinson, Paul, and Martyn Hammersley. "Ethnography and Participant Observation." In *Handbook of Qualitative Research,* ed. Norman K. Denzin and Yvonna S. Lincoln, 248–61. Thousand Oaks, CA: Sage, 1994.

Banks, James A., and Cherry A. McGee Banks, eds. *Multicultural Education: Issues and Perspectives.* Boston: Allyn and Bacon, 1989.

Barber, Benjamin. *Strong Democracy.* Berkeley and Los Angeles: University of California Press, 1984.

Baynes, Kenneth. "Liberal Neutrality, Pluralism, and Deliberative Politics." *Praxis International* 12 (1992).

Bellah, Robert N., et al. *Habits of the Heart: Individualism and Commitment in American Life.* Berkeley and Los Angeles: University of California Press, 1985.

Benhabib, Seyla. *Critique, Norm, and Utopia: A Study of the Foundations of Critical Theory.* New York: Columbia University Press, 1986.

————. *Situating the Self: Gender, Community and Postmodernism in Contemporary Ethics.* New York: Routledge, 1992.

————. "Deliberative Rationality and Models of Democratic Legitimacy." *Constellations* 1, no. 1 (April 1994): 26–52.

————. "The Democratic Moment and the Problem of Difference." In *Democracy and Difference: Contesting the Boundaries of the Political,* ed. Seyla Benhabib, 3–18. Princeton: Princeton University Press, 1996.

————. "Toward a Deliberative Model of Democratic Legitimacy." In *Democracy and Difference: Contesting the Boundaries of the Political,* ed. Seyla Benhabib, 67–94. Princeton: Princeton University Press, 1996.

Bierlein, Louann and Lori Mulholland. "The Promise of Charter Schools." *Educational Leadership* 52, no. 1 (1994): 34–40.

Blits, Jan H. "Tocqueville on Democratic Education: The Problem of Public Passivity." *Educational Theory* 47, no. 1 (1997): 15–30.

Brown, Linda. *The Massachusetts Charter School Handbook.* Boston: Pioneer Institute for Public Policy Research, 1995.

Bryk, Anthony, Valerie E. Lee, and Peter B. Holland. *Catholic Schools and the Common Good.* Cambridge, MA: Harvard University Press, 1993.

Buechler, Mark. *Charter Schools: Legislation and Results After Four Years.* Bloomington, IN: Indiana Education Policy Center, 1996.

Carspecken, Phil. *Critical Ethnography in Educational Research.* New York: Routledge, 1996.

Cavarero, Adriana. "Equality and Sexual Difference: Amnesia in Political Thought." In *Beyond Equality and Difference: Citizenship, Feminist Politics and Female Subjectivity,* eds. Gisela Bock and Susan James, 32–47. New York: Routledge, 1992.

The Center for Education Reform. *Charter School Highlights and Statistics.* Washington D.C.: The Center for Education Reform, 1997.

Chapman, John W., and Ian Shapiro, eds. *Democratic Community: NOMOS XXXV.* New York: New York University Press, 1993.

Churchill, Ward. "White Studies: The Intellectual Imperialism of Contemporary U.S. Education." *Integrateducation* 19, no. 1–2 (1982): 51–57.

Clark, Kenneth B. "The *Brown* Decision: Racism, Education, and Human Values." *Journal of Negro Education* 57, no. 2 (1988): 125–32.

Clinchy, Evans. "The Educationally Challenged American School District," *Phi Delta Kappan* 80 (1998): 272–77.

Cohen, Joshua. "Deliberation and Democratic Legitimacy." In *The Good Polity: Normative Analysis of the State,* eds. Alan Hamlin and Philip Pettit, 17–34. London: Blackwell, 1989.

————. "Procedure and Substance in Deliberative Democracy." In *Democracy and Difference: Contesting the Boundaries of the Political,* ed. Seyla Benhabib, 95–119. Princeton: Princeton University Press, 1996.

Cohen, Joshua, and Joel Rogers. "Secondary Associations and Democratic Governance," *Politics and Society* 20 (1992): 393–473.

Coleman, James S., and Thomas Hoffer. *Public and Private High Schools: The Impact of Communities.* New York: Basic Books, 1987.

Coleman, James S., Thomas Hoffer, and S. Kilgore. *Public and Private Schools.* Washington D.C.: U.S. Department of Education, 1981.

Commonwealth of Massachusetts. *Charter School Application.* Boston: Executive Office of Education, 1995.

————. *The Massachusetts Charter School Initiative 1996 Report.* Boston: Massachusetts Department of Education, 1997.

Connolly, William E. *The Ethos of Pluralization.* Minneapolis: University of Minnesota Press, 1995.

Cookson, Peter, ed. *The Choice Controversy.* Newbury Park, CA: Corwin Press, 1992.

———. *School Choice and The Struggle for the Soul of American Education*. New Haven: Yale University Press, 1994.

Cornbleth, Carol, and D. Waugh. *The Great Speckled Bird: Multicultural Politics and Education Policymaking*. New York: St. Martin's Press, 1995.

Crick, Bernard. *In Defence of Politics*. Chicago: University of Chicago Press, 1962.

Dahl, Robert. *Dilemmas of Pluralist Democracy: Autonomy vs. Control*. New Haven: Yale University Press, 1982.

Dale, Angela, ed. *National Charter School Directory 1998–1999*. Washington, D.C.: The Center for Education Reform, 1999.

Delpit, Lisa. "The Silenced Dialogue: Power and Pedagogy in Educating Other People's Children." In *Beyond Silenced Voices: Class, Race, and Gender in United States Schools*, eds. Lois Weis and Michelle Fine, 119–39. Albany: SUNY Press, 1993.

Dewey, John. *Democracy and Education*. 1916. New York: The Free Press, 1966.

Donmoyer, Robert. "Generalizability and the Single-Case Study." In *Qualitative Inquiry in Education: The Continuing Debate*, eds. Elliot W. Eisner and Alan Peshkin, 175–200. New York: Teachers College Press, 1990.

Ebert, Teresa. "Political Semiosis in/or American Cultural Studies." *American Journal of Semiotics* 8 (1991): 113–35.

Erickson, Frederick, and Robert L. Linn. *Research in Teaching and Learning, Volume 2*. New York: Macmillan Publishing, 1990.

Fine, Michelle. *Framing Dropouts: Notes on the Politics of an Urban Public High School*. Albany: SUNY Press, 1991.

Finn, Chester E. Jr., Bruno V. Manno, Louann A. Bierlein, and Gregg Vanourek. *Charter Schools in Action: Final Report*. Washington D.C.: Hudson Institute, 1997.

Finn, Chester E. Jr., Bruno V. Manno, and Louann A. Bierlein. *Charter Schools in Action: What Have We Learned?* Washington D.C.: Hudson Institute, 1996.

Flax, Jane. "Beyond Equality: Gender, Justice and Difference." In *Beyond Equality and Difference: Citizenship, Feminist Politics and Female Subjectivity*, eds. Gisela Bock and Susan James, 193–210. New York: Routledge, 1992.

Fraser, Nancy. "Rethinking the Public Sphere: A Contribution to the Critique of Actually Existing Democracy." In *Habermas and the Public Sphere*, ed. Craig Calhoun, 83–84. Cambridge, MA: MIT Press, 1992.

Fuller, Bruce, and Richard F. Elmore, eds. with Gary Orfield. *Who Chooses? Who Loses?: Culture, Institutions, and the Unequal Effects of School Choice.* New York: Teachers College Press, 1996.

Fullinwider, Robert K., ed. *Public Education in a Multicultural Society: Policy, Theory, and Critique.* New York: Cambridge University Press, 1996.

Garn, Gregg. "The Thinking Behind Arizona's Charter Movement," *Educational Leadership* 56, no. 2 (1998): 48–50.

Geertz, Clifford. *The Interpretation of Cultures.* London: Hutchinson, 1975.

————. *Local Knowledge* New York: Basic Books, 1983.

Geske, Terry, Douglas Davis, and Patricia Hingle. "Charter Schools: A Viable Public School Choice Option?" *Economics of Education Review* 16, no. 1 (1997): 15–23.

Giroux, Henry. "The Business of Public Education." *Z Magazine*, July-August 1998.

Guba, Egon G., and Yvonna S. Lincoln. "Competing Paradigms in Qualitative Research." In *Handbook of Qualitative Research*, eds. Norman K. Denzin and Yvonna S. Lincoln, 105–17. Thousand Oaks, CA: Sage, 1994.

Gutmann, Amy. *Democratic Education.* Princeton: Princeton University Press, 1987.

————. "Democracy, Philosophy, and Justification." In *Democracy and Difference: Contesting the Boundaries of the Political*, ed. Seyla Benhabib, 340–47. Princeton: Princeton University Press, 1996.

Gutmann, Amy, and Dennis Thompson. *Democracy and Disagreement.* Cambridge, MA: The Belknap Press of Harvard University Press, 1996.

Habermas, Jurgen. *Knowledge and Human Interests.* Boston: Beacon Press, 1971.

———. "Three Normative Models of Democracy." In *Democracy and Difference: Contesting the Boundaries of the Political,* ed. Seyla Benhabib, 21–30. Princeton: Princeton University Press, 1996.

———. *Between Facts and Norms.* Cambridge: MIT Press, 1996.

Harrington-Lueker, Donna. "Charter Schools." *The American School Board Journal* 181, no. 9 (1994): 22–26.

Hassel, Bryan C. *The Charter School Challenge.* Washington, D.C.: Brookings Institution Press, 1999.

Henig, Jeffrey. *Rethinking School Choice: Limits of the Market Metaphor.* Princeton: Princeton University Press, 1994.

Jackson, Philip W. "Conceptions of Curriculum and Curriculum Specialists." In *Handbook of Research on Curriculum,* ed. Philip W. Jackson, 3–40. New York: Macmillan Publishing Company, 1992.

James, Susan. "The Good-Enough Citizen: Female Citizenship and Independence." In *Beyond Equality and Difference: Citizenship, Feminist Politics and Female Subjectivity,* eds. Gisela Bock and Susan James, 48–65. New York: Routledge, 1992.

Kasparian, Meline. "Reshape Charter Schools." *MTA Today,* 4 February 1997, 4–5.

Kincheloe, Joe L., and Peter L. McLaren, "Rethinking Critical Theory and Qualitative Research." In *Handbook of Qualitative Research,* eds. Norman K. Denzin and Yvonna S. Lincoln, 138–57. Thousand Oaks, CA: Sage, 1994.

Kochman, Thomas. *Black and White: Styles in Conflict.* Chicago: University of Chicago Press, 1981.

Kolderie, Ted. "Chartering Diversity." *Equity and Choice* 9, no. 1 (1992): 28–31.

———. *A Guide to Charter Activity.* St. Paul, MN: Center for Policy Studies, 1996.

Kronholz, June. "Charter Schools Begin to Prod Public Schools Toward Competition," *The Wall St. Journal*, 12 February 1999, A1 & A8.

Kymlicka, Will. *Liberalism, Community, and Culture.* New York: Oxford University Press, 1989.

————. *Multicultural Citizenship.* Oxford: Clarendon Press, 1995.

Lather, Patti. *Getting Smart: Feminist Research and Pedagogy with/in the Postmodern.* New York: Routledge, 1991.

Le Compte, Margaret D., and Judith Preissle. *Ethnography and Qualitative Design in Educational Research.* 2nd ed. San Diego: Academic Press, 1993.

Lincoln, Yvonna, and Egon Guba. *Naturalistic Inquiry.* Beverly Hills, CA: Sage, 1985.

McLaren, Peter L. *Schooling as Ritual Performance: Towards a Political Economy of Symbols and Gestures.* New York: Routledge, 1993.

Macleod, Jay. *Ain't No Makin' It: Leveled Aspirations in a Low-Income Neighborhood.* Boulder, CO: Westview Press, 1987.

Madison, James. "Federalist No. 10." In *Dogmas and Dreams: Political Ideologies in the Modern World*, ed. Nancy S. Love, 59–65. Chatham, NJ: Chatham House Publishers, Inc., 1991.

Mandel, Michael. "Will Schools Ever Get Better?" *Business Week*, 17 April 1995, 64–68.

Manin, Bernard. "On Legitimacy and Political Deliberation." *Political Theory* 15, no. 3 (1987): 338–68.

Manno, Bruno V., Chester E. Finn, Louann A. Bierlein, and Gregg Vanourek. "How Charter Schools are Different: Lessons and Implications from a National Study." *Phi Delta Kappan* 79, no.7 (1998): 489–98.

Mansbridge, Jane. *Beyond Adversary Democracy.* Chicago: University of Chicago Press, 1983.

————. "Feminism and Democracy." *The American Prospect* 1 (1990).

Marcuse, Herbert. *One-Dimensional Man.* Boston: Beacon Press, 1964.

Margonis, Frank, and Laurence Parker. "Choice, Privatization, and Un-
    spoken Strategies of Containment," *Educational Policy* 9 (1995):
    375–403.

Michelman, Frank. "Law's Republic." *Yale Law Journal* 97 (1988).

Mintrom, Michael. "Local Organizations as Sites for Deliberative Democ-
    racy: Learning from Charter Schools." Annual Meeting of the Ameri-
    can Political Science Association, Boston, Massachusetts, Septem-
    ber, 1998.

Molnar, Alex. "Charter Schools: The Smiling Face of Disinvestment."
    Educational Leadership 54, no. 2 (1996): 9–15.

———. "Why School Reform Is Not Enough to Mend Our Civil Society."
    Educational Leadership (February 1997): 37–39.

Mulholland, Lori A. *Charter Schools: The Research*, Policy Brief. Tempe,
    AZ: Morrison Institute for Public Policy, 1996.

Nathan, Joe. *Charter Schools: Creating Hope and Opportunity for
    American Education.* San Francisco: Jossey–Bass, 1996.

Nathan, Joe, and Jennifer Power. *Policymakers' Views on the Charter
    School Movement.* University of Minnesota: Center for School
    Change, Hubert H. Humphrey Institute of Public Affairs, 1996.

Noddings, Nel. "On Community." *Educational Theory* 46, no. 3 (1996):
    245–67.

Oakeshott, Michael. *Rationalism in Politics and Other Essays.* India-
    napolis: Liberty Press, 1991.

Page, Reba Neukom. *Lower Track Classrooms: A Curricular and Cul-
    tural Perspective.* New York: Teachers College Press, 1991.

———. "Do-Good Ethnography." *Curriculum Inquiry* 24, no. 4 (1994):
    4790–502.

Page, Reba, and Linda Valli, eds. *Curriculum Differentiation: Interpre-
    tive Studies in U.S. Secondary Schools.* Albany: SUNY Press,
    1990.

Patton, Michael Q. *Qualitative Evaluation and Research Methods.* 2nd
    ed. Newbury Park, CA: Sage, 1990.

Peters, R.S. *Ethics and Education.* Atlanta: Scott, Foresman, and Co., 1967.

Phillips, Anne. "Dealing with Difference: A Politics of Ideas or a Politics of Presence?" In *Democracy and Difference: Contesting the Boundaries of the Political,* ed. Seyla Benhabib, 139–52. Princeton: Princeton University Press, 1996.

Pratte, Richard. *The Civic Imperative: Examining the Need for Civic Education.* New York: Teachers College Press, 1988.

Quantz, Richard A. "On Critical Ethnography (with Some Postmodern Considerations)." In *The Handbook of Qualitative Research in Education,* eds. Margaret D. LeCompte, Wendy L. Millroy, and Judith Preissle, 447–505. San Diego: Academic Press, Inc., 1992.

Rawls, John. *Theory of Justice.* Cambridge, MA: Harvard University Press, 1971.

————. "Justice as Fairness: Political not Metaphysical." *Philosophy and Public Affairs* 14, no. 3 (1985).

————. *Political Liberalism.* New York: Columbia University Press, 1993.

Rhode, Deborah. "The Politics of Paradigms: Gender Difference and Gender Disadvantage." In *Beyond Equality and Difference: Citizenship, Feminist Politics and Female Subjectivity,* eds. Gisela Bock and Susan James, 149–63. New York: Routledge, 1992.

Rothstein, Richard. "Charter Conundrum." *The American Prospect,* no. 39 (1998): 46–60.

RPP International. *A Study of Charter Schools: First-year Report.* Washington, DC: U.S. Department of Education, 1997.

Scheffler, Israel. "Moral Education and the Democratic Ideal." In *Reason and Teaching,* ed. Israel Scheffler, 136–45. Indianapolis and New York: The Bobbs-Merrill Company, 1973.

Schlesinger, Arthur Jr. *The Disuniting of America: Reflections on a Multicultural Society.* Knoxville: Whittle Direct Books, 1991.

Schneider, Mark, Paul Teske, Melissa Marschall, Michael Mintrom, and Christine Roth. "Institutional Arrangements and the Creation of

Social Capital: The Effects of Public School Choice." *American Political Science Review* 91, no. 1 (1997): 82–93.

Sergiovanni, Thomas. *Building Community in Schools*. San Francisco: Jossey-Bass, 1994.

Smith, Stacy. "Voluntary Segregation: Gender and Race as Legitimate Grounds for Differential Treatment and Freedom of Association." In *Philosophy of Education 1996*, ed. Frank Margonis, 48–57. Urbana, IL: University of Illinois at Urbana-Champaign, 1997.

———. "Democracy, Plurality, and Education: Deliberating Practices of and for Civic Participation." In *Philosophy of Education 1997*, ed. Susan Laird, 338–347. Urbana, IL: University of Illinois at Urbana-Champaign, 1998.

———. "The Democratizing Potential of Charter Schools" *Educational Leadership* 56, no. 2 (1998): 55–58.

———. "Charter Schools: Voluntary Associations or Political Communities?" In *Philosophy of Education: 1998*, ed. Steve Tozer, 131–139. Urbana, IL: University of Illinois at Urbana-Champaign, 1999.

———. "School Choice: Accountability to Publics, Not Markets." *Journal of Maine Education* 25 (1999): 7–10.

Stenhouse, Lawrence. "A Note on Case Study and Educational Practice." In *Field Methods in the Study of Education*, ed. Robert G. Burgess, 263–71. Philadelphia: The Falmer Press, 1985.

Strike, Kenneth A. "The Moral Role of Schooling in a Liberal Democratic Society." In *Review of Research in Education* 17 (1991): 413–83.

———. "Professionalism, Democracy, and Discursive Communities: Normative Reflections on Restructuring." *American Educational Research Journal* 30, no. 2 (1993): 255–75.

———. "Centralized Goal Formation and Systemic Reform: Reflections on Liberty, Localism and Pluralism," *Education Policy Analysis Archives* 5, no. 11 (1997) [journal online]. Accessed 18 May 1998. Available from http://olam.ed.asu.edu/epaa/v5n11.html.

Taylor, Charles. "The Politics of Recognition." In *Multiculturalism and "The Politics of Recognition,"* ed. Amy Gutmann. Princeton: Princeton University Press, 1992.

Thompson, J. B. *Critical Hermeneutics*. Cambridge: Cambridge University Press, 1981.

Toch, Thomas. "Education Bazaar," *U.S. News & World Report*, 27 April 1998, 35–46.

Tyack, David. "Can We Build a System of Choice That Is Not Just a 'Sorting Machine' or a Market-Based 'Free-for-All'?" *Equity and Choice* 9, no. 1 (1992): 13–17.

Voke, Heather. "Charter Schools: Particularistic, Pluralistic, and Participatory?" in *Philosophy of Education 1998*, ed. Steve Tozer. Urbana, IL: University of Illinois at Urbana-Champaign, 1999, 140–44.

Wagner, Tony. "Why Charter Schools?" *New Schools, New Communities* 11, no. 1 (1994): 7–9.

Walzer, Michael. *Thick and Thin: Moral Argument at Home and Abroad*. Notre Dame: University of Notre Dame Press, 1994.

Weiler, Kathleen. *Women Teaching for Change: Gender, Class, and Power*. South Hadley, MA: Bergin and Garvey Publishers, 1988.

Wells, Amy Stuart. *Time to Choose: America at the Crossroads of School Choice Policy*. New York: Hill and Wang, 1993.

———. *Beyond the Rhetoric of Charter School Reform: A Study of Ten California School Districts*. UCLA: UCLA Charter School Study, 1998.

Wells, Amy Stuart, Alejandra Lopez, Janelle Scott, and Jennifer Jellison Holme. "Charter Schools as Postmodern Paradox: Rethinking Social Stratification in an Age of Deregulated School Choice," *Harvard Educational Review* 69 (1999): 172–204.

White, Patricia. *Civic Virtues and Public Schooling: Educating Citizens for a Democratic Society*. New York: Teachers College Press, 1996.

Wilson, Steven F. *Reinventing the Schools: A Radical Plan for Boston*. Boston: Pioneer Institute for Public Policy Research, 1992.

Wohlstetter, Priscilla, Richard Wenning, and Kerri L. Briggs. "Charter Schools in the United States: The Question of Autonomy." *Educational Policy* 9, no. 4 (1995): 331–58.

Wright, Erik Olin, ed., *Associations and Democracy.* London: Verso, 1995.

Young, Iris Marion. *Justice and the Politics of Difference.* Princeton: Princeton University Press, 1990.

————. "Communication and the Other: Beyond Deliberative Democracy." In *Democracy and Difference: Contesting the Boundaries of the Political*, eds. Seyla Benhabib, 120–35. Princeton: Princeton University Press, 1996.

Yudof, Mark G., David L. Kirp, and Betsy Levin. *Educational Policy and the Law.* 3rd ed. St. Paul, MN: West Publishing Company, 1992.

Zernike, Kate. "Study Rebuts Fears About Demographics at Charter Schools." *The Boston Globe,* 17 July 1996, A1 & A13.

Index

('n' indicates a note; 't' indicates a table)